Copyright © 2023 by Melody Tyden

All rights reserved.

The characters and events portrayed in this book are fictitious. Any similarity to real persons, living or dead, is coincidental and not intended by the author.

No part of this book may be reproduced, or stored in a retrieval system, or transmitted in any form or by any means, electronic, mechanical, photocopying, recording, or otherwise, without express written permission of the publisher.

Cover design by: GetCovers

A CHANGE of HEART

MELODY TYDEN

Chapter One

~Billie~

Beneath the late-summer Texas sky, smoke drifted up from the barbecue in my parents' Houston backyard. My four-year-old nephew, Charlie, squealed as he raced around the yard, pursued by one of his uncles with a water gun, while his younger sister, Jenny, sat at a picnic table, colouring quietly. Their cousin, Randy, had just gone to sleep in his mother's arms where my sisters sat chatting to each other. My dad and his other son-in-law stood at the barbecue, arguing over whether the meat was done yet while I helped my mom bring out some more beers and a jug of fresh lemonade from the kitchen.

The scene would have been idyllic if it weren't for two people missing: one who couldn't be there, and one who had chosen not to be.

"Have you heard from Dex?" I asked my mom quietly, not wanting my sisters to overhear. They seemed to be in a good mood, and I didn't want to bring them down.

Her lips tightened as she shook her head. "Only to say he didn't feel up to coming. Again."

We all wanted to be sympathetic and supportive, but the truth was, we were getting worried. It had been two years since my brother lost his wife to cancer, and rather than getting better, he seemed to be withdrawing more than ever. Grief didn't have a timeline, we understood that, but the situation left us all feeling helpless. My sisters and I had all promised Dex's wife that we'd encourage him to move on and keep living his life, but lately, he hadn't given us much of a chance to.

It must be hard for him to see life going on as our family continued to grow. My sister, Tonia, and her husband, Cam, had two kids, while Laura and her husband, Jesse, had just had their first. As the youngest, I knew how it felt to always be a step behind everyone, but unlike Dex, I'd never lost anyone special to me. I just hadn't found the right guy yet, the one who made me feel the way my sisters did with their significant others. I dated; some might even say I had dated a lot back in college. My sisters often called my taste in men into question, but I didn't think there was anything wrong with them. I was simply waiting for the lightning strike that came with finding 'the one'.

"Billie, come and sit down," Laura called out to me as the argument at the grill got settled and Cam proudly carried over a plate of steaks that were far too well-done, as usual. "You've got to fill us in about your new class."

"There's not much to tell," I answered honestly, grabbing a beer and settling down next to Laura and Tonia. "I've only had two days with them. Half of them are still calling me Mom."

"Any obvious troublemakers?" Tonia asked, glancing over at her own son who had just stolen the water gun from Jesse and was doing his best to shoot his uncle right in the crotch. "After putting up with him, I think we're going to owe Charlie's teacher some therapy sessions."

At four, Charlie was younger than the second graders I worked with, but the previous year, in my first full year of teaching, I'd had a few who were a handful in their own way. Only two days into the current year, I couldn't say for sure about my new students. "No one's stood out just yet. They're all on their best behaviour so far, but by the end of the week, I'll have a much better idea."

"I don't know how you do it," Tonia admitted, giving her husband a kiss as he set down a plate in front of her. My dad was right behind him with food for me and Laura while our mom bustled around with a big bowl of potato salad. "I can barely handle one kid that talks back. Thirty at the same time would be a nightmare!"

I gave them a shrug as I took a drink from my beer. "The good ones outweigh the bad, and most of the time, they don't mean to cause trouble. Just like Charlie doesn't mean to turn Tonia's hair grey."

"Hey!" My older sister's outraged interjection before she furtively glanced at her blonde hair nearly made me snort my beer back through my nose.

When Laura and I stopped giggling, I elaborated a bit further. "Honestly, they're full of life and that's a good thing. I just need to harness that and help them enjoy learning, and we can all have a good time together."

"You've got far more patience than I do," Laura stated. "I'd hate to imagine the person who could push you too far."

"Let's hope we never meet them," Tonia agreed. "But speaking of meeting people..."

I groaned as my sisters dove into their favourite topic: my love life. Since they were both married and settled down and Dex couldn't be further from wanting to date anyone, that left me as the only Callahan sibling still on the market, and they'd decided they were going to live vicariously through me to experience the single life. Not that I'd had much time for dating since I started teaching and moved into my own house. Between work, family, and taking care of things around the house, I fell into bed alone most nights.

"It'll happen when it happens," I reminded them both as we all dug into our food. "Just like it did for the two of you."

Almost two hours later, I pulled up in front of my house as the sun disappeared from the sky. My keys jangled in my hand as I left my truck in the driveway and headed to the front door. Just before I reached it, however, a flash of movement at the end of my flower bed caught my eye.

"Is someone there?"

Although no reply came, a distinct rustling sound in the hibiscus plant let me know I hadn't imagined it. My heart rate immediately kicked up as I tried to imagine why someone would be hiding. Had they been trying to break in? I didn't have any kind of weapon with me, but I didn't want to turn my back and open the door either in case they tried to follow me in. Better to confront them and figure out what I was dealing with.

"I can hear you," I warned my intruder as I stepped closer. "Come on out of there."

The rustling grew louder as I got nearer, accompanied by a soft, quiet sound that almost sounded like...giggling?

More confused than ever, I rounded the corner to find a small girl pressed up against the house beside the plant, doing her best to blend in.

"Well, howdy," I exclaimed in surprise. "Where'd you come from?"

I knew most of the neighbourhood kids, but this one didn't seem familiar. I couldn't see her clearly in the dimming light, but she must have been about seven or eight, the same age as my students. Her long, dark hair hid her face as she turned away from me, still giggling, as if we were playing a game.

Maybe that *was* what she thought? Perhaps I could get a response from her if I played along; it seemed worth a shot. "Found you! Now it's my turn to hide."

As I hoped, her face turned towards me, eager to keep playing, and in the streetlamp, I could make out the almond-shaped eyes and slightly flattened face that were characteristic of a child with Down Syndrome. It confirmed that I definitely hadn't seen her around before, and I quickly glanced around, looking for anyone she might belong to, but besides us, the street appeared empty.

"Count to ten!" she squealed in excitement, still focused on the game. "One... two..."

Before I could ask her more about who she was or where she lived, or do anything at all, a door banged shut on the other side of my truck and a man's voice called out, laced with panic. "Adele? Adele!"

I couldn't see the man the voice belonged to beyond my truck but I suspected his frantic cry might have something to do with the little girl in front of me. "Honey, is your name Adele?"

"Three... four..." She carried on counting, her hands over her eyes, ignoring both me and the shouting from down the street.

"No, no, no... Adele!" The man's bellowing grew louder and even more distraught and I tried to take a step back while still keeping my eyes on the little girl in my bushes. I still couldn't see him, but I called out anyway.

"Sir? Are you looking for a little girl?"

He didn't reply to me directly, but a moment later, a large figure came barrelling around the back of my truck. I barely had a moment to take in his solid frame and his agitated expression before he'd walked right up to me and grabbed me by the arm so roughly that I winced. "Where is she?"

With my free arm, the one he wasn't holding onto, I gestured towards the little girl in the flower bed, still counting to ten with her eyes closed. "Is this Adele?"

"Ten!" With another squeal, she pulled her hands away and clapped in excitement when she saw me there. "Found you!"

"What the hell?" the man next to me muttered, looking between me and the girl I had to assume belonged to him. "Were you *playing* with her? What's wrong with you?"

"I didn't know where her home was," I pointed out, trying to keep my voice level even though his grip dug into my arm more tightly by the second. "I just came across her two minutes ago. Is she your daughter?"

"Daddy!" Adele exclaimed, running up to him in answer to my question. "I found her."

Finally, he let go of my arm so he could scoop the little girl up as if she weighed nothing at all. I could see relief on his face, but when he turned back to me, his expression turned colder, his green eyes turning steely beneath the streetlight. "Stay away from her."

What exactly did he think had gone on? That I'd gone to his house and lured the little girl away? His overreaction seemed extreme, but I cut him some slack since he had just thought he'd lost his daughter. Anyone would be a little stressed by that. "Are you moving in next door?" I asked instead.

The house next to mine had been vacant ever since I moved in. It would be nice to have some new neighbours, especially one as sweet as the little girl seemed to be. Hopefully, her father was just having an off day. Maybe her mother and I could be friends.

"It's none of your business," he muttered, his big hands cradling his daughter protectively. "Don't bother us and we won't bother you."

"Nobody was bothering anyone..." I tried to protest, but it had no effect. He turned and walked away without another word while Adele waved goodbye to me over his shoulder.

With a shrug, I headed for my own house, brushing off the unpleasant parts of the encounter. No one could be that naturally brusque. I'd go take them some cookies the next day to welcome them to the neighbourhood and we'd get off on the right foot instead. After writing myself a reminder on my kitchen calendar, I headed to bed so I could be well-rested to face my class again the next morning.

~**Grey**~

My heart continued to pound furiously as I took Adele back inside our new house. She chattered away, completely unaware of the danger she'd put herself in, and I took a deep breath to calm myself before I set her down in the hallway inside. Anger didn't work with her; she would shut down and tune me out, so I needed to keep my emotions in check. Kneeling down, I got to eye level with her and spoke as calmly and clearly as I could.

"Do you remember what I told you this afternoon, sweetheart?"

Those sweet, trusting eyes looked up at me in puzzlement. "Afternoon?"

Licking my lips, I tried again. "We stay inside the house unless I say we can go out. Remember? That's the rule for the new house."

It would take some getting used to. In the small town we'd been living in, she could go outside and play in the yard on her own. The mostly-elderly neighbours were usually at home and would look out for her. We lived on a quiet cul-de-sac with no traffic to speak of, and the danger had been minimal.

Houston was a whole other story. Even though I'd chosen the quietest residential area I could find among the houses I viewed, it still felt too busy. Scary. I didn't want to lock her in the house, but I might have to start, considering just how easily Adele had managed to slip out while I'd been setting up her new bed in her room.

Thank God she hadn't gone very far or come across someone who wanted to hurt her. The possibilities were terrifying and if I let myself dwell on them too long, I'd never be able to sleep that night.

"Remember," Adele confirmed in response to my question, though I didn't think she really did. Sometimes, she simply didn't understand, and other times, she heard only what she wanted to hear. In her world, everyone was a friend, so why should she worry?

As if to prove my point, her face brightened as she giggled, grabbing my arm with her chubby little hand.

"What the hell?"

The words sounded both ridiculous and wrong in her little voice, and I stared at her in utter bewilderment. "What did you say? Where did you hear that?"

My reaction only amused her, and she repeated the words again before letting go of my arm, turning and running down the hall to her room. It took me a second to piece it together: she must have been mimicking the way I'd spoken to our new neighbour and the way I'd grabbed her arm too.

I shouldn't have spoken like that in front of Adele. Hell, I probably shouldn't have said it at all, but honestly, what had the woman been thinking? Who played hide-and-seek with a child they'd never seen before out in the dark? People in Houston could be strange, and it would be better for us to keep our distance, no matter how pretty she might be.

Where had *that* thought come from? I hadn't noticed any woman in that way in quite a while, and I definitely didn't need to start. Those blue eyes beneath the streetlight had taken me by surprise, that was all, and after locking the front door behind me, I headed back to Adele's room.

"Time for bed now, sweetheart. You've got school tomorrow," I reminded her, standing in the doorway as I watched her trying out her new bed by lying down on it and trying to make a snow angel on it. At least, it looked that way to me as her arms and legs slid over the new unicorn comforter I'd bought her. I'd spent a lot of money on her new room, but I figured the more new, fun things she had, the less she'd notice the things we left behind.

Like her mom, for one.

"Yay! School!" With the same enthusiasm she had for everything in life, Adele hauled herself back to her feet and pulled back the covers, ready to climb in.

"Hold on, we still gotta get you into some pajamas first. I think there's some in this box over here."

The move had obviously thrown her off her routine, as it had thrown me off mine, but with a little trial and error, we would figure it out. Eventually, I got her into her pajamas, brushed her teeth and made up a story since I couldn't remember which box her books were in. I'd be up unpacking late into the night, but I didn't mind. As long as Adele was safe and happy, nothing else mattered. Keeping busy helped to keep the more desperate thoughts in my head at bay anyway.

It had passed four o'clock by the time I finally fell into bed, face-planting on the mattress on the floor in my room since I hadn't set up my own bed yet. The alarm that went off two hours later made me groan, but I pulled myself out of bed anyway and got ready first so I could help Adele when she woke up. She would already be starting school a few days later than everyone else, not to mention the extra attention that her appearance would generate; she didn't need to be late on top of everything else.

With that in mind, we arrived at the local elementary school half an hour before school started. The entrance looked bright and sunny, with coloured footprints leading to the front door, all the colours of the rainbow, and Adele insisted on stepping on each one before we could go inside.

The receptionist gave me a warm smile from the other side of the desk as we approached, but I didn't miss the way her eyes widened when she glanced down at Adele. I'd grown far too accustomed to that reaction since she'd been born; the surprise and the recognition that she was 'different'. In the best-case scenario, that surprise was as far as it went, and people treated her normally afterwards. In the worst case... well, that had been part of what brought us to Houston in the first place.

"Can I help you?" the women behind the desk asked primly and politely. Her dark hair pulled back in a bun made her look older than she was. She couldn't be all that much older than me.

"I sure hope so. This is Adele Wright, she's starting with y'all today."

"Oh." The woman glanced down at a file on her desk that clearly had Adele's name on it. I could see it from where I stood. "Oh dear."

"Is there a problem?" Though my nostrils flared, I did my best to keep my voice level. After my outburst the night before, Adele didn't need to see me losing control again. Besides, maybe the woman didn't mean that the way it sounded.

"It's just... the information we received didn't say anything about her... additional needs. Does she have an IEP?"

Heat rose in my neck as I tried to remember what those letters stood for. Individualized Education Plan sounded right to me, but whether or not Adele had ever had one, I couldn't say. "I don't think so. She's been home-schooled until now. This is her first day at a proper school."

I hoped the woman could hear the unspoken plea in my voice, the desire to make the transition as easy and straightforward as possible for the little girl at my side who looked around eagerly at all the bright colours and the other children out in the hall behind us who were starting to trickle in. She was itching to go and play with them, I could tell by the way she'd started to bounce beside me.

"Well, there's a whole process that has to go on before she can start. If you'd let us know ahead of time, we could have begun it, but now we'll have to delay her start until..."

"Can I speak to the person in charge here, please?" I cut her off, firmly but still as politely as I could. I'd promised my daughter she'd be starting school that day, and if I had to spend the whole day filling out forms, I would. I'd do anything I could so I didn't have to walk back out of there with her and have to explain to her why she couldn't just go to school like everyone else.

The woman's lips pursed but she got to her feet, asking me to wait a moment as she went into an office behind her that must belong to one of the school's administrators. A couple of minutes later, we were ushered into that same office, where an older woman with shoulder-length dark hair, greying at the temples, sat behind a desk. She gave Adele a warm smile and said hello to her first as we walked in, which I appreciated, but my guard remained up until I found out what she had to tell us.

"Good morning, Mr Wright. My name is Mrs Harris, I'm the vice-principal here. I understand there's been some confusion about Adele's transfer."

"Honestly, I don't know, ma'am. We just moved here. My wife... ex-wife... Adele's mother, she looked after the school side of things before. I went online a few weeks ago and filled out the form for a new student and I got an email that said she could start today. So, here we are. She's got all the supplies on the list, I told her she could start today."

My voice started to rise in panic towards the end, and the vice-principal gave me a sympathetic smile. "Alright. Well, as Ms Johnson told you out on the desk, we'll need to start the process on an IEP, but let's see if there's something else we can do in the meantime. Give me just a moment, please. Adele, there are some books on the table there if you want to read while you wait."

My daughter perked up at the sound of her name, and her eyes lit up when she saw the table of books, and I gave Mrs Harris a grateful nod as she walked past us out the door. Distracted by her books, Adele didn't seem to notice the time passing, but my eyes stayed fixed on the clock, each second that ticked by putting us closer to the start of the school day and closer to Adele not getting to have the start I wanted her to.

Finally, the door opened again, and Mrs Harris walked back in. I got to my feet, the nervous energy too much to keep still anymore, but she gestured back to the chair I'd been in. "Please, have a seat. I've just spoken with Ms Willis, the teacher in the class that Adele was meant to be in. I'm afraid she's not comfortable with taking Adele without some additional support in place."

"She ain't gonna hurt anyone or break anything," I protested, my indignation rising despite my best efforts to stop it. "She's the sweetest kid, you can see for yourself."

Right on cue, Adele looked up and gave us both a big, toothy grin, and Mrs Harris couldn't help smiling back at her. No one with a heart could resist.

"I understand, Mr Wright. Please, let me finish. We've got three second grade classes, so while Adele had originally been assigned to Ms Willis' class, I've spoken to Ms Callahan, one of our other second grade teachers, and she's happy for Adele to start in her class today instead. It's fine with me too, as long as you sign a release stating you understand that we can't devote any additional resources beyond what the other children get until an IEP is in place."

"Yes. Fine. Sure." I would sign anything I had to rather than have to explain to Adele why she couldn't stay at school that day.

"In that case, I'll get the papers ready, and I'll have Ms Callahan come and meet Adele right now."

She picked up the phone receiver on her desk to give some instructions while I glanced up at the clock again. Although it had felt like a lifetime, only twenty minutes had passed since we arrived, so there were still ten minutes until class started. Hopefully, Adele could still be in the classroom before the day got started. At last, I felt I could breathe again.

Or at least, I had been able to, until the door opened and a familiar pair of blue eyes walked in. In the bright school lighting, I could see her much better than I had the night before, but I recognized her immediately anyway: the woman who lived next door to our new house, the one I'd been less than polite to.

And now, apparently, the woman in charge of making sure my daughter had a good school year.

What were the fucking odds?

~**Billie**~

I had just started to welcome students into my classroom for the day when Debbie Harris appeared at my door. "Ms Callahan, can I speak to you for a moment?"

My teaching assistant gave me a nod to confirm she could keep an eye on things in my absence, and I quickly followed the vice-principal to an empty classroom. "What's going on?"

One of the things I enjoyed about teaching was the fact that no two days were alike. Each day threw up its own challenges and rewards, but the words out of her mouth were ones I definitely hadn't expected when I arrived at work that morning: "Can you take a new student in your class this morning?"

Based on the fact that she was asking me fifteen minutes before class began, I had to assume it had come as a surprise to her too. "Of course," I replied without any hesitation. Of all the school administrators, Debbie had to be my favourite. Diplomatic and practical, she didn't stand on ceremony and procedure like some of the others did. If she had come to me urgently, she must have had a good reason. "Just for today, or permanently?"

"Permanently, I think. She's transferring here from another district and she was meant to be in Carol's class, but we weren't aware that she has Down Syndrome and Carol doesn't feel comfortable taking her without any preparation or additional support. I don't want to send the family away since they're already here, not if there's a way we can make things easier for them."

There was no judgement in Debbie's voice regarding Carol's decision, making it clear that if I were to refuse, she wouldn't hold it against me either. However, I had no intention of refusing. Between me and my teaching assistant, we could certainly handle one more child. On top of that, I'd spent a term during my placement in college working with students with additional learning needs. It didn't intimidate me in the least.

I also couldn't help flashing back to the little girl I'd met outside my house the night before. If she and her family were new to the neighbourhood, it could well be the same child. "What's the girl's name?"

"Adele Wright," Debbie told me, confirming my suspicions, and I couldn't help smiling at the memory of the little girl's grin. She seemed like a sweetheart, and it would be wonderful to have her in my class. "I'll go and let the father know, and then I'll call you in to meet her. Just wait at reception until you hear from me."

So, her father was there too. Hopefully, he'd calmed down since the previous evening. Would he recognize me, I wondered? I wouldn't say anything about it unless he did, but my curiosity continued to grow as I waited for the signal from the receptionist to go into Debbie's office.

When it came, I walked in to find Adele flipping through some board books at Debbie's table while her father perched anxiously on the edge of his seat. He leapt to his feet the moment he saw me, and I could have sworn I saw a flash of recognition in his eyes, followed quickly by a look of uneasiness, no doubt brought on by the memory of the way he'd spoken to me the night before.

For the first time, I got a proper look at him. He was broad and solid, as I'd already noticed the night before. Above his green eyes, which were still intense even in the morning light of the vice-principal's office, his hair was so dark, I would have called it black. Stubble ran down his jawline and over his upper lip, and he wore a t-shirt and jeans, suggesting whatever he did for work didn't involve sitting at a desk all day.

I held out my hand to shake his firmly and confidently. "Good morning. I'm Billie Callahan. You must be Mr Wright."

I heard the way it sounded as the words came out of my mouth, and I could only thank God my sisters weren't there to have heard that. If I told them a literal Mr Wright had moved in next door to me, I'd never hear the end of it.

"Grey," he introduced himself, engulfing my hand in his large, rough grip. "Grey Wright. Thank you for taking Adele into your class at the last minute, I really appreciate it."

So, he did have some manners after all. That was good to know.

"It's no problem, I'm glad to have her." I glanced down at the little girl, still happily reading her book, paying no attention to anything else around her. Stepping around Grey, I crouched down to be eye-level with her. "Good morning, Adele. I found you again!"

Just like her father, a flash of recognition crossed her face as she looked up at me, but unlike him, it quickly morphed into a look of delight. "Bush lady!"

Okay, I definitely didn't want her calling me that in front of anyone else. "My name is Ms Callahan. Can you try saying that for me?"

She repeated it back to me a couple of times until she had it mostly right, and I got back to my feet, turning back to the other adults in the room. Debbie gave me a nod of approval while Grey's expression remained intense and impossible to read.

"I should get back to class. I can take Adele's things with me if you like?"

It took Grey a second to register that I was speaking to him, but when he did, he quickly handed over her school bag and jacket. "Her lunch is in there. If it's not right, let me know and I can change it for tomorrow."

It sounded like he'd never packed a school lunch before, making me even more curious about their situation when combined with the last-minute change of classroom, but we had no time for any questions right then. "Thank you. We'll have a great day, won't we, Adele?"

Nodding enthusiastically, the little girl took my hand, waving goodbye to her daddy without any kind of separation anxiety as she walked next to me down the hall. The bell rang as we reached the classroom door, and when we walked back into the classroom, everyone turned to stare.

Luckily, one of our students was out that day for an appointment, so I had an empty chair at the large rectangle of tables already and extra sets of all the activities for that day. I'd have to make additional arrangements for the next day, but I could put it out of my mind for the time being. When class began, I always tried to leave the rest of my worries behind, focusing entirely on the little people entrusted to me.

I led Adele to the empty seat before taking my place in the empty space in the middle of the tables, where all the children could see me. "Good morning, everyone. We've got a new friend joining us today. This is Adele and she'll be in our class from now on."

Adele waved happily to everyone, almost bouncing in her seat with excitement. Whatever challenges she might have, a lack of confidence definitely wasn't one of them.

In that, we seemed to have something in common.

A few of the children waved back at her but others looked less certain, and finally, one little boy asked the question that many of them must have been thinking: "Why does she look funny?"

Thirty pairs of eyes turned to me for a response, full of curiosity. That was both the best and worst thing about working with children:

they wanted to know everything and they weren't afraid to ask it. In that situation, the worst thing I could do would be to treat the question as wrong or taboo. Teaching children they couldn't talk about certain things made them think there was something wrong with those things, and if we couldn't talk about Adele's condition, the implication would be that there was something wrong with it too.

Therefore, I had to answer the best I could off the top of my head, to encourage discussion but also to remind them that the words they chose mattered. It could be a teachable moment if I approached it right.

"I think you mean she looks a little different. Is that right?" Pretending that she didn't wouldn't do any good when they could see it with their own eyes. When the child nodded, I carried on with my answer. "All of us look a little different from each other, don't we? My hair is brown but Kyle's is blonde and Alice's is black. Do you know why that is?"

A few of the children shook their heads but one hand shot up. "It's because of the way our parents look."

I gave the boy a warm smile. "That's right, Jayden, very good. Our parents give us something called genes. They're like an instruction book that tells our body how to develop. Has anyone ever used an instruction book to set up a new TV or to learn how to play a game?"

"My dad does," a couple of the kids said. Most nodded in understanding.

"So, this instruction book of genes tells our bodies whether to give us blue eyes or brown eyes, or how tall we're going to be, or what the colour of our skin is. It also tells our bodies how to help us learn and how to do things like run really fast and sing really well and whether we're going to be naturally strong. Those kinds of things, we can all work at to get better at, but some things are easier for some people than they are for others, and that's because of their instruction book. Does that all make sense?"

Most of the children nodded again, so I pressed ahead, hoping I hadn't lost them and they weren't just humouring me.

"When Adele's body got her instruction book, it had an extra page in it by accident, and that extra page changed a few things. It makes her face look a little bit different, and it makes some things a little bit harder for her to do. It doesn't mean she can't do them, just that it might take her a little bit longer. But do you know what that instruction book doesn't control?"

No one had an answer for that. I hadn't really expected them to, but I always liked to give the students a chance to contribute, even if they were just guessing.

"It doesn't decide if you're a good person or not. It doesn't say if you're kind or giving or a good friend. Those things, we get to decide for ourselves. And that's why we never judge a person by how they look, because the way they look doesn't tell us anything about what kind of person they are inside."

Pausing for a second, I let that sink in, hoping they'd already heard something similar at home, though I could never be sure of that. When I thought they'd had time to process it, I added a simple summary to try to get their buy-in.

"So, we're all going to treat Adele just like we treat anyone else, right?"

They promised me they would, thirty earnest little faces staring up at me, and I breathed a sigh of relief as I returned to my regular lesson plan for the day. Hopefully, the rest of the day would be a little more predictable than the beginning of it had been, but no matter what happened, I'd find a way through. A Callahan always did.

Chapter Two

~Grey~

Mrs Harris pulled the classroom door closed as the class settled down to start their day. "I hope that helps to set your mind at ease, Mr Wright."

As we had watched Adele and her teacher walking away to the classroom, the vice-principal must have seen something in my face that gave away how anxious I felt about the whole situation, because she offered to take me to the door to watch how the class reacted to Adele. My daughter was such a good-hearted kid, she wouldn't even necessarily know if people were being mean to her. Schools all said they'd watch out for bullying, but as a parent, it seemed impossible not to worry. That had been the main reason my ex-wife had decided to teach Adele at home, or so she'd claimed at the time. Given more recent events, I had to wonder how much had been about protecting her own feelings instead.

Mrs Harris opened the door a crack so we could hear what was said without being noticed, and when the boy asked why Adele looked funny, my whole body tensed. For a moment, I was tempted to burst into the room and pull her right out of there, no matter how much she'd been looking forward to it and how difficult it would be to explain to her why I'd done it.

However, as Ms Callahan gave her answer, speaking to the kids in terms they could understand but not talking down to them, my tension began to ease. Not only did she seem to have a good grasp on Adele's condition considering she'd only found out ten minutes earlier that Adele would be in her class, I got the feeling she wouldn't tolerate any kind of mean behaviour, not only towards Adele but towards any of the children. For someone so young, she seemed to have it all together, and the kids responded well to her.

I had to admit I was impressed.

Adele probably couldn't have ended up with anyone better placed to look out for her, and that took a huge weight off my shoulders as I thanked the vice-principal for her help and headed out to work for the day.

Just like living in Houston would be an adjustment for us, working there also meant some big changes for me. In the small town where we'd lived before, I had my own plumbing business. People called me directly when they needed help. With my ex-wife not working, relying on my payments to support her, she'd been flexible on our shared custody of Adele so I could work overtime when necessary and not have to worry too much about keeping to a precise schedule.

Hopefully before long, I could arrange some kind of child care that would give me a little more leeway in that regard again, but with us having just arrived, my hours were limited to the time Adele spent in school. On top of that, I was going to have to get used to how long it took just to drive around the city to get between jobs and make sure I had enough time to get back to the school at the end of the day. For that reason, I'd signed up as a subcontractor with a large plumbing business. They had an app where individual plumbers could claim jobs as they became available. I could work as little or as much as I liked, so long as the work was done well. The savings I'd managed to put away since my divorce provided a bit of a cushion if it took a while to find my rhythm, but I'd never been one for sitting around. I'd squeeze in as much as I could during the time I had, and as soon as I got back to my van, I pulled out my phone to look for my first job of the day.

A nearby business had a clogged drain in their staff restroom, so I grabbed that job, plugged the address into my satnav, and headed out. The small building I pulled up in front of belonged to an insurance brokerage, and the receptionist's eyebrows raised as I walked in with my toolbox in hand.

"Howdy. I understand you've got a plumbing issue."

Her eyes drifted down my body to the box in my hand, a little more slowly than necessary. Once upon a time, I would have been flattered. I might have even flirted for a while, leaning against her desk casually, simply to brighten her day and mine, but those days were gone. I had a job to do, and each second wasted was one less I could spend on the next one.

"Where's the toilet, ma'am?"

My blunt question and brusque tone seemed to snap her out of her distraction. "Just through here. Follow me."

She led me through a door and through an open-plan office space, attracting even more attention as we walked past men and women in suits at their desks. My jeans made me stand out even without the toolbox in my hand, but I kept my eyes ahead, focused on the job as she pointed to the door of the womens' restroom.

"Make sure everyone knows it's out of order until I'm done," I instructed her before stepping inside. I didn't need any distractions or interruptions.

Although it made sense that they would have tried a plunger themselves before calling a plumber, I'd learned never to assume that. I gave it a try myself first, but when that didn't work, I pulled out my drain auger instead, a cable that could be threaded through the pipe to break up the clog. Forty-five minutes later, the toilet was draining smoothly again. On my way out, the receptionist asked for my number so they could call me again if they ran into trouble, but I told her to go through the main contracting company instead to get the quickest service. Ignoring her look of disappointment that suggested the request hadn't been entirely professional, I headed out to the next job.

I'd made my own lunch that morning along with Adele's, and I ate my sandwich in my van between calls so I didn't waste any time. After finishing another job at 1:30, I scrolled through the app again to look for any jobs that wouldn't take too long. Adele would be finished at 3:00, which didn't give me a lot of time to play with, but I didn't want to waste an hour of working time either. Finally, I found one that should work: a leaky kitchen tap, not too far from the school. I pulled up to the house just before two o'clock, feeling pretty optimistic about being in and out of there in hardly any time at all.

The woman who answered the door was dressed in an even fancier suit than the people in the insurance office that morning. "It's about time," she muttered as she turned around and walked down the hall, leaving me scrambling to get my shoes off and follow after her before I lost her in the big house. When I caught back up to her in the large, spotless kitchen, she pointed to the offending tap with distaste. "I'm in a virtual meeting right now. Try to keep it down."

With that, she walked away again, leaving me alone as I placed my toolkit down on the pristine white countertop. The tap was a ceramic disc one, so after turning off the water, I took the tap apart to look for the problem. Sometimes, a screw just needed to be tightened, but in that case, the disc had actually cracked so it would need to be replaced. I made a note of the type of disc needed and went out to check my van to see if I had any in stock. Unfortunately, I didn't, and I didn't have time to go out to get one. In that case, I would have to update the app with the part required, and another plumber would pick up the job to get the item needed and finish the repair.

Heading back inside, I put the tap back together, making sure to leave everything as clean as I'd found it, and went in search of the homeowner. Voices drifted out from behind a closed door, so I knocked quietly and opened the door a crack to get her attention.

The woman sat at her home office desk, focused on the computer in front of her. She didn't even glance over at me, so after waiting a moment, I knocked again, a little louder. Her eyes did flit over to me then, in annoyance, but she immediately turned her attention back to the computer, ignoring me.

I didn't have time for this. I needed to get back to the school, so I cleared my throat. "Ma'am, I've done as much as I can..."

"I'm so sorry, excuse me one minute," she said to the people on the screen before clicking a few times, no doubt putting herself on mute. When she stood up and walked over to me, her eyes flashed in anger. "I told you I was busy. If you're done, just go."

Nothing frustrated me more than people who believed they had the right to talk down to others, whether that be in relation to Adele or because of my profession, and my own anger flared in response. "My time is just as valuable as yours. I'm not here to chat."

"Spit it out, then," she commanded, not backing down an inch.

I kept my explanation short. "You need a new part. Someone else will bring it by as soon as possible."

"It's not fixed, then?" She sounded so outraged that it would have been comical if I weren't already so annoyed. Anyone would think the world was ending than a little water dripping down the outside of her tap.

"No, it ain't. That's why I needed to speak to you, so you didn't think I fixed it when I hadn't."

"Ridiculous," she muttered under her breath, glancing back over at her computer. "I don't have time for this."

"Neither do I."

Turning on my heel, I left before I could say anything I regretted, already anticipating the 1-star review she would leave for my services. Just what I needed as a brand-new contractor with the company. By the time I made it back to my van, the clock read 2:45 and I swore in frustration as I put in the directions to the school and it showed the street I'd been intending to take backed up with traffic. The alternative suggested route would put me at the school at 3:05.

In reality, I made it to the school at 3:03, but finding somewhere to park provided a whole new challenge. It seemed half of Houston had descended on the area to pick up their children, so by the time I finally made it to the schoolyard, most of the kids were already gone. Adele stood outside, holding her teacher's hand as she looked around for me, and guilt added to the irritability I already felt over the stress of the day.

"Daddy!" My little girl's eyes lit up as she saw me approach, not seeming to care that I'd made her wait long after the others had been picked up. She deserved better than that, especially on her first day.

"Hey, sweetheart," I mumbled, bending down to pick her up as she threw herself into my arms. I could hardly bring myself to meet Ms Callahan's gaze as she walked over, holding onto Adele's bag, but I grunted an apology anyway. "Sorry I'm late."

"That's alright. It always takes a while to settle into a new routine." Her cheery response only made me feel worse, as if she didn't think I was capable of doing any better. "Adele had a great day. I've put a few notes in her bag, nothing to worry about, just some things you should know."

"Okay, thanks." I snatched the bag from her with a little too much force, making her jump in surprise. "See you tomorrow."

"Wait, Mr Wright..." she called out after me as I began to walk away, but I didn't stop. I was barely holding things together already, and one more kind word from someone so sweet and pretty who had no idea what it felt like to be on the verge of losing control might just break me.

~Billie~

So much for the manners I thought I'd seen that morning. As Grey stomped away from me with Adele in his arms, just as he had the night before, I let out a sigh of frustration. He didn't seem to take me seriously, which was going to be a problem when we'd need to work together to get Adele caught up with the other students as much as possible. That started with the IEP application which I still held in my hand since he hadn't given me the chance to pass it over to him.

Debbie told me over my lunch break that Adele had been home-schooled by her mother the previous year, so I also needed to talk to her and find out exactly what they'd worked on. With that in mind, my plan to bake some cookies and welcome my new neighbours to the area would now have an ulterior motive; Grey could try to run away from me all he wanted, but I knew where he lived.

First, though, I had to return to my classroom and get ready for the next day. I found an extra chair for Adele and rearranged the seating to put her between two students I'd already identified as being ahead of the class and eager to help. They could provide a first level of support for Adele if the teaching assistant and I weren't immediately available. Then, I went through my lesson plans for the next two days to make sure I had enough materials for an extra student, and I sat down at the class computer to do a bit of additional research on Down Syndrome. Although I knew the basics, living with it day-to-day was completely different. After reading through a few medical websites, I found a great one-page explanation for kids that I could adapt to give my class a better understanding too. With that finished and printed out, I could finally head home for the day.

After growing up on the family ranch, which always had people bustling about, and then living on campus for four years when I went to college, coming home to an empty house still felt strange. I got a good deal on the house because it needed some work, and a year on, the improvements were starting to add up, but I still had work to do.

In fact, as I headed to my bedroom to change out of my work clothes into something more comfortable, I could already hear the steady dripping from my shower that had started just a couple of days earlier. That needed to be sorted out, but first, I needed to eat. I could get supper on the stove and cookies in the oven all within half an hour if I set my mind to it.

By seven o'clock, I stood outside the Wright house with a plate of fresh chocolate-chip cookies in one hand and the IEP paperback in the other, wearing jeans and a t-shirt, my hair still up in its ponytail and a friendly smile on my face as I pressed the doorbell.

A few seconds ticked by with no response, and a few more. A large, white van sat on their driveway, so I figured there must be someone home, but as the seconds continued to pass, I wondered if my timing might be off. Maybe they were still eating and didn't answer the door during dinner. Maybe Adele was having a bath and they couldn't leave her. Maybe…

My imaginings of domestic life inside the house were cut off as I heard the lock pulling back, and a second later, the door opened and Grey appeared, his green eyes suspiciously taking in the sight of me. "What do you want?"

A tiny little spark of annoyance flared up inside me at his blunt, unfriendly question, but I pushed it down. All day long, I dealt with seven-year-olds who hadn't learned to express their feelings yet. I could handle one grumpy thirty-year-old man.

"Hello to you too." I flashed an even brighter grin at him to show him I wasn't going to be intimidated. "I'm here with two hats on. The first one is as your neighbour, with a 'welcome to the neighbourhood' offering."

I held up the plate of cookies, hoping that might entice him to invite me in, but when his expression remained unchanged, I pulled out the bigger guns instead.

"The other is as Adele's teacher. I have some information about the application for her education plan."

The papers in my other hand were of much more interest to him, but he still didn't step aside. Instead, he held out his hand for them. "Thanks.

I'll take a look at them."

It seemed he expected me to just hand them over, but that hadn't been my intention. "I can help you with them, if you like. There are some things that would be good for us to discuss together."

Whether that might have persuaded him, I never found out, because before he could answer, a cheery face suddenly appeared from behind Grey's legs. "Ms Cally-lan!"

Not exactly my name, but close enough. My smile grew wider and a lot more natural at the sight of the little girl. "Hi, Adele."

Her eyes zoomed in on the plate of cookies in my hand with that sixth sense that seemed to apply to kids and sugar. "Cookie?"

Eager, puppy-dog eyes looked up at Grey, and not even Mr Wet Blanket himself could resist. "Yes, you can have one cookie."

Reluctantly, he moved to the side to let her pass and Adele immediately grabbed my hand, pulling me inside, to her father's dismay.

"We just moved in," he mumbled in explanation of the boxes that lined the front room. "We ain't set up for visitors yet."

Maybe *that* explained why he hadn't wanted to invite me in, so I did my best to set his mind at ease. "I've seen worse, trust me."

Slipping my shoes off, I let Adele lead me to a bright but slightly run-down kitchen. The appliances needed to be replaced and the cabinet doors were scuffed and marked. It looked a lot like my kitchen had when I moved in, the houses both having been built around the same time. Boxes sat on the counters, but a small table had been set up in the corner. Adele pulled out a chair to sit down before finally helping herself to a cookie from my plate. Placing the plate down on the table next to her, I remained standing.

Grey followed us into the room, looking even more uncomfortable than he had out on the front step. "I can meet you at the school, before or after class, if that's easier for you to talk about the form."

He *really* didn't seem to want me there. "This is just as easy for me, unless you're busy. Is Adele's mother here? I'd like to speak with her too."

His entire body got even more tense. "No. She doesn't live here."

I forced myself to keep the smile on my face even as I kicked myself internally. *Way to stick your foot in your mouth, Billie.* Now that I looked for it, my gaze darting furtively to his hands, I could see he didn't have a ring on. I shouldn't have made the assumption, and that was usually something I looked up on all my students' files so I didn't do something thoughtless like ask a child about their dad when they didn't have one. Adele's unexpected addition to my class had thrown me off my regular routine, and it showed.

Still, it didn't change the fact that speaking to the woman would be helpful, so I tried to brush off my mistake. "Could I get a phone number for her, then? Mrs Harris said that Adele's mom had been homeschooling her, and I'd like to find out exactly what they worked on."

Grey's nostrils flared. "You could try calling her but I don't think it'd do you much good."

Oh, shit. My stomach sank even further as I realized what he must mean. For someone whose sister-in-law had recently passed away, I could really be dense sometimes. Grey's overall unhappiness suddenly made a lot more sense, and I cast a sympathetic glance down at Adele, even though she seemed oblivious to our conversation as she helped herself to another cookie off the plate. "I'm so sorry, I didn't know you'd lost her. Was it recent?"

The words made me wince as soon as they came out of my mouth. Of *course* it must have been recent if she'd been teaching Adele last year. I really needed to learn to think before speaking.

Grey's brows furrowed at my question and he shook his head. "No, that's not what I..." He trailed off for a second before addressing his daughter. "Adele, why don't you go get Jenny to show Ms Callahan?"

Whoever Jenny was, that prospect seemed to thrill Adele and she immediately hopped up off her chair to go and get her. As soon as we were alone, Grey stepped closer to me.

"That came out wrong. She's not dead."

"Oh." That both relieved and confused me. "So... I *can* talk to her?"

Grey glanced back over his shoulder, making sure his daughter hadn't come back yet. "Last time I spoke to her, she made it pretty clear that she didn't want to have anything more to do with Adele. You're welcome to call her if you want, but I can't guarantee she'll talk to you. That's what I meant."

That made even less sense to me. Who wouldn't want Adele in their life? Before I could figure out what to say next, the girl in question returned, her face lit up with an excited smile as she held out a well-loved doll that had to be Jenny for my inspection.

Crouching down next to her, I exclaimed over the doll and asked Adele questions about her, all while my mind raced. Every signal Grey was sending me seemed designed to push me away, but after what he'd just said, I had to wonder how much of it was simply a defense mechanism. Maybe he really just needed a friend, and someone who had Adele's best interests at heart.

Maybe he needed me. He just didn't know it yet.

~Grey~

I took a step back as Ms Callahan knelt down to look at Jenny with Adele. Telling her about my ex-wife hadn't been on my agenda for that evening, or for any time, actually, but I couldn't let her think Donna was dead. She had a valid reason for wanting to talk to her, and I felt I had to give her a heads up about how it might turn out. Even though Adele hadn't seemed to be listening, I sent her out of the room anyway; she had a habit of picking up on the one thing I didn't want her to hear, and to hear that her own mom had put her freedom ahead of being in Adele's life was something I never wanted her to realize.

Adele adored Donna. That came as no surprise; she loved everyone, but Donna had never felt that same pure, unconditional love when it came to her own daughter.

"I thought you tested for that," were Donna's first words when the doctor told us our newborn daughter had Down Syndrome, when what was supposed to be the happiest day of our lives because one of the most confusing as the tiny little girl was whisked off to the neonatal intensive care unit. Apparently, she had a heart defect, and as I sat in a hard plastic chair in the hospital room next to my wife who had just gone through hell giving birth, I'd never felt so useless.

The doctor tried to reassure her. "We did, but the tests aren't 100% accurate. Sometimes, they don't pick it up. This seems to be one of those cases."

I cared a lot less about some test that didn't matter anymore than I did about the little girl we were talking about. "What's happening with her heart?"

He used some big words I didn't recognize, but I got the gist of it: Adele had a hole in her heart that was letting the blood go where it shouldn't. I might not know much about hearts, but as a plumber, I understood the damage a burst pipe could do.

"What do we do? How do we fix it?"

Thankfully, he had a clear answer for that. "She'll need to have surgery when she's a little bit older. It's too risky right now, but when she's about five months old, we can do a repair on it."

"Is she always going to look like that?" Donna asked from beside me. The doctor's lips tightened, but I knew she didn't mean it the way it sounded. She was just in shock. We both were.

"I'll get you some information about the condition in general," he offered. "You can go and see her when you're ready, they should be finished the tests on her by now."

I thanked him, and as he left the room, I turned to Donna, whose face had begun to crumple. "Hey, don't cry, sweetheart." Getting out of my chair, I sat down on the edge of her bed so I could put my arms around her. "She's gonna be okay."

"No, she's not," Donna sobbed against my chest. "She's not ever gonna be the little girl we wanted."

Over the following weeks and months, I did my best to reassure her. No, we didn't plan for it, but now that it had happened, we had to make the best of it. Adele was still our little girl. With enough love, we could deal with anything. The surgery was tough, but our little fighter made it through. When the doctor came out to give us the good news, I turned to Donna to share my joy and relief, and in her eyes, I saw something that chilled me to the bone.

Disappointment. Almost as if she hadn't wanted her to make it after all.

Things got better when Adele started to walk and talk and get more interactive. There were days when we would have passed for a normal, happy family, but deep in my heart, I never forgot that look. Maybe it made me pull away from her. Maybe she pulled away all on her own. I couldn't say for sure, but one day just before Adele's second birthday, Donna told me she'd had enough. "This isn't the life I wanted," she gave me as a reason for asking for a divorce, and since it wasn't the one I wanted anymore either, I gave her what she wanted.

The split was pretty amicable as divorces go. We agreed to share custody. She'd look after Adele during the day while I worked, and I'd take her overnight and on weekends. That way, we didn't need two bedrooms for her, or two sets of everything, and I'd pay for Donna's rent and other expenses. It made sense to me, and I was happy to have evenings with her. It was almost the same as it had been, since I hadn't seen her during the day while I worked anyway. The only difference was Donna's absence, but we quickly adapted to life without her.

I'd hear stories about Donna going out and getting drunk at the local bar. She had the odd fella who would stay overnight. In a small town, nothing stayed quiet for long, but every day, I'd go to drop Adele off and she'd be there to take her, and every day when I picked her up, Adele seemed happy and healthy, so I thought things were fine. Maybe not the life I'd imagined, but still a pretty good one, as long as I got to take that sweet little girl home with me every night.

When the time came for Adele to start school and Donna said she wanted to homeschool, I hesitated. "You always hated school," I reminded her. We'd been high school sweethearts and I remembered her skipping class almost more often than she went.

"This is learning the alphabet, not algebra," Donna pointed out. "I think I can handle it."

The hours coincided with the hours of her custody anyway, and I didn't have a strong enough reason to try to overrule her, so I gave in and signed the piece of paper she put in front of me to say that we'd agreed homeschooling would be best for Adele.

Life might not have been perfect, but I thought things were working, until out of nowhere, Donna announced she wasn't happy once again.

"Okay, Adele, I think she's seen all of Jenny now. Can you go and play in your room for a spell? Ms Callahan and I need to talk about some grown-up stuff."

Adele put on one of her famous pouts, the one that worked on everyone in the world but me. Her bottom lip came out and her eyes turned watery while I stood there, unmoved. Her grin had me wrapped around her little finger, but I never gave in to a pout.

Ms Callahan, on the other hand, nearly melted at the sight of it. "Oh, I don't mind if she stays a little bit longer."

I wouldn't have thought a teacher would be so easily manipulated. "Don't let her fool her, it's all a big show. Watch this: Adele, you can take one more cookie if you go to your room."

Instantly, the lip went back in, replaced by a cheeky grin as she scampered back to the table to grab a cookie. She waved cheerily to us both before heading back down the hall to her room, and Ms Callahan laughed in surprise as she stood back up. "Well, I'll be damned."

"Rookie mistake," I sympathized. "You'll learn."

Her blue eyes met mine with a look of such sincere amusement that I almost smiled back, until I remembered what she'd actually come there to talk about.

"So, Ms Callahan…"

"Billie," she interrupted me.

"Excuse me?"

"You can call me Billie. I'm your neighbour and your daughter's teacher, you're going to be seeing a lot of me. Ms Callahan will get old pretty quick."

"Billie's a boy's name," I couldn't help pointing out, unable to stop my eyes from wandering downwards to her chest in her t-shirt, which definitely did not belong to a boy. Not that I'd noticed her chest before that very moment, I hastened to remind myself.

"And Grey is a colour. What's your point?"

Again, I almost laughed. She had me there.

"Let's take a look at these papers before the cookie monster comes back," I suggested, gesturing at the table in the corner. "Please, have a seat."

Chapter Three

~Billie~

After that night, making friends with Grey got added to my to-do list, very close to the top. Although he remained gruff and stoic as we reviewed the paperwork together and I gave him advice on how to fill it out, I'd seen a hint of humour in his eyes earlier, enough to let me know that a happier guy lurked somewhere behind his stony facade. Why would he have moved next door to me if I wasn't meant to help him find that person again? It felt like providence.

On Thursday, I had to stay in the classroom at the end of the day so I didn't see Grey during the student pick-up. When I arrived home, though, Adele was playing happily with a big, soft ball in the front yard while Grey sat nearby on a folding chair with his laptop in his lap, his brow furrowed in concentration.

They both looked over as my truck pulled into the driveway, and Adele ran over as soon as my door opened, despite Grey trying to call her back.

"Ms Cally-lan! Come and play!"

"She just got home, sweetheart," Grey told his daughter before shooting me a tight-lipped nod of greeting. "Sorry. The backyard ain't cleared yet, it's getting done this weekend. After that, we'll hang out there so she doesn't see you every time you come or go."

"That's fine. I can play for a few minutes."

Leaving the work that I'd brought home for the evening on the seat of my truck, I tossed and rolled the ball back and forth with Adele for five minutes, with Grey keeping his attention focused entirely on the laptop screen, his lips moving as he read things out loud and his expression growing darker by the minute.

Eventually, my curiosity got the better of me. "Are you working on the IEP?"

He glanced up with a scowl. "I know you said to focus on her weaknesses, but it's depressing as hell."

I could sympathize with that. "We want her to get the full support she's entitled to, so it's no good looking on the bright side or painting an unrealistically optimistic picture. You and I both know Adele has plenty of strengths. I can look it over before you submit it, if you like?"

His internal struggle was clear, fighting between wanting the best for Adele and not wanting to accept any outside help, no matter how freely I'd offered it. Finally, his fatherly instincts won out. "Sure. I ain't done yet, though."

"No problem. You know where I live. Just knock on my door when you're ready."

With a friendly smile, I waved goodbye to Adele and headed inside.

The next day, my teaching assistant handled the pick-up again, but it took her a while to come back. "Mr Wright was late," she told me when I asked what took so long. "He's a bit of a grouch, isn't he? Looks like Adele got all the happy genes in that family!"

I couldn't disagree, but Grey being late again got me thinking. He'd told me that Adele's mother didn't live with them, and if he was on his own, maybe work made the pick-up time difficult. That might be something I could help with to ease their transition to their new home.

I didn't get a chance to talk to him about it that evening, though, as there was no sign of them outside their house when I arrived home and I couldn't think of a good enough excuse to simply go over again. There was a fine line between being neighbourly and being overbearing, so I held myself back Friday evening, no matter how much I wanted to get involved.

On Saturday, I had a different distraction. My sisters and I had agreed to check in on our brother, Dex, at random intervals, since he kept skipping out on the family barbecues. Tonia had gone over to his house on Thursday, and I had promised to visit the gallery on Saturday morning.

A talented artist, my brother had his own gallery in a slightly run-down downtown neighbourhood. His wife had helped him set it up and run it, and since her death, he'd been managing it on his own. Whenever we asked him how things were going, a curt "fine" was all we'd get. When I walked in that morning, though, there were no signs of any other customers, nor any sign that anyone worked there. The whole gallery was empty, but before I could call out to see where everyone was, a loud, frustrated cry came from the workshop in the back, followed by a crash.

Instantly, my feet carried me to the workshop door, my heart racing. "Dex! Are you alright?"

My brother stood in the centre of the room, black paint splattered across his blue t-shirt. On the ground, a tripod had fallen over, a canvas lay face-down next to it, and a black paint tin was still rolling away, leaving a trail of paint in its wake.

"Billie?" He stared at me in confusion, as if I might be some kind of apparition, but seeing as he seemed to be unharmed, I immediately set to work in preventing any further mess and cleaning up what had already taken place. Working with second-graders, I'd dealt with my fair share of paint spills. The can got scooped up first, followed by wiping up as much of the paint on the floor as I could. The floor of the workshop had been left as concrete in anticipation of a mess, so I was less worried about that than I was about my brother.

"Shirt off," I commanded, holding my hand out for it. "I can get those stains out."

"Leave it, Billie. It's fine."

"It's not fine. Your shirt will be ruined, so take it off and give it to me."

"I said: leave it."

His raw growl sounded so unlike my once-easygoing brother that I took a step back. Regret flashed in his eyes, but he didn't take it back. He didn't say anything at all, so I bent down to keep cleaning up his supplies instead. After righting the tripod, I picked up the canvas. On the other side, he had painted a beautiful, haunting scene of a woman staring into the mirror. The lighting was dim, as if he caught her at dusk or in the early morning, illuminated by a lamp to her side, and set at a distance, as if the viewer were glimpsing it through an open door, the woman unaware that anyone was there. Her hand reached up tentatively to her bald head, her body frail but her eyes defiant.

It was utterly gorgeous and captivating… and completely ruined by the black paint sprayed across it.

My eyes moved back to my brother who stood there watching me, his fists clenched and his nostrils flaring. Had it been an accident, or had he destroyed it on purpose?

His next words answered my question. "I can't get it right. I can't do her justice."

In his voice, the edge of grief was still so raw, it almost felt like it would cut me if I stepped too close. I couldn't imagine what it must be doing to him on the inside.

From past experience, I'd learned that he didn't want to talk about it, though. He'd rather focus on practical things, so no matter how much he hurt, or how much I hurt for him, I tried to do what he'd want me to do.

"Where's your staff?" I asked him, putting the canvas back on the tripod as if there were nothing wrong with it. "There's nobody out front."

"I gave them weekends off. We're not that busy anyway."

"You're going to serve people all day looking like that?" I glanced down at his paint-splattered shirt. "I don't think so. I'll work the front today."

"Billie." His voice went low in warning. "You work hard all week. It's your day off."

"And when's the last time you took a day off? I assume it's been a while since you're too busy to come and see us."

My eyes met his in challenge, two Callahans just as stubborn as each other, and to my relief, Dex blinked first. "Fine. You can stay."

"Good. You finish cleaning up the rest of the mess, I'll go out front."

Leaving him there, I went back to the gallery, where I propped the front door open to make it seem less intimidating for people walking by to stop in. The sun shone brightly as people popped in and out all morning, maybe not to buy anything but at least to look around. If they saw something they liked, they might come back later and buy it then. I might not be a businesswoman like my sisters, but I understood that much.

By the afternoon, Dex's mood had improved and he ran out to get us some sandwiches for lunch, which we ate together in the workshop. He asked about my class and we talked about our niece and nephews, and for a while, it felt almost normal.

Only when I told him a little about Grey and Adele did Dex's expression cloud over again. "Tread lightly, Billie. Not everyone needs to be fixed. He may have a good reason for wanting to keep his distance."

On that point, we disagreed. People might not *want* to be fixed, but they might need it all the same.

By the time I got home, most of the day was gone and I hadn't even begun to tackle my own to-do list for the weekend. First up would be fixing that pesky dripping shower. It had begun to work its way into my dreams, and not in a good way; more like a metronome of doom, ticking away over me.

It only took a bit of searching on YouTube to find a video about how to fix the problem. It suggested starting with the showerhead itself, so I removed it and put it to soak in vinegar, as the video suggested. In the meantime, I put together a big pot of chilli, one of my go-to weekend meals. It would give me leftovers to take for lunch during the week and I could leave it bubbling away while I went back to the shower issue.

Unfortunately, the clean showerhead made no difference. The dripping started again almost immediately when I reattached it, and with a sigh, I moved onto the next suggestion. However, as soon as I started to unscrew the next component, a concentrated spray of water suddenly hit me square in the chest.

"Oh, fuck!" Clamping my hand over it, I tried to reattach the pieces, but the pressure was too strong. I couldn't get it back together again. "Shit!"

Reaching over to the towel rack, I was able to grab one of my big, fluffy towels, and wrap it around the pipe to stop the water from hitting me directly. Unfortunately, that wouldn't buy me very much time, as the water quickly started to soak through it. Frantically, I went back to the online video, trying to figure out what I'd done wrong, but before I could figure it out, a loud knock sounded at my front door.

"Billie? Are you okay?"

~Grey~

The guys I hired to clear out the backyard did a great job, starting at nine o'clock that morning and working nearly straight through to five, taking only a short break for lunch. From beneath the tangle of weeds and long grasses, a lawn appeared. Hidden in the back right corner, they found a small vegetable patch, its wooden borders rotting, and they dug it out and restored it. The small shed in the left corner became accessible for the first time since we got there. The house had been vacant for a while before we moved in and it showed, but the yard had been even worse. With the clear-out, it finally started to feel more like a real home.

Adele found the whole process fascinating. I set her up on the deck with some books and snacks and a promise not to leave the deck on penalty of extreme tickling, and she happily kept an eye on the whole procedure like a queen surveying her kingdom. After watching her surreptitiously for a while from the back window, until I felt confident she understood my instructions, I took the opportunity to get more of the house unpacked, including finally setting up my bed. Maybe I could get a decent night's sleep that night. Things were starting to come together, and the underlying panic I'd felt ever since I sold our old house on the spur of the moment and decided to move us to Houston finally seemed to be receding.

I could have done the yard by myself, but it would have taken me at least twice as long and the end result wouldn't have been as good. The guys I got had the experience and the equipment necessary to do the work in the most efficient way possible, and as a tradesman myself, I understood the value of that. Some things were worth paying for.

"Well, Adele, should we try out the barbecue for supper?" I asked her once the men had packed up and gone. They'd even set up the backyard furniture I bought, at no extra charge, so we had a table where we could eat outside. "We could have burgers or hot dogs…"

Before she could choose, a loud shriek rang out from next door, from Billie's house. If we'd have been in the house, we wouldn't have heard it, but in the yard, it sounded clear as day through one of her open windows. "Oh, fuck! Shit!"

Although the language made me wince, knowing Adele could hear it, my main concern at that moment was for Billie. Cussing like that meant something had to be wrong. Maybe she'd hurt herself? I hadn't seen any signs that anybody lived in the house with her, so if she was on her own and injured, she might need help.

Making up my mind in a matter of seconds, I scooped Adele up in my arms and jogged over to the house next door, banging on the door with my fist. "Billie? Are you okay?"

Her response came back muffled, but clear enough. "I could use some help!"

Her tone suggested just what she said: help would be appreciated, but the situation wasn't life or death. Not having any idea what I might be walking into, I let myself in through the unlocked front door, straight into a bright, sunny living room. The spicy, savoury scent of whatever she was having for dinner drifted out of her kitchen, making my stomach grumble involuntarily. The house layout almost mirrored my own, and sizing things up, I placed Adele down on the sofa, turned the TV on to her favourite kid's channel, and went off in search of the homeowner.

"Billie?"

"In here," her voice came from down the hall, towards the rear of her house. "The bedroom at the back. I'm in the bathroom."

Following the sound of her voice and her instructions, I found myself in a pretty, feminine bedroom, the queen bed covered with a floral comforter. The room smelled of her, of flowers and sunshine, but I kept my eyes focused on the bathroom door, wondering, for a fleeting moment, if she'd be fully dressed when I got there. What exactly was going on?

The scene that greeted me made things a bit clearer. Billie stood in the shower, holding a big towel against the pipes that led to her showerhead, her yellow t-shirt soaked with water and a chagrined smile on her face. "Hey. I don't suppose you know anything about showers?"

Between the tools on the floor and the state of her, I sized up the situation pretty quickly, having been called into enough plumbing 'emergencies' to take an educated guess at what had happened. "What were you trying to do?"

"Stop a drip," she admitted, glancing down at her drenched clothes. "It's a little more than that now."

It never failed to amaze me how little people understood about the water system in their houses. "Let me guess: you didn't turn the main water off first?"

"The video said to turn the water off, but I thought it just meant to make sure the shower was switched off." She offered me another sheepish smile, but I didn't smile back. She could have done some real damage, especially since I suspected she wouldn't know the answer to my next question.

"Where is your main water valve located?"

Exactly as I expected, Billie shrugged apologetically. "I'm not sure."

"Wait here." With a sigh, I left her there holding the towel while I headed back to the front door. Adele was caught up in an episode of My Little Pony, curled up on the sofa among the soft pillows there, making herself completely at home, so I left her there while I ran next door to grab my toolkit. Luckily, the valve was right where I expected to find it, in the flowerbed at the front of the house, and I turned it off before returning to Billie's bathroom.

"Water's off. Go and get cleaned up," I instructed gruffly, placing my tools down on the vanity counter. "I'll fix it."

Hesitantly, she pulled the towel back from the pipes, as if she didn't believe me. When she saw the flow had indeed stopped, she took a deep breath. "Looks like you know what you're doing."

She meant it as a joke, but I didn't smile, focused on pulling out the tools I needed. The gasket or the washers were the likeliest cause of a leak and although it wouldn't take long to fix, it wasn't something to be rushed either. "This is what I do for a living. I left Adele out in your living room, so maybe after you change your shirt, you could check up on her."

"Right. Sure." She stepped out of the shower, grabbing another towel off the wall to press against her wet shirt as I tried not to watch her out of the corner of my eye. When she reached the door, she paused for a second. "Thanks, Grey."

I grunted in acknowledgement, keeping my gaze down as I went to work.

Half an hour later, the washers had all been replaced and after showing Billie where to find her main water supply valve, I turned the water back on so she could test it out. Reaching into the shower, she turned the tap on and let it run for a few seconds before switching it back off.

Nothing came out, but she tried it again, just to be sure.

"Thank you," she repeated, her face relaxing into a relieved smile. The shirt she'd put on to replace her wet one had polka dots on it and a scooped neckline that showed off her collarbones. Her light, brown hair was pulled back in a ponytail, as usual. She probably wore it that way to keep it from getting in the way in the classroom, but for a fleeting second, I wondered what it would look like down. "I should have just hired you in the first place."

"You should have," I agreed, the words coming out a little rougher than I intended as I tried to clear my mind of the unexpected thoughts that had just popped into it. "Or any licensed plumber. Some things are worth having a professional do."

My gruffness didn't seem to put Billie off. Did *anything* fluster her, I wondered? "Well, I need to pay you now that I've taken up so much of your time, and on your day off, too."

"That ain't necessary. You're helping with Adele, that's more than enough."

"That's *my* job," she reminded me. "Which I get paid for."

Technically, that might be true, but she didn't get paid to come over to my house and help me with the application. I understood that, even if I might not be the best at showing my gratitude for it. "Forget it, Billie. Just do me a favour and call a plumber next time, alright?"

Picking up my toolkit, I started to make my way back down the hall, but Billie followed after me, not giving in. "At the very least, can I offer you supper? Have the two of you eaten? It's getting late and I've taken up a lot of your time."

Whatever she had cooking *did* smell pretty good, and I hadn't actually started on anything yet at home. When I hesitated for just a moment, Billie took it as an agreement.

"Perfect. I'll go and set the table. Won't be a moment."

She walked past me into the kitchen as my eyes followed her, several different emotions warring inside me. I'd made up my mind before we came to Houston not to get close to people. My confidence in my ability to judge someone's character had been completely shot by everything that happened with Donna. Knowing that I'd fallen in love with and put my complete faith in someone who turned out to only have her own interests at heart made me doubt whether I really knew anyone at all, and with Adele as my top priority, I didn't want to open either of us up to any further disappointments.

That had been my plan until Billie Callahan showed up like a force of nature, a hurricane that seemed to have blown into our lives and turned me around, leaving me feeling completely off-balance. Getting out of her orbit seemed to grow more challenging by the day, and even worse, *much* worse, I wasn't even entirely sure I wanted to.

~**Billie**~

Apparently, having to rescue me from a plumbing emergency was *not* the way to improve Grey's mood, but I didn't let it bother me. If I hadn't already been convinced I was meant to become his friend and help him adjust to his new life in Houston, I'd just been given another sign; why else would he turn out to be a plumber right when I needed one? No one could argue with that.

Maybe he didn't *technically* accept my offer of supper, but he didn't say no either, so I planned to take full advantage of the ambiguity. Getting two extra place settings on the table didn't take much effort, but Grey followed me into the dining room to supervise anyway.

"What're you planning on having?" he asked me warily.

"Chilli. It's almost done, and it's not too spicy. It should be fine for Adele." I added the last bit in case that had been his reason for asking.

A grimace crossed his face as he looked down at my cream-coloured carpet. "I don't know if that's the best idea. She can feed herself - insists on it, actually - and most of the time she's pretty dang good at it, but sometimes, things still go flying."

Ah, so *that* was the problem. He didn't want me to end up with chilli all over my dining room. That could almost be considered thoughtful. "Not a problem. We can improvise."

At the back door, I had a long rubber mat, and it only took a minute to grab it and place it under Adele's chair.

"There. Problem solved."

Grey looked unconvinced. "You ain't seen how far she can throw yet."

"Well, if it gets any farther than that, I have cleaning supplies. I'm not afraid of a little mess, Grey." He seemed determined to make me want to rescind my invitation, but I had no intention of it. Maybe we could finally sit and have a conversation that didn't revolve entirely around Adele's education. Maybe I could actually learn a thing or two about him in the process. "Go and get her and sit down. I'll bring the food out."

I left the room before he could protest, grabbing three deep bowls from the cupboard and filling them from the bubbling pot on the stove. Into Adele's, I put a bit of sour cream to cool it down, just in case. When I returned to the dining room with the bowls for myself and Grey, they were just sitting down, taking seats across the table from each other and leaving the head of the table empty for me. I offered Grey a beer, but he declined, his jaw tight. I could have sworn he wanted one but wouldn't allow himself to accept it.

Why did he have such a hard time saying yes?

When I came back with Adele's bowl and some juice, I also brought an apron for her to wear, since Grey seemed worried about spills. It had colourful flowers on it, and as I hoped, she eagerly accepted it, looking down at it across her stomach and lap while brushing her fingers over it almost reverently.

"She loves clothes," Grey told me as we watched her, his voice taking on that special tinge of affection it held whenever he talked about his daughter. "I never go shopping without her, she knows exactly what she wants."

"Does she pick yours out too?" I teased gently. His grey t-shirt might match his name, but it didn't seem like something a sunny 7-year-old girl would choose.

"Not yet," he muttered, but I could hear his amusement at the idea, even though he tried not to show it.

There we were, talking about Adele again, though. I'd rather know something about him. Work seemed like a pretty safe topic to begin with. "So, how did you become a plumber? It's not something kids usually say when you ask them what they want to be when they grow up."

As soon as the words came out of my mouth, I could hear how they sounded. I had simply meant to say that although plumbers were vital, people didn't automatically think of it as a career, but it almost sounded like I thought no one ever willingly chose it.

By the way Grey's shoulders tensed, he obviously heard it too. "It pays well," he answered tersely, as if I had suggested it didn't.

"I'm sure it does, but what about it appeals to you?"

Again, that didn't come out right. It sounded almost like I found it impossible that anything about it might be appealing, which wasn't what I meant at all. I just wanted to know if he enjoyed his work.

Grey shoved a forkful of chilli into his mouth, as if he couldn't eat fast enough. "The best thing is not having to talk to people all day long."

Obviously, he included me in 'people'. A quick glance over at Adele confirmed she was fully occupied with her meal, and not getting the chilli anywhere other than a little on her face so far, so while she was still distracted, I decided to approach my questions from a different angle. "Is that why you moved to Houston? For work?"

From Adele's file, I knew that she'd previously been registered under a rural school district, but that was all I knew about where they'd previously lived. Why they moved, I had no idea.

He gave me a look that could only be described as disbelief. "You think only people in Houston need plumbers?"

Oh, come on. That one hadn't even been that bad. "I didn't say that. I just noticed that you've been late to pick up Adele a couple of times this week already, and I wondered if you were finding the schedule difficult to coordinate with your new job."

Well, I certainly hadn't meant to blurt *that* out. I had indeed been wondering that, but I had intended to bring it up a little more tactfully. Maybe my sisters had a point when they claimed my verbal filter was broken.

Entirely predictably, Grey took that in the worst possible way, his face somehow growing even more tight. If he turned any more rigid, he might just turn to stone. "It's an adjustment but I'm trying."

I knew that. That was why I wanted to help, and since he seemed determined to take everything I said in a negative light, I laid all my cards on the table. "Look, Grey, I'm not trying to make you feel bad. I know it's tough when there's a lot of change all at once. I just wanted to know if there was something I could do to help."

"Why would you wanna do that?" He sounded so suspicious that it almost made my heart ache. What had happened to make him so untrusting?

"Because where I come from, that's what people do. They help each other out when they need it. Just like you came and fixed my shower, right? You knew how to do it and I didn't, so you helped me out. So, if you need help and there's something I can do that you're struggling with, I'd like to do it. That's all. It's not an insult."

He didn't meet my eye, appearing to be thinking that over while he reached for his glass and took a drink of water, so I took a moment to ask Adele how she liked her supper. She just nodded at me, still fully intent on eating, which I took as a good sign.

When I turned back to Grey, he'd put his glass down and picked up his fork again. He still didn't look at me, but at least he spoke again. "Where do you come from?"

That had to be the first time he'd actually asked me something about myself, and I took that as another positive development. "A little town called Sandy Creek. My family had a ranch there that I grew up on."

"Do they still have it?"

Two questions in a row? I hit the jackpot, it seemed. "Not exactly. My sister's still there, but only because my dad sold the ranch and she married the guy he sold it to... it's kind of a long story."

"I can imagine." It didn't seem like there were any more questions coming, but at least he didn't seem quite as closed off anymore. His green eyes looked a touch less clouded than before when he finally looked back over at me, and when he returned to our previous discussion, he sounded a bit less defensive. "My new job doesn't have set hours. I'm trying my best to make sure I'm at the school on time, but I know I haven't been doing a great job at it. I'll try harder."

"Well, maybe you don't have to."

My words took both me and him by surprise. "What do you mean?"

What *did* I mean? An idea had occurred to me but he might think I was overstepping or interfering, or any of those other words commonly used to describe pushy women. However, since I sincerely wanted to help, I shared my idea with him anyway.

"Adele's no trouble. If she wants to stay with me after school while I finish up my day there, I can bring her home with me and drop her off with you then. If you're not home yet, I can bring her back here and you can come pick her up when you get home. That way, you're not rushing to try to get to the school on time. It can be a bit more flexible, at least until you find something else that works for you. What do you think?"

Chapter Four

~Grey~

Billie seemed to have invited me to stay for supper just to insult me. Having people look down on my job, and me by extension for doing it, was nothing new. I'd grown accustomed to the offhand comments or immediate lack of interest whenever I answered the question about what I did for a living. Even Donna, at our own wedding, had made a comment to one of her extended family about how I went into it only for the money. "He could do something else if he wanted to," she added. "He's actually really smart."

As if plumbing and intelligence didn't normally go together.

Since bringing up how well it paid usually shut people down the fastest, that had become my default defense, but it didn't stop Billie. Nothing seemed to stop her. And when she explained that she was asking because she'd noticed me being late to the school, I nearly got up and walked out right then, even if Adele was treating her meal like some kind of religious experience. She'd never been so quiet and absorbed in *my* chilli.

I knew I'd been late and my tardiness embarrassed me, as if it suggested I just didn't care as much as other parents, which couldn't be farther from the truth. I was well aware of my own shortcomings and I didn't need my chatty, pretty neighbour to remind me of them.

However, when she mentioned wanting to help me because of where she'd been raised, she managed to pique my curiosity enough to stay. Learning that she came from a small ranching town made things a lot clearer to me, including her apparent lack of boundaries. I'd always heard people in the city kept to themselves, but Billie couldn't be more the opposite, and with that piece of new information about her, I had a better understanding about why.

So, I stayed in my seat while she made her suggestion, a suggestion which couldn't have been any better suited to what would help me the most, at least in the short term. I still needed to arrange child care on a long-term basis, I knew that, but trusting someone I'd never met before to care for Adele seemed almost impossible. That probably explained why every time I sat down at my computer to start looking at providers in the past few days, I ended up walking away in frustration.

I knew Billie, though. Maybe not well, but enough to know she cared for Adele and would look out for her. As a teacher, she obviously had a way with kids. Her location right next door to our house couldn't be better. From my perspective, I really couldn't see any down sides, but something still held me back, that warning in my head telling me not to get involved with her any more than I already had.

"It's too much to ask," I said out loud, reluctantly. No matter how much it would help me, it would be a huge imposition on her. "You already work a full day and you've got a life of your own."

Billie brushed that objection aside. "You're *not* asking. I'm offering, and I wouldn't offer if I didn't want to."

That might be true, but she didn't know the whole story. Maybe if I gave her a few more details, she'd change her mind. "In plumbing, things often take longer than you think they will. I've had jobs that ran hours longer than I expected because I needed to pick up additional parts, or the thing I thought would fix the problem didn't and I had to do some detective work to find the true issue. It varies enormously from one day to the next. There's no bell to tell you when the day's gonna end."

Billie's blue eyes watched me intently as I spoke. "Detective work, huh? Is that what you like about it?"

"Yeah, actually." It surprised me that she'd picked up on that. Most people didn't. "There's always a solution, I just have to find it, taking into account time, cost, and long-term effects."

Billie nodded as if she really understood. "It must be satisfying when you find the answer. A lot of the time in teaching, I never know if what I'm doing will have any impact or not. It can take days, or weeks, or even years before it makes a difference. It would be nice to turn a tap on and see whether the water comes out or not."

Her smile let me know she was kind of joking, but not entirely. "Your job has to be the most important one, though," I pointed out. "The influence you have in kids' lives is huge."

Billie kept smiling but shook her head at the same time. "I don't think there's a 'most important' job. At the time that you show up to fix a flooded basement, I bet you're the most important person to the person who's knee-deep in water. If I've got a toothache, my dentist is pretty damn important. And I spent all day today with my brother, who's an artist, which some people think is useless, but I've seen the joy his work brings to people. No one profession is inherently better than any other one. As long as it makes *you* happy, it's important."

That perspective was incredibly refreshing, and completely contradicted what I thought she'd been implying about my work earlier. Maybe I had jumped to conclusions? I had to admit that was possible. Sometimes, it felt easier to assume the worst of people; that way, I wouldn't be let down. "Anyway, my point is: my work is job-based. It's a balancing act to try to figure out when I finish one job if I can take on the next one in the time I have left. Sometimes, I get it wrong."

"I understand that, Grey," she assured me. "Maybe not all the details, but I get the gist of it. Flexibility is important to you and I can help with that. If I have plans in the evenings, they're usually after supper, and I can let you know in advance if there are exceptions to that. On Tuesdays, for instance, I have a standing engagement for supper, but we can work all that out. You've got all the stress of moving and Adele starting a new school and you starting a new job, and I just want to help. Please let me."

The eagerness in her expression made it feel like I'd be doing *her* a favour by accepting rather than the other way around, and my resolve began to weaken. "Adele really wouldn't be in the way at school while you finish up your day?"

"Not at all. There are a hundred things in the classroom she could keep busy with. Look at her, she's eaten her whole supper by herself without making a peep. I hardly know she's here..."

Billie just had to tempt fate. No sooner were the words out of her mouth than Adele's spoon somehow flew out of her hands, straight across the table, directly at me. The spoon itself hit me square in the chest while chilli splattered across my face, and the table and, to my horror, down onto the light-coloured carpet behind me.

Fuck. Now, I would have to feel guilty about that too, even though I warned Billie it might happen.

However, rather than flying into a panic as Donna would have, Billie began to laugh. "Those spoons are slippery, aren't they?" she asked Adele, immediately ensuring that my daughter didn't feel bad about what happened. Reaching over, she picked up the spoon that had fallen onto the table after hitting me and handed it back to Adele. "There you go."

Adele immediately returned to eating, as if nothing had happened, while Billie turned to me.

"Uh, Grey, you've got a little something..."

She gestured to pretty much the whole of my face, still grinning, and I had to fight back a smile myself. "Just a little, huh?"

Grabbing the napkin next to my plate, I wiped my face off as best I could, though by the sparkle in Billie's eyes, I suspected I hadn't quite got it all.

"Take your shirt off," she suggested next, looking down at the large red spot where the spoon had hit me. "I can treat it for you before it sets."

I could do my own laundry. "That's fine, I'll do it when I get home."

For the first time since I'd met her, Billie almost snapped at me. "For the love of... why are you men so stubborn?! It's better to treat it immediately. Just take the shirt off!"

Her reference to 'you men' made me think her reaction was fuelled by more than just my dirty shirt. There must be more to the story, but rather than ask, I gave in, pulling my t-shirt off over my head before she got any angrier.

"Thank you." Exhaling loudly, Billie took the shirt and walked out of the room.

Left on our own, I looked over at Adele, who grinned up at me, thoroughly enjoying herself. "It's pretty good, huh?" I asked her as I took another bite of my chilli.

The food *was* damn good, but that wasn't entirely what I meant. For the first time in months, things were actually starting to feel okay again.

~Billie~

I hadn't meant to use my 'teacher voice' on Grey, but his refusal to let me treat the stain on his shirt, after Dex had been the same way that morning about the paint on his, pushed my patience just a little too far. Why ruin a perfectly good shirt just to prove his self-sufficiency? Especially after we'd actually been making some progress towards letting me help with Adele. Why did men find it so hard to just admit they could use a little help?

Whereas Dex had dug in deeper, though, Grey gave in, and when he pulled the shirt off over his head and handed it to me, I immediately regretted asking for it in the first place. Whatever I thought might have been beneath his shirt, not that I had given it *any* real thought, it would not have prepared me for the real thing.

With his shirt on, Grey's chest looked broad and solid in a strong yet still neighbourly and fatherly way. With the shirt gone, it veered strongly and instantly into fantasy territory. His muscles were more defined than I had expected, tattoos lined one of his sides and across the front of his chest, and most unexpectedly of all, a shiny barbell pierced through one of his nipples.

My sisters had always laughed at my fondness for body piercings, but I couldn't help it: I found them incredibly sexy, and for a moment, all I could do was stare as he shook the shirt out and handed it to me. Gripping it tightly in my hands, I ran out of the room before he noticed me drooling over him.

In my laundry room, running the shirt under cold water, I shook my head, trying to dislodge the image from my memory. Up until that point, although I obviously knew that Grey was a man, I truly hadn't thought of him *that* way. His grumpiness and his position as one of my students' fathers had put a barrier between us, not to mention the fact that I'd originally assumed he must be married. Objectively, in an academic way, I'd noticed his attractiveness, but I'd never thought about it in a personal way. It hadn't had any relevance to me at all.

It still didn't, I quickly reminded myself, pouring out some vinegar and water into a bowl to soak the stain. He was still my student's father, which made any kind of relationship between us a terrible idea, not to mention that he hadn't shown a single ounce of interest in me. He barely tolerated me. I'd set myself the goal of breaking down his walls to become his friend, but anything further than that felt wildly optimistic at best and downright delusional at worst.

I would just have to forget what I saw and my reaction to it; I had no other choice. Leaving the shirt to soak, I grabbed my carpet stain remover next and returned to the dining room to deal with the flecks of sauce on the carpet.

"I can do that," Grey immediately offered as he saw me kneel down to scrub the cleaner into the floor.

"No!" I protested, a little too loudly. As long as he stayed sitting in the chair, he was mostly hidden from my view and that seemed safer all round. "No, that's fine. Please, finish your supper. It'll only take a second, I just want to do it before it has a chance to dry."

"Well, I think Adele's already done eating," he told me drily, thankfully following my instructions and staying where he was. "She devoured that."

"It's my mama's recipe." I kept my eyes down, scrubbing vigorously at the floor. The spots were coming out just fine, as I expected, but I kept scrubbing at them anyway. "She'll be delighted to hear it made such an impression."

"I watch more Pony," Adele declared from the other side of the table. Now that she'd finished, she was eager to get back to the TV.

"Not so fast, sweetheart. We're gonna get on home in a minute. Can you say thank you to Ms Callahan for your supper?"

I stood up in time for Adele to flash me an adorably wide grin. "Thank you, Ms Cally-lan!"

"You're so welcome." With my eyes fixed on her, I could almost relax again until, against my will, my gaze dropped to Grey in front of me, and *more* tattoos on his back that I could just see over the back of the chair. My heart rate immediately kicked up again as I tried not to panic. "I'll be right back."

Retreating to the safety of my laundry room, I took his shirt out of the bowl, wrung it out, and sprayed it with a stain pretreatment, using a brush to work it into the fibres of the fabric. The stain had started to come out already, and I felt certain that the shirt could be salvaged.

"Billie?"

Grey's voice nearly made me jump, and my head swivelled around, looking over my shoulder to find him standing in the doorway, his bare torso on full display and his jeans sitting dangerously low on his hips.

"I think you've done enough there. I'll take it home and wash it."

It took me a second to realize he meant the shirt in my hands and I immediately dropped the brush, as if I'd been doing something wrong. "Sure. Just give it a regular wash, immediately, and it should be good as new."

"Thanks." He stepped closer to me to take the shirt from me, making the laundry room feel smaller, almost as if it were closing in around me with each step he took. "And thanks for supper. We're gonna go, she's getting a bit restless and I don't want her to watch any more TV tonight, but, uh... listen. If you're really, entirely sure that you don't mind bringing Adele home with you after school, just until I get some other arrangements made, it would be a huge help. I would really appreciate it."

Well, that was good news, even if I felt a little too distracted to fully enjoy my victory.

"Yeah. Of course." Every word out of my mouth sounded a little too bright as I kept my gaze focused on his face and his green eyes. "We'll start on Monday."

"And you said you got plans on Tuesdays, right? I can make sure I finish up a bit early those days so you're not waiting on me."

My head nodded, feeling awkward. "That's right. It's just a family thing every Tuesday. Not a date or anything."

The words made me wince as they came out of my mouth. *Honestly, Billie?* He hadn't asked me what I was doing; why did I feel the need to clarify that I did not, in fact, have a single soul interested in me?

"Okay. Enjoy the rest of your weekend, then." Holding up his shirt and giving me a nod of acknowledgement, Grey turned around and walked away down the hall while I exhaled in both relief and embarrassment.

Monday was two days away: two days before I would see him again, and two days in which to figure out how to learn to control this new and unwanted attraction towards Grey Wright before I completely humiliated myself. On top of everything else, I didn't want him to think I had offered to watch Adele simply to get close to him, because I had some kind of schoolgirl crush.

Somehow, I needed to go back to the way I had seen him before, before it was too late.

~**Grey**~

All the next day, Billie kept popping into my mind at random times. Adele and I went grocery shopping, which always took three times longer than if I went on my own because she wanted to be the one to put everything in the shopping cart. Even though it would have been quicker to go by myself, she always had so much fun that I couldn't let her miss it. While we picked out the ingredients to make our own chilli, my mind kept drifting back to sitting at Billie's table the night before.

At the park where we went after dropping all the groceries off at home, Adele tried to play with some of the other kids on the play equipment. A few of them made half-hearted attempts to include her but most of them ignored her, and I couldn't help remembering the way Billie had spoken to the other kids in Adele's class about the differences between them.

My preoccupation made some sense to me. It had been a long time since I got to know *anyone* new. In the small town we'd lived in, the people around me never changed: neighbours I'd known for years, clients I was on polite terms with, and former friends from high school who drifted away after Adele was born and Donna and I broke up, who gave me a friendly nod if I ran into them on Main Street, but nothing more. Moving to Houston, I expected more of the same: some acquaintances, people I'd recognize but never really know, and a lot of strangers.

Instead, I'd gotten Billie.

That had to be part of why I kept thinking about her, but it also had to do with the way our supper had ended. Though she said she didn't mind the mess Adele might make, once it happened, her whole demeanour seemed to change. She wouldn't look me in the eye anymore, and she disappeared to the laundry room for so long that eventually, I had to go and find her there. Something seemed to have shifted, but I had no idea what or why.

While she'd been gone, I had more time to think over her suggestion about watching Adele and everything she said about it, and I realized I'd be an idiot not to agree. No one was going to make me a better offer, and most people would have already withdrawn it after how ungrateful I'd come across. So, I swallowed my pride and accepted it as gracefully as I could, expecting her to be pleased. Instead, she just seemed to want me to leave as soon as possible.

I had no idea what to make of any of it, except that people were confusing and unpredictable. All except Adele, who wore her heart on her sleeve and every emotion close to the surface. I always knew exactly how she felt and why, and I hoped to God that never changed.

When we arrived back home, Billie's truck was gone. "No Ms Cally-lan?" Adele asked, noticing the missing truck the same as I did.

"Not today, sweetheart. You'll see her tomorrow at school."

Adele accepted that and moved on, while I found myself wondering where Billie had gone and what she was doing. Could she be on a date? She'd made a point of telling me that her Tuesday obligation was not a date, maybe because she thought I wouldn't like the idea of Adele being around a man I didn't know? I almost wished she hadn't brought it up. By saying it, she made it clear that she *did* date, and somewhere deep inside me, a tiny little flame of jealousy stirred.

Jealousy towards the men that got to spend time with her, sure, but also something deeper and more nebulous; in a strange way, I felt jealous of the man I used to be. The one whose marriage *didn't* fall apart, the one who could get a babysitter on short notice to take a woman on a date because their child was just like everyone else's, the one who trusted people enough to believe that each of us had a happy ending in store.

The one who might have taken a woman like Billie Callahan on a date, if the situation had been different.

All the problems I thought I had earlier in my life paled in comparison to going to cardiologist appointments with my child, worrying about people mistreating her, and worrying about what would happen to her if something happened to me. Most of all, I was jealous of the version of myself who didn't know what those kinds of worries were like.

"Time to talk to Auntie June, sweetheart," I told Adele once we'd settled back in the house. Every Sunday, we had a video chat with my sister in California, the only family I had left besides the little girl at my side. Our father had skipped town when we were both young; if he was still alive, I had no idea where and I didn't care. Our mother passed away in my last year of high school. June, five years older, had already moved to the coast, and though she offered to let me go and live with her, I'd never really been tempted. I already had a job with a local plumber that he'd promised to turn into an apprenticeship as soon as I graduated. I had Donna and all our friends. My whole life was there.

When I told her Donna had given me full custody earlier that summer, she'd asked me once again to consider moving to California to be closer to her, but I still couldn't imagine it. Texas was my home, I told her. She said I just couldn't admit I might need some help.

Maybe we were both right.

"Della!" June greeted my daughter through the phone screen, completely ignoring me. "How's school? Show me your new house!"

Only after Adele had shared all her news and taken the phone on a tour of the entire house did she finally hand the phone over to me. My sister's face filled the screen, her eyes the same shade of green as mine.

"Hey, June. How are you? How's Richard?"

Richard was June's boyfriend. She called him her partner, and they'd been together for six years but had no interest in getting married or having kids. June always joked that she wasn't the maternal type, even though she'd always been an amazing aunt to Adele.

"We're fine, nothing new here. You're the one with all the big life changes. How's it going? How's Houston?"

I filled her in on my work and the admin side of Adele's school. Since Richard was a lawyer, June offered to have him look over the IEP application that I'd almost finished filling out, but I told her not to worry. "Adele's teacher is helping me with it. She lives next door, as it turns out."

"Next door, huh? And is this teacher young? Attractive? Single, maybe?"

"Why the hell would you jump to that conclusion?" For all she knew, Adele's teacher might be a 60-year-old woman with grandchildren of her own. It seemed like quite a leap to make, even if she'd hit the nail directly on the head.

June crowed in triumph. "I'm right, aren't I? You've got a tell, Grey. You've had it since you were a kid. Whenever you're interested in someone, you do the same thing. It's how I knew you were serious about Donna in the first place, before you admitted it to anyone."

"That's ridiculous." I had no idea what she was talking about, but damn it all if she hadn't made me curious anyway. "What is it?"

My sister looked far too pleased with herself. "I'm not telling you. If I do, you'll stop doing it and I'll never get any information out of you. So, what's the deal with you and the teacher?"

"There's no deal." I made every effort to keep my face completely neutral, trying not to do whatever action she thought I'd been doing. "She's offered to help with Adele. Adele likes her. That's all."

"You still haven't gone on a single date since you and Donna split up, have you?"

That had nothing to do with anything. "You ain't matchmaking from two thousand miles away, so let go of that idea right now."

"Just let me say one thing and I'll let it go, I promise."

Against my better judgement, I gave in. "What is it?"

"You can still be a good dad and have a life of your own. You're still young, Grey, but you're not getting any younger. This move is a fresh start, and I think it'll be really good for you, as long as you don't just hide in your house. Get out there, talk to people, make some friends. It's not too late."

"That was a lot more than one thing," I pointed out, but when she started to protest, I gave in again. "I'll think about it, I promise."

We hung up and Adele and I spent the rest of the day playing in the backyard and making a blanket fort in the living room before I put the extra sheets away. When I told her to get ready for bed because she had school in the morning, she couldn't have looked more excited as she babbled on about the other kids in her class and 'Ms Cally-lan' and all the fun things they were going to do.

For that reason alone, moving to Houston had been the right call. Adele had never been so excited about going to Donna's, and as long as my daughter was happy, nothing else really mattered.

Chapter Five

~**Billie**~

It always amazed me how quickly new things could start to feel routine. On Monday, I took Adele home with me after school for the first time. As I expected, she caused me no trouble in the classroom after everyone else left. As soon as I gave her some paper and crayons and asked her to draw a picture for her dad, nothing could have distracted her.

First thing that morning, I spoke to Debbie, the vice-principal, about my arrangement with Grey, just to make sure I hadn't inadvertently gone against any school policy by agreeing to provide after-school care to Adele. She assured me I hadn't, but suggested that I have Grey sign a release form as a precaution, relieving the school of any liability if anything happened to Adele while in my care outside of school hours.

It didn't take her long to locate an appropriate form on her computer and make a few changes to make it relevant. "Since you never know how people will react, we have to cover ourselves," she explained as she handed me the form off her printer. "That said, I think it's really generous of you, Billie. I'm sure Mr Wright appreciates it."

I didn't tell her how I'd practically had to beg him to let me help. "It's got to be challenging for him on his own."

"I'm sure it is," she agreed sympathetically. As I headed for the door, she added one more thing. "Just FYI, there's no policy against teachers dating students' parents either."

Immediately, the image of Grey's tattooed, pierced, muscled chest that I had been trying so hard to push down came rushing back to the front of my thoughts as I stuttered out a response. "I didn't say anything about…"

"I know. Just putting it out there." She gave me a conspiratorial smile. "If I were twenty years younger and single, it definitely would have crossed my mind."

Grey's van sat in his driveway when we pulled in after school, so I took Adele straight over there. She proudly held up her drawing to show Grey as he answered the door. "Look, Daddy! It's you!"

He immediately crouched down to take a better look as Adele giggled. "It sure is, sweetheart. Where'd you get a picture of me from?"

"I draw it!"

"You? No way! This is a photograph." He took the paper from her hands and held it up next to his face. "See? It's just the same."

My hand went to my mouth to cover my smile. The only real resemblance was the big green circles Adele had made for his eyes, but the way he praised it had the little girl beaming. How could he be so sweet with her and so brusque with everyone else?

As if to prove my point, when those green eyes finally looked over at me, they immediately grew more guarded and he quickly stood back up again. "Thanks for bringing her home."

Lowering my hand, I gave him a friendly, neighbourly smile. "No problem. I'm sorry to throw more paperwork on you, but the school asked me to get you to sign a form about me watching Adele."

He snatched the paper from my hand without glancing at it. "Sure. I'll take a look."

He seemed eager to get the door closed, but I had one more question. "Speaking of paperwork, how's the IEP application going?"

"Actually, I was going to ask you about that. Would it be okay if I sent it to you to review before I submit it? I tried to follow your advice, but I mighta missed something."

I wanted to say that I could look it over with him rather than on my own, but sitting next to him might test my resolve a little too much. His suggestion made more sense. "Sure. Email it over and I'll take a look tonight."

We said goodnight and I headed home alone. After supper, I grabbed myself a beer and went through the application. Overall, Grey had done a good job, and he obviously *had* tried to incorporate my suggestions. I made a few more notes and sent them back to him, which earned me a reply of "Thanks" and nothing else.

On Tuesday, Grey was out mowing the lawn when we came back. He had his shirt on, thankfully, but it clung to him anyway, making the contours of his body far more visible than usual. "Have fun with your family," he said before returning to his work after Adele went inside, and it pleased me more than it should have that he actually remembered I would be seeing my family that night.

At the barbecue, Tonia and Laura asked me again how school was going, and although I told them about the new addition to my class, I said nothing about Adele's dad or how they lived next door. I knew my sisters; there would be follow-up questions for days, and I wasn't ready to face them just yet, not until I felt more settled about things myself.

On Wednesday, the Wright driveway was empty when we got home, so I took Adele into my house instead. Together, we made a big taco salad, and I sent half of it home with Adele, despite Grey's protests. "She helped make it, it's half hers," I stated firmly, not taking no for an answer.

By the time Friday came around, the drop-off felt so familiar that the thought of not seeing Grey on the weekend, even just for the time it took to say hello and goodbye, felt a little strange. "Do y'all have any big plans for the weekend?" I asked him conversationally after Adele had gone inside.

"We ain't really the 'big plans' type," he told me bluntly. I almost thought he would close the door right then, but almost reluctantly, he returned the question. "What about you?"

I actually did have plans, though he might not consider them exciting. "I'm babysitting my niece and nephew tomorrow. My sister and her husband have a wedding they're going to. You might see us out in the backyard, or hear us, anyway. Charlie's a bit of a tornado at times."

"They're coming here?" He glanced in the direction of my house almost nervously.

"Yeah. Is that a problem?"

"No, of course not. No. It's fine." With that overcompensating denial, he said goodbye and closed the door.

Well, we weren't quite friends yet, but all in all, the week hadn't gone too badly. He seemed a little less stressed and Adele had enjoyed herself, so I would count it as a win.

One thing I hadn't mentioned to Grey, however, was my plan for that evening. After trying all week to get a hold of Adele's mother, texting and calling her with no response, I'd made up my mind to go and visit her in person. She'd find it a lot harder to ignore me if I were standing right in front of her.

Only an hour and a half outside of Houston, the town where Grey and Adele used to live was exactly as I expected to find it. Main Street with its flag poles and flower baskets, the churches, the well-kept lawns and the single-level brick school all looked so familiar, it could have easily been a clone for my own hometown. Only the people were different.

Though I didn't know for sure if Donna still lived at the last address that had been filed with Adele's old school district, I figured it would be the best place to start. Even if she'd moved, the new residents would likely know where to find her.

The white-sided house looked much the same as the others on the street, all built in the 70s or 80s, each with a big lawn and flowerbed. A car sat in the driveway, which I hoped that meant someone would be home. The time had just passed seven o'clock in the evening.

The ring of the doorbell brought a man to the door, around thirty years old and not wearing a shirt. His chest wasn't anywhere near as appealing as Grey's, I couldn't help noticing. "Yeah?" he asked, keeping the screen door shut as he looked me up and down.

"Howdy. I'm looking for Donna, is she at home?"

"Who's asking?"

His response suggested she did still live there, so I gave my name. "Billie Callahan."

I didn't say anything else about who I was or why I'd come. She'd read my texts, I could tell she had, so she ought to recognize my name.

With a grunt, he wandered back into the house, and a moment later, a woman came to the door, her eyes almost panicked. "What are you doing here?"

Nice to meet you too, I thought. She was pretty, with long, dark hair that Adele had clearly inherited. Obviously, I had the right woman, but I said her name anyway just to be sure. "Donna? You didn't return any of my calls or texts. As I said in them, I need to speak with you about Adele's schooling."

Glancing over her shoulder, she quickly let herself out the door, stepping onto the front step as I took a step back. Only once she'd closed the door behind her did she speak again. "Look, I'm moving on, alright? My new husband doesn't want to be reminded of my previous marriage. That's all in the past."

Her *daughter* was in the past? Instantly, my indignation flared, but I took a deep breath to keep myself under control. Grey hadn't mentioned that she'd remarried.

"I'm not here to cause any trouble for you and your husband. I just need to know what you and Adele were working on together, and what works or doesn't work for her in terms of how she learns. It won't take long, and we could have just done it over the phone if you'd returned my calls. She's already been in my class for a week and a half."

"So you decided to come and stalk me at home? How did you get my address? Is this even legal?"

A sharp retort sat on the end of my tongue, but something made me pause. Behind her belligerence and defensiveness, I caught a brief glimpse of something else, and it reminded me, God help me, of my brother, and the way he'd been withdrawing and lashing out over the previous months.

Maybe, behind all her bravado, sat a pain that she'd never fully acknowledged. Maybe the way to get her cooperation wouldn't be through threats or admonishments, but through understanding instead?

With that in mind, I swallowed down my comeback and made her an offer instead: "Do you want to go out and get a drink somewhere?"

The bar Donna took me to looked just like every other small-town bar I'd ever been to. We sat down at a table near the back, away from the men gathered around the bar to watch the football game, and presumably where no one could hear our conversation, as if we'd gone there to discuss something illegal or shameful.

"You got kids?" she asked me bluntly after taking a long drink from her bottle of beer.

My drink was non-alcoholic, since I still had to drive back to Houston that night, but it gave me something to do with my hands as I sat there, and I shook my head in response to her question. "No. Not yet."

"How old are you?"

I hadn't gone all that way to talk about myself, but I hoped that the more I opened up to her and set her at ease, the more she'd be willing to share with me, so I answered her question honestly. "Twenty-three. Twenty-four next month."

"Married?"

"No. Not in a relationship at all, actually."

Her bottle returned to her lips. "So, you have no idea. You don't know what any of it's like."

My grip tightened around my own bottle, the condensation cool against my hands, but I kept my tone even. "I'm just here to talk about teaching Adele. I have no interest in passing judgement on anything about your life. I don't know what it's like in your shoes."

"No, you don't." With a sigh, she put the bottle back down on the table. "What did Grey tell you?"

Hearing her say his name so casually, reminding me of how intimately they'd once been involved, sent an unexpected spike of jealousy through my body, completely irrationally.

I pushed it back down to focus on more important things. "He said you looked after Adele's kindergarten and first grade curriculum from home. That's why I want to speak to you, about what methods you used and what she responded best to..."

Donna cut me off before I could finish. "I mean: what did he tell you about me?"

He really hadn't said very much at all, other than that it might not be easy to talk to her. He definitely had that right. "I don't really know Mr Wright very well. Mostly, we just talk about Adele."

She seemed almost put out by that, as if she should come up all the time. "What about Adele? What does she say about me?"

The truth was that I'd never heard Adele mention her mother. Though I answered honestly, I did my best to soften that news. "She doesn't really talk about anyone unless she's directly asked about them. I haven't asked her about you."

"You must think I'm a horrible mother. A horrible person." Her eyes darted furtively around the bar, as if someone else might be listening, even though no one else seemed to have even glanced at us since we sat down.

"I told you: I'm not here to judge you. I don't know anything about you. I'm just here to talk about Adele and..."

"If I'd found out what was wrong with her during my pregnancy, I would have had an abortion. That's why they do the test, isn't it?"

My blink lasted longer than usual as I tried to figure out how on earth to respond to that in a way that wouldn't trigger her. "I don't think that's *why* they do the test, but I know many women do make that choice. It's a very personal decision."

Donna nodded bitterly. "A decision that I never got to make because the doctor didn't do the test right. We didn't know until she was born, and by then, it was too late."

"I didn't know that." Grey hadn't mentioned it, and why should he?

Donna was just getting started. "Grey was so damn determined to see the bright side. He kept talking about how we would adjust and adapt to everything, but I didn't want a pep talk. I wanted to grieve. The little girl I thought we were going to have, the one I carried in my heart for nine months during my pregnancy, I lost her that day. It felt like she died, and no one ever acknowledged that. Instead, I was supposed to just accept the fact that we had to spend the rest of our lives looking after this other child, a child who could never care for herself."

Obviously, she needed to get these things off her chest, so I didn't interrupt.

"He kept saying it would get better and that eventually, it would feel normal, but it didn't. Everyone talked about us. They'd whisper and stare when we went out with her, and Grey didn't care. He didn't understand how I felt. He never even tried."

"People have different coping mechanisms," I pointed out as non-judgmentally as I could. "It probably wasn't easy for him either, he just dealt with it differently."

She continued as if I hadn't spoken. "All my friends had their perfect kids and their perfect lives, and I had a broken daughter and a husband who hated me."

"I'm sure he didn't hate you." The words came out almost as a reflex, though of course, I couldn't speak for Grey.

Donna disagreed anyway. "He did. I could see it in his eyes. He used to look at me like I was the most precious thing in the world. He used to have a wicked sense of humour. He used to laugh all the time."

Grey laughed all the time? The image couldn't quite take shape in my mind, it seemed so unlikely. I'd barely seen him smile, other than when he looked at Adele.

"Things changed. He looked at her the way he used to look at me, and he turned so cold toward me. He snapped at me all the time. So, I left. What else could I do?"

Without being a marriage counsellor, I really couldn't answer that question. Besides, none of what she said had anything to do with the reason I had come to talk to her, so I tried to steer us back towards the subject I really needed to discuss. "You stayed in Adele's life, though. You decided to home school her."

"How could I send her to school?" she asked me bluntly. "Everyone else had their Instagram-perfect first day of school pictures. What did I have?"

A sweet, loving, wonderful little girl, I replied in my head, but out loud, I pushed ahead with my official line of questioning. "So, what did you teach her at home? She knows most of her letters and numbers, which is great. How did you teach her those?"

Finally, she answered me. "She watched Sesame Street a lot. Dora. Alphabet videos on YouTube. There are all kinds of educational videos on there."

Although I had an answer, it wasn't exactly the one I'd hoped for. It sounded like Donna had let the TV do most of the teaching for her. "What about flashcards? Board games to help with counting? Anything like that?"

She shook her head. "No one told me how to do any of that."

Frustration bubbled up inside me, even more than before. "That's why there are courses for you to take when you apply to home school a child. You must have had visits from the school district? Didn't they tell you about them?"

Donna shrugged. "The woman who came said kids like Adele would never catch up anyway, so I should just do the best I could do."

Unfortunately, I knew that attitude still persisted among a lot of people, but all I could think was how badly Adele had been let down. She'd lost out on two years of school where she could have not only been learning but having the social interaction she craved so much. Instead, she'd been stuck at home in front of a TV with a mother who resented her.

"Why did you decide to stop teaching her?" I asked, trying to close out the conversation now that I knew I wouldn't be getting any of the useful information I'd hoped for.

"I met my new husband." For the first time, something that could almost be called hope showed up on her face. "He wanted to get married and he wants a family of our own. He didn't want to be Adele's stepdad. She always liked Grey better anyway, so I gave him full custody and they moved away. She'll be happier without me."

Did she truly believe that, or did she convince herself of it so that she could carry on with the rest of her life as if her daughter had never existed at all?

I'd heard enough. "Alright, I think I've got what I need. Thanks for your time, Donna."

I got to my feet, pushing my chair back firmly while she looked up at me in surprise. "That's it?"

"Yeah, that's it. Unless you have anything else to tell me about Adele's education?"

As I expected, she didn't. "You said you wouldn't judge me," she reminded me sullenly, making it all about her again. "But you are. I can tell."

My frustration finally bubbled over. "I can't judge you as a mother or a wife. I haven't had to walk in your shoes. But as a teacher, I can tell you that you did that little girl more harm than good. She's capable of so much more than you gave her credit for. Luckily, her dad is going to make sure she gets what she needs."

There was so much more I could have said, but I'd made my point. Leaving her sitting in the bar alone, I headed back to my truck and back home, a little more knowledgeable about the whole situation than I'd been when I arrived, and a little sadder about it too.

~Grey~

The news that Billie would be babysitting at her house on Saturday put an idea in my head, one that I couldn't shake no matter how much I tried to convince myself I should just mind my own business like I'd been intending to all along.

What she'd done for me with Adele that week had been more helpful than I could have imagined. Knowing I didn't have to worry about getting to the school on time took a huge weight off my shoulders. I could take on more jobs and do them better, and by the time Adele got home, I'd had a moment to decompress rather than still carrying the stress of the day with me. Honestly, it made me a better father, more like the one Adele deserved.

I'd also gotten the IEP application submitted, taking another worry off my plate, and thanks to Billie's suggestions, I felt it did a really good job of describing Adele's needs and strengths. Because I got home before she did nearly every day, I'd also had time to finish unpacking the rest of our boxes. The house had started to feel like home, and although it still needed a little fixing up here and there, for the most part, things felt under control again.

I had Billie to thank for just about all of that, and maybe inviting her and her niece and nephew over to our place for a barbecue might be a good way to show my appreciation.

It meant spending more time with her, but surely, with three kids to look after, things wouldn't get too personal. It'd be a simple thank you, and we could go straight back to our separate lives afterwards.

It felt like the right thing to do.

Adele took her job as party planner very seriously when I explained it to her at the grocery store. "You can pick out one bag of chips for everyone to share and one dessert."

Carefully, she studied the pictures on each bag, asking me for my favourite flavour, and Billie's favourite flavour, which of course I didn't know, before finally settling on plain ripple chips since no one could dislike that. At the bakery, I thought we might have to pull up a chair because she stared at the different cakes for so long before finally deciding on an apple pie.

Back at our house, I set her the task of creating an invitation to take over to Billie. Having Adele deliver the invitation would make her more likely to say yes, I figured. I had to make use of the advantages I had.

When she had it finished, we walked next door where Adele rang the doorbell while I stood back, there as backup but wanting to stay out of the spotlight.

"Good morning!" Billie exclaimed as she opened the door, looking fresh and casual. Her light brown hair hung down over her shoulders for a change and she wore a blue-and-white striped top with navy capris, ready for the warm late summer day that had been forecast. The blue colour seemed to highlight her blue eyes, and her feet were bare as she bent down to get eye-level with Adele. "How did you know I was missing you?"

Adele's grin couldn't get any wider. "We barbecue!" she announced, shoving her hand-drawn invitation into Billie's face. "You can come."

Billie's eyes flitted over to me for the first time, curious and slightly confused. "What's happening?"

"We're gonna have a barbecue out in the backyard tonight," I explained. My hands suddenly felt awkward, like I didn't know what to do with them, so I shoved them into the pockets of my jeans. "You said you got kids coming over, right? You can bring 'em and I can cook. Unless you already have other plans."

It hadn't occurred to me until right that second that she might have already cooked something, or at least planned something out. I already knew she was a good cook, so it didn't seem like a stretch.

Surprise flashed across her face before she looked back down at the invitation. "Is this you and daddy in the backyard?" she asked Adele, who nodded vigorously as Billie pointed to figures on the invitation. "And this is me?"

"And kids!" Adele added. She seemed just as excited about the idea of having someone to play with as she did about the dessert she'd bought, though I didn't have any idea how old Billie's niece and nephew were or if they would be comfortable playing with Adele.

Billie seemed genuinely charmed by the drawing. "Well, I can't say no to such a beautiful invitation. We'd love to come."

Adele squealed in excitement before turning around and running back towards our house.

"Where are you going?" I called out after her.

"Toys!" she yelled back as Billie laughed.

I gave her a sheepish shrug. "I should go and keep an eye on that."

"Yeah, of course." She smiled over at me as she stood back up, still holding the invitation in her hands. "What time should we show up?"

"Whenever you want." Wincing at how indecisive that sounded, I tried again. "I mean, whenever the kids need to eat. We'll be out back so just come on over."

"Sounds good. See you later, then." She gave me one more smile before going back inside her house, while I jogged after Adele who'd already made it to our front door.

I soon realized that by 'toys', she meant preparing the toys that she wanted to share with her guests later that afternoon. She went through nearly everything in her toy box, lining them all up and organizing them into piles, until I realized she actually wanted to take them *all* to the backyard.

"Pick three," I told her, which drew the pouting lip out of hiding. She even stomped around the room a little bit in frustration, but when I didn't give in, she eventually settled on her three picks to share.

Just after five o'clock, we'd already moved outside when a little blonde-haired boy came barrelling into the backyard. I'd left the gate open for Billie, so it came as a relief when she followed soon after, holding a little girl in her arms.

"Charlie, say hi before you start playing," she called after the boy, who had already started running circles around the lawn. "This is Mr Wright and Adele."

Charlie immediately changed course, heading to Adele. "Hi! Chase me!" Turning around, he took off again, and Adele immediately followed after him, not missing a beat.

"Simple as that, huh?" I marvelled as I watched them running after each other as if they'd known each other their whole lives. "Kids have it easy sometimes."

"They do," Billie agreed with a laugh as she walked up the steps to join me on the deck. "Can you imagine if I just walked up to you the first time we met and ordered you to chase me?"

Completely unbidden, my mind immediately conjured up images of chasing after Billie, her shrieks of laughter, adrenaline running through my body, and the feel of her in my arms when I caught her.

Where the hell did *that* come from?

"That would... that would be weird," I agreed weakly before clearing my throat. "So, the one running around is Charlie. Who's this?"

The little girl in Billie's arms turned away as soon as I glanced down at her, burying her face in Billie's neck.

Billie smiled down at her affectionately. "This is Jenny, who might be the only shy Callahan in existence. No one knows where she got it from, but definitely not from her mama. I told her that Adele probably has some colouring books she could play with?"

"I'm sure she does. Let me go and find one."

After grabbing a colouring book and some crayons from Adele's room, I made my way back, pausing for just a second as I reached the back door. The scene outside could hardly look more idyllic: food laid out, Billie and Jenny standing on the deck watching Adele and Charlie chase each other around the yard. For a brief second, I got a flash of the life I used to dream about, with a big family and a beautiful, caring wife who loved both me and our kids fiercely.

I'd given up on that dream a long time ago. Life had other plans for me, it seemed, but standing there at that moment and watching them, it suddenly didn't feel quite so out of reach as it once had.

Chapter Six

~Billie~

Grey's invitation came as a surprise, and the actual barbecue was an even bigger one. While I wouldn't have called him friendly, necessarily, at least he behaved hospitably. It helped that he seemed to have a genuine soft spot for kids and not just his own. Even though Jenny refused to look at him, he made an effort to put her at ease but also knew when to back off and give her some space.

Charlie was a lot easier to win over. As long as a person wanted to play with him, they were his friend, simple as that. Before we went over, I gave him a quick explanation about Down Syndrome, appropriate for a 4-year-old, just so he wouldn't be surprised by Adele's appearance, but he seemed supremely unconcerned about any of it. "Does she play?" was his only concern, and when I assured him she did, that was good enough for him.

While the kids played and coloured, Grey barbecued some hot dogs and burgers. Ahead of time, he'd already prepared a salad, though he didn't insist that the kids eat any if they didn't want to. A bag of chips and some lemonade rounded out the meal, served with plastic plates and cups that no one had to worry about dropping. Dessert was apple pie and ice cream, proudly served by Adele, and from the silence that descended over the picnic table as they devoured it, it couldn't have gone over any better.

Clearly, the man knew his way around children, and I found that far more attractive than I should have.

We didn't have time to say much to each other before or during the meal, since the kids were the focal point, but after we'd finished and he'd taken all the dishes inside, assuring me he could clean them up later, he returned to the deck with a beer for each of us.

Jenny had overcome her shyness around Adele enough to run around on the lawn too. Although she didn't take part in Charlie and Adele's game, which seemed to be some kind of cross between Hide and Seek and Tag, she didn't avoid them either. Standing side-by-side on the deck as we watched them, Grey and I both took a drink.

"You've got a pretty tight-knit family, then?" he asked, keeping his eyes on the activity on the lawn. "Y'all seem pretty close if you have supper every week."

"Yeah, I guess so." It just seemed normal to me, but I knew not all families were the same. "It used to be every two weeks, but now that we've got the kids, it's gone to every week so they can get to know their cousins. I've got one brother and two sisters. I'm the youngest. What about you?"

"I'm the youngest too, but I've only got one sister. She lives out in California."

That might have been one of the most personal things he'd shared with me, and I tried to encourage him to tell me more without pushing too hard. "I can't imagine my family being that far away. What about your parents?"

"Not around."

That could mean a number of things, but I managed to bite my tongue to keep from asking. From his tone, I could guess he had nothing else he wanted to say on the subject. Instead, I shared more about my own family, hoping that by being open with him, he'd feel more comfortable sharing with me in return.

"My parents moved to Houston a few years ago. Daddy had a heart attack and had to retire, so he and my mom came here. My brother, Dex, is the oldest, and he lost his wife to cancer a couple of years ago. Then there's Tonia, she's married to Cam, and Charlie and Jenny are their kids. My sister, Laura, lives out on the ranch we grew up on, married to Jesse and they run it together. They have a baby now, but they still come into the city for our family supper most weeks. And then there's me, and you know all about me."

Grey glanced over at me, his lips twitching almost as if he wanted to smile. "Ain't no way I'm going to remember all that."

"Don't worry, there won't be a quiz until next week." I gave him a teasing smile, and I thought I caught a hint of a smile in return on his face before he turned back to the yard, his eyes finding his daughter again.

"I also wouldn't say I know all about you. All I really know is that you're a teacher and you're..."

He trailed off there, leaving me in suspense. "I'm what?"

Pushy? Intrusive? Too talkative? It could be any number of things.

"Nothing." He shook his head sharply before taking another drink from his beer. "What made you want to be a teacher?"

I shrugged as I brought my bottle back to my lips, the cool glass feeling refreshing in the evening heat. "A lot of the reasons most people do, I guess. I like kids, I like helping them learn. Since I had no younger siblings of my own, I used to set up all my dolls around the room and teach them classes. It's what I always wanted to do."

"I guess some people are more naturally suited to it," he mused.

"And some aren't," I agreed, my mind flashing back to my conversation with Donna the night before. I hadn't mentioned to Grey yet that I had been to see her, but I probably should. I didn't know how often they were in touch, but if Donna mentioned it to him, I didn't want him to feel I'd kept it from him. Since he'd given me an opening, I decided to bring it up then. "On that subject, I spoke to Donna about Adele's education."

Grey almost choked on the drink he'd just taken, coughing a couple of times before he could swallow again. My hands itched to reach out and rub his back, but I didn't know if he wanted me to touch him. I didn't know if it would be a good idea from my point of view either. The vision of him shirtless was still very strong in my mind; I didn't need to know what it felt like too.

"She actually talked to you?" he asked in surprise once he'd got himself back under control.

"Well, I didn't give her much choice," I admitted. "I went to her house."

"You... what?" I had his full attention by that point, those green eyes of his staring at me in complete bewilderment.

Trying to hold his gaze calmly, I filled him in. "She wasn't answering my calls and I wanted to talk to her, so I went there. We had a drink together and she told me what she'd done with Adele. I can add that information into the IEP review when the school responds to your application."

He blinked at me slowly a couple of times, still trying to wrap his head around it. "What did you learn?"

He sounded nervous, as if Donna might have told me things about him he would rather I didn't know, but I stuck to the topic of his daughter in my response, being as diplomatic as I could be. "It doesn't seem like she did a lot of formal teaching. Based on what Adele picked up, it probably means she's a visual learner and my aide and I can use that to adapt the way we teach her."

Despite my attempt at diplomacy, Grey caught my meaning immediately. "Donna sat her in front of the TV all day, you mean?"

I'd been trying *not* to say that, and though I didn't deny it, I still tried to put a positive spin on it. "At least she chose some educational programs to show her."

Grey's jaw clenched, his grip tightening around the bottle in his hand. "You must think we're horrible parents for not putting her in school before."

I certainly hadn't thought anything like that, and especially not about Grey. "There are a lot of factors that go into a decision like that. You said you didn't know exactly what they worked on, so I'm guessing you thought there was a bit more teaching going on than there was."

"I shouldn't have assumed."

The self-recrimination in his voice made my heart ache. From everything I'd seen of him so far, he always had Adele's best interests at heart. He must have been convinced that keeping Adele at home would be best or he wouldn't have done it.

The comfortable, companionable atmosphere that had presided over the rest of the barbecue dissipated as Grey's body grew tenser, much more like how he'd been the first few times I'd met him. I could almost see him closing himself off again.

It came as no real surprise to me, then, when he called an end to the entire evening. "It's getting late," he stated bluntly. "I've got to get Adele ready for bed."

That seemed like a stretch. Still running around the yard with Charlie, she didn't look close to tired, not to mention that there was no school the next day.

However, we were his guests, so if he wanted us to go, we'd have to go. I didn't want to overstay my welcome, so I placed my half-full beer down on the deck railing. "Alright. Thanks for having us."

I almost thought I saw a brief flash of regret in his eyes in response to my cool tone, but only for a second. Soon, his expression closed off again as he called down to Adele to tell her to say goodbye. All the kids protested, but Grey had made up his mind, so I went down to pick up Jenny and try to corral Charlie.

Grey stood by the gate to close it behind us after we left, and though he tried to avoid my eye when I walked past, I stopped anyway, speaking quietly enough that the kids wouldn't hear me. "You're a great dad, Grey. Don't be so hard on yourself."

I didn't expect an answer, so I didn't wait for one. With my niece and nephew in tow, I returned to my house with my heart heavier than it had been. It seemed like every time I made any progress with Grey, we immediately took an even bigger step back. What would it take to break through his walls once and for all?

~**Grey**~

Billie's words kept ringing in my head as I tried to sleep. *Don't be so hard on yourself,* she told me, but she had no idea. It had become second nature for me to second-guess my actions; my only real regret from that evening was that I took out my frustration on her rather than keeping it inside where it belonged.

Once upon a time, before Adele was born, I thought I'd done everything right. My dreams weren't big. Wealth and fame didn't appeal to me. All I really wanted was a steady job and a family like the one my friends had: one where money wasn't a constant worry, one where the dad *didn't* leave, where the parents loved each other and their kids enough to stick it out through the hard times.

It didn't seem like all that much to ask.

Every major decision I made had been with that goal in mind, including my choice of career. Plumbing provided a steady, reliable income, not subject to extremes of supply and demand. I didn't care about a fancy title; I wanted dependability, and people would always need a plumber. I didn't propose to Donna until I had enough put away to make the down payment on our house, and we didn't start trying for a baby until I had a savings plan in place for that child's education. I never jumped into anything, never made any impulsive decisions. Hell, we never even had sex without a condom until I felt sure we could afford it if her birth control failed.

In Donna, I thought I'd found someone with the same dreams. June called her lazy, but she'd never spent much time with her in person. I saw someone content with what we had, who kept an immaculate home and took pride in it. Sure, she spent a bit more than I would have liked on home decor to post on her social media, but it made her happy. I didn't begrudge her that happiness. The simple pleasures made life worth living, I'd always believed that, and when she was happy, no one shone brighter. She made me feel damn lucky to have her.

The nursery had been her biggest project of all. For months, it consumed her as she spent hours making sure everything would be perfect in time for our baby's arrival. With the same crib that celebrities had and a closet full of clothes that would match and complement Donna's own wardrobe, she did a live tour of it online the week before Adele arrived. All her followers exclaimed over it, commenting about how jealous they were, and in some ways, I could understand why that pleased her. Though I didn't feel the need to show it off, as far as I was concerned, life felt pretty much perfect.

After we brought Adele home, things changed. All the pretty clothes in her closet went untouched. The planned mother and daughter photoshoot got cancelled, and gradually, I began to see how our entire relationship had been an illusion in the first place. When Donna was happy, everything felt right with the world, but when she wasn't, our home became oppressive.

I'd seen her in a bad mood before; everyone had bad days, but usually, buying her something would help to pull her out of it. Not that time, though. A cloud descended over us that no amount of effort on my part seemed to dispel, and gradually, I began to see that she'd never been the woman I thought she was in the first place. Adversity shows you what a person's really made of, and it showed me that the whole life I'd built for myself had been based on a mirage.

That came down to me. I had to bear the blame for letting myself be so completely blinded to the truth, and the fact that she hadn't been doing anything to teach Adele properly didn't surprise me nearly as much as it should have. I had wanted to give her the benefit of the doubt, even though she hadn't earned it, and so I left it all in her hands.

I should have fought harder for my little girl. That thought was the one that hurt most of all.

In the morning, Adele babbled excitedly about her guests from the night before, asking me again and again over breakfast when we could see Charlie and Jenny again.

"I don't know, sweetheart. I'm not sure where they live. They were only visiting Ms Callahan." She looked so disappointed, not with her fake pout but genuine disappointment, that I quickly amended my answer. "I'll ask her next time we see her."

How I would do that, I didn't quite know. After all but kicking Billie out the night before, I couldn't imagine she would be thrilled to see me again.

It came as a complete surprise, then, when someone knocked on my door just after lunch. When I went to open it, a man in jeans and a t-shirt stood there, wearing a friendly smile.

I'd never seen him before in my life.

"Yes?" I kept my greeting polite but brusque. Maybe he was another neighbour, or maybe he just wanted to sell me something. I had no idea why someone would be knocking on my door in Houston.

"Howdy. You're Grey?"

The fact that the man knew my name only made me more confused. "Yes. And you are?"

"Cam Bailey. Nice to meet you." He stuck out his hand to shake mine, and though I accepted the handshake, I still had no idea what was going on. Thankfully, his next words made things a lot clearer. "I understand you met my kids last night: Charlie and Jenny."

That would make him Billie's brother-in-law, which did explain a few things, though not exactly why he was on my front step. "Yeah, we did. They're great kids. Adele's already been asking to play with them again."

"How about now?" he offered, and when my brow furrowed in confusion, he laughed. "Long story short: I've got tickets to the Astros game this afternoon. My wife and I were supposed to go while Billie had the kids, but Tonia had a bit too much fun at the wedding last night. She forgets she's not twenty-one anymore."

The affection in his voice as he spoke about his wife made it abundantly clear he found her behaviour endearing rather than frustrating.

"Anyway, she'd rather skip the game, so Billie suggested you might want to go instead while Tonia stays with her. Adele could go over to Billie's and play with the kids while we're gone. If you ain't already got plans, that is."

I could mostly follow that, but it felt completely out of the blue. "You really want to take a stranger to the game?"

Cam laughed. "Once you're in with one of the Callahans, you're no longer a stranger. And yeah, as long as you know something about the game, I'd rather go with you than alone. You'd be doing me a favour."

It had been a long, long time since I'd gone out anywhere without Adele. I worked all day and I spent my evenings and weekends with her. Friends were a luxury I didn't have time for, and eventually, all the ones I used to have stopped trying. I couldn't blame them when I kept turning them down.

I had no real reason to turn Cam down, though. We had no plans. Obviously, I already felt safe leaving Adele with Billie, and Adele would be thrilled at the chance to see her new friends again. I couldn't really understand why Billie would have suggested it after the way I behaved the night before, but I appreciated that she had.

The more I thought about it, the more I liked the idea. "That sounds great, actually. Let me get Adele ready and I'll bring her over."

"Perfect. See you soon."

Cam headed back next door while I went to tell Adele the good news. The weekend was turning out to be a lot more eventful than I had anticipated, all thanks to my irrepressible next-door neighbour.

~Billie~

Tonia turned eagerly towards the front door as Cam came back in. "Well?"

"He's coming," Cam replied. "Said he'll be over in a few minutes."

That news both delighted and surprised me. I'd been half-afraid Grey would slam the door in Cam's face or just refuse to answer the door at all. More likely, I thought he'd find an excuse for why he couldn't go to the ball game. The chances of him actually agreeing had seemed pretty small to me, but I couldn't be happier that he had. Grey needed a chance to relax, and Cam was good at setting people at ease. They should get along well.

Maybe that was why he'd agreed? Because Cam asked and not me? Maybe he only found *me* annoying? That thought dampened my excitement just a touch, but I was still glad he'd accepted.

Tonia, on the other hand, had other matters on her mind. "That's not what I meant. Is he hot?"

I rolled my eyes, trying not to flush at the memory of Grey's bare chest and just how attractive I found him, while Cam chuckled. "Not sure I'm qualified to be the judge of that, Sugar. You can see for yourself when he gets here."

"Men," Tonia complained good-naturedly, shaking her head as Cam walked past us through the living room. She called out after him as he headed down the hall to the bathroom. "If you asked me to check out a woman for you, I would do a much better job."

"Good to know!" he called back before shutting the door behind him.

Left on our own again, I turned to my sister. "Tonia, I'm begging you: don't go embarrassing him when he gets here. I'm serious. He barely tolerates me."

It hadn't been my idea to bring up Grey at all when Tonia and Cam arrived, explaining that they'd decided not to go to the game that afternoon because Tonia couldn't handle the bright sunshine with her headache. Charlie had been the one to let the cat out of the bag, telling them all about the barbecue and his new friend, Adele.

Reluctantly, I explained about both Adele and Grey, and Tonia immediately latched onto the 'single' part of single dad, as I knew she would.

Next thing I knew, she had decided that Adele should come over to play with her kids while she recovered, and Cam and Grey could have a 'playdate' of their own. Once Tonia got an idea in her head, very little would stop her, and Cam barely put up a fight, mostly since he still wanted to go to the game.

I really hadn't thought Grey would say yes.

"Don't be silly! He'd be a fool not to appreciate you," my sister replied firmly and protectively. "And the fact that he's the dad of your student makes it even better! It's a little taboo, which you like, but it's not entirely inappropriate."

Although I narrowed my eyes at her, she did have a point. I often fell for the guys I knew I couldn't have, like my TA in college or the teacher I'd been assigned to assist during my first placement. Hell, I'd even had a not-so-secret appreciation for Laura's husband when they first got together. I didn't like them *because* they were off-limits though, it just worked out that the men who appealed to me were often unavailable.

Grey certainly fit that bill, not because of the school connection, since the vice-principal had informed me it would be allowed, but because he'd made himself emotionally unavailable. For my own sake, I needed to focus on him as a friend and nothing more, since anything further seemed doomed to end in disappointment. At that point, even getting him to regard me as a friend seemed like a tall order.

When the knock at the door came, Tonia sprang up off the sofa remarkably quickly for someone who claimed to be nursing a hangover. Though I scrambled up after her, she beat me to the door by a couple of seconds, opening it to reveal a very excited-looking Adele and an uncomfortable-looking Grey. He had his usual jeans and t-shirt on, along with a pair of ridiculously sexy sunglasses. They hid his green eyes but gave him an almost irresistible air of mystery.

It didn't take much to see that my sister appreciated the view too.

"Hi!" Adele greeted us both brightly. "I'm here to play!"

"Of course, sweetie, go right on in," Tonia invited, as if it were her house rather than mine. "Charlie and Jenny are at the table in the dining room."

Adele remembered exactly where that was from her previous visit, which Tonia obviously noticed. I would have to answer some questions later, I already knew, but for the time being, she turned her full attention to Grey.

"It's good to meet you, Grey. I'm Tonia, Billie's sister."

"Nice to meet you, ma'am." He stepped forward to offer his hand, and I could practically see Tonia assessing the strength of his grip along with every other part of him. "You've got some great kids. Adele sure had fun with them yesterday."

His manners were back, and though he still didn't look entirely comfortable, he seemed to have regained his composure from the night before.

"They had fun with her too," Tonia assured him. "It's the first thing we heard about when we got here. It's a good thing, too; otherwise, we wouldn't have known you existed."

She shot me a pointed look while I tried not to react. "I hope you have a good time this afternoon," I said to Grey, ignoring my sister.

With the sunglasses on, I couldn't tell which of us he was looking at, but he nodded in my direction. "Thanks for keeping an eye on Adele."

"Well, you know, it's a real hardship when she's such a handful," I teased him gently. "Are you an Astros fan?"

I had no idea what kinds of things he enjoyed or what he did for fun. It had never come up.

"I used to be. Haven't followed them much lately." He didn't say why not, but I had a good guess. All his attention had been focused elsewhere. "It'll be nice to go to a game."

It sounded like he meant that, and Cam came up behind us right then, gently moving his wife out of the way. "Alright, we're off, then. You ladies have a fun afternoon."

"You too. Don't do anything I wouldn't do." Tonia gave him a kiss before he headed out the door.

"That leaves our options wide open, then," Cam assured Grey, throwing Tonia a teasing look, full of affection.

The two men headed out to Cam and Tonia's SUV while my sister and I stood at the door, watching them go.

"Thank you for not putting him on the spot," I murmured to her. All things considered, she'd been incredibly restrained.

"If you want the same treatment when he comes back, you're going to answer *all* my questions before then," Tonia stated sweetly, as if what she just said didn't qualify as blackmail.

"There's nothing to tell," I tried to protest.

"Then why are you blushing?" Tonia grinned as my cheeks turned even redder. "Come on. Let's go make sure nothing's getting destroyed in there, and then you can start from the beginning. I want to know *everything*."

Chapter Seven

~Grey~

Cam let me buy him a beer and a hot dog since he got the tickets for the game, and as we took our seats on the third base line in the warm afternoon sun, I felt more at peace than I had in months. Maybe even years.

When I moved to Houston, my expectations were pretty low. Basically, I just wanted to get away from Donna. She made it clear that her new boyfriend didn't want anything to do with Adele, and therefore, she didn't either. The idea of running into her while out grocery shopping or playing at the park, Adele getting excited to see her mom and Donna ignoring her or worse, broke my damn heart. I wouldn't put her through it, and so I uprooted the only life I'd ever known and moved somewhere where we didn't know anyone because it seemed better than the alternative.

However, rather than feeling isolated and alone like I expected upon moving to the city, we were quickly finding a better life than the one we'd left behind. The new house was coming together and so was my job. At first, I thought I'd miss working for myself, but in a way, I was still my own boss, just without the headache of managing all the bookkeeping. The client from my first day had left me a bad review, as I expected, but the guy who'd signed me up told me not to worry.

All my other reviews so far had been good and he cared more about the average than one petty complaint. Even more important, Adele was getting settled at school and making friends, and for the first time ever, she had someone else looking out for her other than just me. I had no idea why Billie had gone out of her way to help us. Lord knew I hadn't given her any reason to. When I went to drop Adele off at her house, I wore my sunglasses to hide my awkwardness, knowing she had every right to be annoyed with me, but instead, she acted as if nothing had happened, as if I'd done nothing wrong even though we both knew I had.

Did anything ever get her down?

Before I could try to figure out a way to ask the man sitting next to me, Cam brought her up himself. "How long have you been living next door to Billie?"

"Just a couple of weeks. It seems to have been a stroke of good luck to get her as a neighbour, and not just because of the free baseball tickets."

Cam grinned, taking a drink of his beer as we watched the pitcher throw a perfect strike. "Billie's great. You couldn't ask for a more loyal friend than a Callahan. Long as you stay on their good side, that is."

"Does she have a bad side?" I honestly hadn't seen one yet.

Cam's grin turned into a laugh. "She's probably the least prickly one. They're all stubborn and blunt and will tell you exactly how it is, but out of all of them, I'd say Billie's the least likely to go off on someone without a reason. You know what they say about still waters, though: she feels things deeply. She'll give you the shirt off her back if you need it, but if you cross her, there's no coming back."

I would definitely have to keep that in mind. How close had I come to the line already, I wondered?

In any case, I didn't want to make the afternoon all about me. "How long have you and Tonia been together?"

"That's kind of a long story. We were together for years in high school, then apart for almost six years, and then we got back together for good."

"Sounds complicated," I observed, which made Cam laugh again.

"I s'pose so, but worth it in the end." The affectionate gleam in his eye whenever his wife was mentioned made it clear he meant it. "What about you? Any chance you'd get back together with your ex?"

I nearly choked on my beer. "No. None."

"That bad, huh?" He gave me a sympathetic smile, but didn't push for any further details, which I appreciated.

After a few more minutes of watching the game, the crowd around us buzzing as the home team took an early lead, I tentatively brought the conversation back around to his sister-in-law. "Billie's been helping me out with Adele, which has been a godsend, but I need to make some other arrangements. If you or your wife have any recommendations for good childcare options, I'd feel better with a personal referral."

"Tonia's totally hooked into the working-from-home mom scene. I'm sure she could have a list for you by the end of the day. Has Billie said she wants to stop?"

I quickly shook my head. "No, not at all. I just don't want to take advantage of her generosity."

Cam snorted. "Trust me, if a Callahan doesn't want to do something, they won't. If she's doing it, it's because she wants to."

"I don't know why she would," I admitted, surprising myself as the words came out of my mouth. I hadn't meant to dump any of this on him, but he was surprisingly easy to talk to. "I mean, she and Adele get along great, but I've been kind of a jerk to her. A few times. I don't know what it is, the nicer she is, the more defensive I get."

Cam nodded like that made sense, even though I knew it didn't. "Sometimes, accepting kindness can be hard, especially if you're used to something else. But I mean it: if Billie's helping, it's because she wants to. She's got no hidden agenda, no ulterior motive. She's just a good person. They still exist, even if it doesn't always seem that way."

We moved on to other, less personal topics, and when the game ended, I could hardly believe how quickly it went by or how comfortable it had been. Cam took my number so we could do it again sometime, and I believed he meant it.

Back at Billie's house, he walked straight in while I lingered on the front porch, waiting for Adele to come out. However, after a minute, Tonia appeared at the door instead.

"Adele wants to stay and have supper here with the kids. Is that alright?"

"Uh, sure, I guess." It didn't sound like I was invited, and I didn't really deserve to be. I tried not to take it personally. "I'll head on home and you can bring her over as soon as she's done."

"Wait," Tonia called out as I turned to go. "Cam and I were supposed to go out to eat after the game, but my stomach's still not 100%. Since we've already got the kids here, why don't you and Billie take the reservation instead?"

"Excuse me?" Was she really suggesting I take Billie out to dinner, just the two of us? Alone?

"She's been dying to try this place," Tonia added, lowering her voice as if it were a secret. "She's too shy to ask you for a favour, but I know she'd love it. It's better than eating on your own, right?"

Shy? That had never been a word I'd applied to Billie before. Something didn't seem entirely right, but if Billie really did want to go and Adele was taken care of, it might not be such a bad idea. I owed her an apology anyway, and maybe I could actually get through a whole meal without saying the wrong thing or losing my temper.

"Sure. If that's what she wants. I guess I should get changed?"

I glanced down at my jeans and t-shirt, and Tonia nodded firmly. "Something a little dressier would be perfect. She'll be ready in a few minutes."

She closed the door before I could change my mind, leaving me standing there with my head spinning and my heart beating a little faster than it had before. Nothing about that day had gone to plan, so what difference would one more surprise make? Maybe it would even end up being another good one.

Stranger things had happened.

~Billie~

Adele and I had found ourselves a perfect hiding spot beneath my overturned wheelbarrow when my sister outed us. "Charlie, look under the wheelbarrow!"

A moment later, we were exposed, my nephew's little face suddenly appearing as he lay on the grass to peer beneath the metal covering us. Adele took it all in stride, shrieking in joy as she scrambled to her feet to chase after Charlie, but I glared over at Tonia as I lifted the wheelbarrow up. "Snitch!"

"Had to be done," Tonia replied unapologetically. "You have to go get ready."

"Ready for what?" Dusting myself off, I got back to my feet, a lot slower than Adele had, and started to make my way back over to the deck where Tonia stood, tapping out something on her phone.

"Grey's taking you out for dinner."

I nearly tripped over the grass, stumbling to keep my balance as my stomach fluttered in surprise. "What?"

Her words made absolutely no sense to me, but my sister's self-satisfied grin told me I hadn't misheard her. "He just went to get changed, so you need to do the same. A dress, Billie. Hurry up."

"Hold on, I need a little more information than that." Playing with the kids, I hadn't even realized Cam and Grey were back, and I couldn't think of a single plausible explanation for Grey suddenly deciding to take me to dinner, other than the woman standing right in front of me. "What did you do?"

"Me?" she asked as innocently as possible, still tapping away on her phone. "What makes you think I... hey!"

She cried out as I snatched the phone from her hands, holding it up above my head. The extra two inches in height I had on my older sister came in handy sometimes.

After clawing at my arm uselessly for a few seconds, she gave in. "Alright, I'll talk, but give me my phone or you won't have a reservation and then he'll know the whole thing was made up."

"*What* did you make up?" I asked as I handed the phone back to her and crossed my arms to try to prepare myself.

"It's clear that you two need a chance to talk, away from Adele, away from the school and away from broken pipes. You want to be friends, right? This is your chance to get to know him better."

I'd told her about my shower and Grey coming to the rescue. I'd told her about almost everything since she would put a bloodhound to shame once she got on the trail of something she wanted to know. The only thing I'd left out was the chilli sauce and seeing him without his shirt on. That would have given her the wrong idea, since I had stressed multiple times that I only saw us being friends.

"What did you tell him?" She still hadn't explained anything.

"I said that Cam and I had dinner plans but that I still wasn't feeling well so you two should take them instead. Adele can stay here with us. It worked for the ball game, so I figured: why mess with a winning formula?"

"And he agreed, just like that?" Knowing my sister, she had still left some things out.

"Close enough. I believe his words were something along the lines of: 'if that's what Billie wants, then I'd love to.'"

That didn't sound like Grey at all. "But you *didn't* have dinner plans," I pointed out. They were supposed to come pick up the kids after the ball game. I had been planning to feed them unless they wanted to get home. We were going to play it by ear.

"Which is why I need to make the reservation now to make it look like we did." She held up her phone as if that explained anything at all.

"Now, go get ready! He'll be back any minute."

Knowing that arguing with Tonia would be a lost cause, I gave in and went inside. If Grey really had agreed, it must mean he didn't completely hate the idea. He wasn't the kind of guy to do something he didn't want to do. He could have made up an excuse to get out of it if the thought completely repelled him.

In my bedroom, I gave myself a quick glance in the mirror. Dirt was smudged across my face and arms from playing on the ground, and my knees had grass stains on them. *Perfect.* I looked like a big kid myself. With no time for a shower, I grabbed a washcloth and cleaned myself up as best I could before swapping my shorts and t-shirt for a knee-length floral dress with long sleeves, in case the air conditioning at the restaurant made it chilly. The surplice neckline crossed over my breasts, cinching in at the waist, and I paired it with a pair of cowboy boots left over from my days on the ranch. My hair had been up in a ponytail all day, but I let it down and brushed it out so it fell over my shoulders and finished touching up my makeup just as Tonia appeared at my door.

"He's here," she announced gleefully before giving me an appreciative look. "Good choice. He'll definitely notice you in that."

"Tonia." I put on my best teacher voice to try to convey my seriousness to my sister. "This is not a date."

"No, of course not." Although her words agreed with me, her tone conveyed the complete opposite. "Come on, time to go! Oh, and by the way, he thinks you've been dying to try this restaurant, so try to act excited when you get there. I sent the address to your phone."

"What?" I snatched my phone up from the dresser where I'd left it to get ready. "Tonia! I've never even heard of this place."

"Sorry, I think Charlie's calling me!" She disappeared from view while I took a deep breath, not sure whether to laugh or groan. Somehow, when I'd been the one interfering with my sisters' love lives, it seemed a lot funnier than it did on the receiving end.

The kids must have still been outside since the house was quiet as I walked down the hall towards the front door. When I reached the living room, Grey stood at the front door, looking even more nervous and uncomfortable than he had earlier that day.

For the first time since I met him, he wasn't wearing jeans. Instead, he wore khaki pants with a slate-grey polo shirt that stretched dangerously across his chest, so tight that I could see his piercing through the fabric.

Fuck. That wasn't going to help me stay focused.

He caught sight of me just a second after I saw him, his green eyes widening ever-so-slightly as they took me in. "Hey, Billie."

"Hey." I smiled at him, trying to cover my own nerves and the staccato rhythm of my heart. "Sorry for the last-minute invitation. I hope Tonia didn't guilt you into this too badly."

"She's..." He trailed off for a second before deciding on the right word. "Persuasive."

"That is one word for her," I had to agree. "Well, should we go? We don't want to miss the reservation."

"Absolutely. After you." Like a true gentleman, he held the door open for me as I stepped out into the early Texas evening with absolutely no idea of what the night might have in store.

~**Grey**~

The square black building I pulled up in front of didn't look much like a restaurant. Driving by, I never would have pegged it as any kind of business that actually wanted people to come inside. The blacked-out windows and lack of any kind of sign certainly didn't help. "This is the place?" I asked Billie, just to be certain.

"Uh, yeah, must be." She sounded a little unsure too, but her sunny smile stayed fixed on. "I've heard good things about it. Hopefully, they were all true."

I hoped so too, for her sake. The idea of her being disappointed didn't sit right with me.

Inside, we were immediately plunged into darkness as the door closed behind us and the bright Texas sunshine gave way to dim candles and floor lighting. It took our eyes a moment to adjust, but gradually, the entryway began to take shape around us.

"Yes?" a voice asked from ahead of us, belonging to a dark-haired woman dressed all in black. Black certainly seemed to be a theme.

"We have a reservation under Tonia Callahan," Billie answered, and after checking the tablet in her hand, the woman led us inside to a small, cozy table with the narrowest chairs I'd ever seen. Half a butt cheek hung over either side as I tried to centre myself to keep my balance.

As far as I could see, only one other table in the whole place was filled. "I'm not sure the reservation was necessary," I pointed out after the waitress had left us alone.

Billie snickered, covering her mouth with her hand. "No, it doesn't look that way. This is... different."

She had that right, and not just because of our surroundings.

It had been a long, long time since I went out to dinner with a woman. While I got dressed, I reminded myself over and over again that whatever this evening was, it certainly wasn't a date. However, sitting at the table with the soft candlelight between us and Billie looking as stunning as she did in her pretty dress, it kind of started to feel like one.

"So, what's supposed to be good?" I asked after cracking open the menu and being confronted with a whole lot of words I had never seen before. Squinting in the dim light, I tried to make out the first item. "What's an emulsion, other than a kind of paint?"

Billie tried to hide her laugh again. "I'm not sure. I'm beginning to think Tonia did this as a joke."

I had no idea what she meant by that. "I thought you were dying to try it?"

"Honestly, I've never heard of this place before."

Clearly, I had missed something. "Then what are we doing here?"

Billie sighed as she placed her menu down, looking a little sheepish. "My sister means well but doesn't really understand boundaries. She thought we needed a chance to talk alone so she made up the whole thing about having a reservation and me wanting to try this place. I had no idea about any of it until you'd already agreed. She only made the reservation just before we left, and I guess this was one of the only places she could find that had room available."

"I wonder why." My sarcastic tone made Billie smile as I tried to process everything she'd just said. "What are we supposed to be talking about? She's not trying to set us up, is she?"

As the words came out of my mouth, it actually didn't sound all that bad, especially if Billie had agreed to it. Maybe she didn't dislike me quite as much as I'd feared?

However, she quickly dashed that hope, shaking her head vehemently. "No, nothing like that. She just thought we could use a child-free opportunity to get to know each other a bit better, and she didn't trust that as adults, we could figure it out ourselves. As I said: no boundaries."

So, Billie definitely didn't consider it a date. Strangely, that rather disappointed me.

"I'm sorry for dragging you here," she continued. "I should have told you right when you showed up, but I thought maybe you were looking forward to it. Sometimes, it's nice to have dinner out, even with your annoying neighbour."

"I never said you were annoying." My words came out a little huskier than I intended as shame rushed through me. She didn't really believe I thought that, did she? Had I honestly been *that* much of a jerk?

Billie's gaze dropped, a pink colour rising in her cheeks that only made her more appealing. "Not in so many words, but I understand if you think so. The lack of boundaries thing kind of runs in my family. I know I've been a little pushy."

"Billie." Acting completely out of instinct, I reached across the small table to take her hand so that my words carried more weight. I wanted her to believe they were true. "I don't think you're annoying. I think you're... well, kind of amazing, actually."

Her blue eyes looked up at me in surprise before dropping down to my hand that still covered hers. It felt nice there, warm and safe, but I pulled it back anyway, recognizing that it had probably been a step too far.

Fuck, it had been a long time since I'd done any of this. What *was* I even doing? Honestly, I had no idea.

Billie swallowed, still looking down at her hands for a moment before she finally looked back up at me. When she did, the surprise on her face had gone, replaced by a rather mischievous, conspiratorial expression. "What do you say we sneak out of here? I know a taco truck nearby that does the best dirty tacos. We could go eat 'em over in the park?"

Glancing back down at the menu, I sighed in relief. "That sounds perfect."

We both pretended to look at the menu again until the waitress disappeared into the back, at which point we hurried back out onto the street, wincing as we stepped back out into the bright sunshine.

"I think I'm going to get Tonia and Cam a gift card to that place for their anniversary," Billie giggled as we climbed back into my van. "Now, let's go get some real food, please."

"With pleasure." Following her directions, we pulled up next to a good-sized neighbourhood park. The taco truck sat just outside the park on a busy corner, and at least a dozen people already stood in line.

"I told you it's good," Billie reminded me as we took our place in the line, considerably more dressed up than anyone in front of us. While we waited, she gave me a run-down of every item on the menu, and my mouth was watering by the time we finally got our food and bottled lemonade.

In the park, we found an empty bench beneath some trees, not entirely private but a little bit sheltered, and as we ate, we talked, just as Tonia wanted us to.

Billie told me more about her family and asked about mine. I found myself talking about June and her partner and their life in California, going into way more detail than I expected to. I even told her how June had invited me to go live out there with them but it had never appealed to me.

"That would be a tough call," she mused. "If my whole family moved, I'd have to go with them, but I'd sure miss Texas. I love that Laura's still on the ranch so I've still got the connection to our hometown along with all the perks of living in the city. It's the best of both worlds. Does Adele like horses? Maybe we could take her out to the ranch sometime."

"She's never been riding but I'm sure she'd love it. She loves all animals." I didn't say anything directly about her invitation to go to her sister's ranch, not wanting to assume too much when she said 'we'.

"What about you? Did you ride growing up?"

I gave her my answer without fully thinking it through. "I did a bit when I was younger but I haven't been since getting pierced. I'd have to do some research about how to protect myself before I got back on a horse again."

"Pierced?" Billie repeated the word curiously, her gaze dropping first to my chest before she put it together and her eyes moved lower, down to my lap.

Just the fact that she must have been thinking about my cock made it stir, completely against my will. "Sorry, that was probably too much information."

I had no idea why I'd just mentioned it. Neighbours didn't usually discuss genital piercings with each other.

"No, it's fine," Billie quickly assured me. "I like piercings. I mean, I'm interested in them. I don't have any of my own, other than my ears, but I noticed yours the other day."

She meant my nipple piercing, but instead of gesturing to my chest, she indicated her own, drawing my attention down to the swell of her breasts beneath her flowery dress, which did nothing to help the situation in my pants.

"What... uh, what kind do you have?" Her eyes moved downwards again, as if she could tell just by looking at my clothes. My hips shifted as my body reacted even further to the unexpected attention she was giving it. Suddenly, the evening air felt a whole lot warmer.

"That's classified," I told her, trying to make a joke out of it even as the new tension between us continued to rise. "It's shared on a strictly need-to-know basis."

Billie's eyebrows raised in challenge. "And what, exactly, would qualify me as needing to know?"

Well, fuck it. I'd gone that far, I might as well say what was on my mind. "I suppose you'd need to know if you were planning to use it."

Chapter Eight

~Billie~

Something shifted between me and Grey on that bench in the park, the same way it had when I saw him without his shirt on in my house.

Except that this time, I was pretty sure he felt it too.

Up to that point, we'd been having a friendly, neighbourly evening. Enduring the disaster of Tonia's restaurant reservation together had forged a new sense of camaraderie, and as we ate our tacos and chatted in the park, it felt like Grey finally started to relax. He didn't snap at me. He wasn't constantly looking away like he had something more important to be doing. It might not have been anything big, but it felt significant anyway, like after a few weeks of awkwardness, we'd finally started to lay the foundation of a real friendship.

And then he had to go and mention his cock.

Not just mention it, though that would have been bad enough, but he brought up the fact that he'd had it *pierced*. No matter how much the warning signs in my head were flashing, the sirens blaring to tell me to change the subject before I said or did anything I regretted, I couldn't help it. My eyes kept moving back to his lap, wondering what it would look like. *Imagining* it. Imagining what he would *do* with it.

Suddenly, nothing about our evening together felt neighbourly at all.

In typical Callahan fashion, I couldn't help blurting out my question, wondering what kind of piercing he had done. As I told him, I considered myself a bit of an enthusiast. I knew the names and locations of the most common piercings, though I'd never been with a man who actually had one.

Grey refused to answer me though, telling me I only needed to know if I intended to 'use it'. Didn't he know he should never, ever give a Callahan woman a challenge like that?

"So, what if I *were* interested in making use of it? Is there an application process, or…?"

I trailed off there, leaving the words hanging between us and the ball firmly in his court. He could pretend I meant it as a joke and brush it aside, or he could take it as a serious question. Before that conversation, I wouldn't have put any money on him being in the least bit interested in me in a sexual way, but as I said, something had shifted. As surely as I couldn't take my eyes off him, he'd started looking at me much more thoroughly too.

When he answered me, his voice sounded tighter than before. "You ain't really that curious about seeing it."

He stated that as a fact, but I could hear the question behind it. He wanted to be wrong, hoped that he was, and knowing that made me even bolder.

"Grey, can I be completely honest with you?"

His green eyes had never looked more intense as he nodded. "Go right ahead."

With a deep breath, I let it all out, everything that had been swirling around my head ever since that night I really noticed him for the first time, and everything that, if I had any common sense at all, I would never, ever say to the father of one of my students.

"I think you're a very sexy man. I know your life is complicated with your daughter and your ex and all the rest, so you're probably not looking for anything serious right now. That's okay. At the moment, I happen to be single too. I have been for a little while, actually. And I am very, *very* curious about your piercing. So, if you wanted to spend the night together, just a one-time thing, to help satisfy my curiosity, I'd be open to it. On the other hand, if you aren't attracted to me at all in that way, we can pretend I never said anything..."

"No."

His blunt, almost growled word stopped me in my tracks, and disappointment immediately gripped me as I tried to guess what he meant. No, he didn't find me as sexy as I found him? No, he wasn't interested? I must have misread his signals, and though it would be awkward between us for a while, at least I knew for sure. I would have to take comfort in that.

However, Grey hadn't finished yet. "I mean: no, I don't want to pretend you didn't say it."

That sentence had a lot of negatives in it. "What *do* you want?"

He looked away from me, his jaw tight, as doubts continued to linger in my mind. I'd just out-and-out told him I wanted to have sex with him, so how hard could it be to say it back if he felt the same? His hesitation made no sense to me unless he didn't want it and just didn't want to hurt my feelings.

"If you're not interested, Grey, I won't be offended. I promise. Disappointed, yes, but not offended. If you're not attracted to me, then you're not, you can't force..."

He didn't let me finish. A strong, rough hand slid along the side of my neck, his fingers curling around the back of it and gripping it firmly as he pulled me closer to him. Almost before I realized what was happening, his lips were on mine.

Nothing in his kiss was hesitant. His mouth moved against mine firmly and confidently, his fingers pressing into the back of my neck and his clean, masculine scent filling my nose. Warmth spread through me, warmth and longing, satisfaction and desire, and a deep, aching need.

Who had I been kidding when I thought I could ignore my body's reaction to him? With his kiss, he blew that lie apart, making me realize just how deep my attraction to him had grown. With the proof that he didn't find me completely off-putting after all, with the possibilities that his kiss seemed to promise, my anticipation grew even stronger.

Eventually, he pulled back, leaving me gasping for breath. "Does that answer your question?"

"What question?" I could barely remember what we'd been talking about.

Grey's lips curled upwards into what I would almost call an actual smile. It had to be the closest I'd seen from him anyway. "You asked what I want."

"Oh. Right." It came back to me slowly, drifting through the haze of my arousal. "Well, it seems like we're on the same page, then. Does that mean you'll show me your piercing?"

A deep groan rumbled in his throat. "If you're sure that's what you want, Billie. I don't want to take advantage of you."

I had to laugh at that idea when I had been the one to proposition him. "I'm pretty sure I'm taking advantage of you, not the other way around. You're the one with the unique offering."

His green eyes looked darker than I'd ever seen them before. "There's plenty that's unique about you. But I don't know… I mean, how should we…"

He didn't seem to know how to phrase his question, but I knew what he meant: logistically, how would it work?

Luckily, I already had it all planned out, the pieces falling into place in my head in an instant. "We go back home and act like nothing has changed in front of my sister. You can even act like you had a terrible time if you want. You'll take Adele home, and when she's in bed and my sister's gone, you can text me when you're ready for me to come over. You'll give me my demonstration and I'll go back home afterwards. No one will know."

It might not be very romantic, but we weren't talking about romance. What I felt at that moment, and what I could see reflected in Grey's eyes, could only be called pure and undiluted lust.

"And it ain't gonna make things weird between us afterwards?" Grey asked, sounding truly concerned that it might, and it flattered me to know that he would be worried about that. It must have meant I had made some progress on turning him into a friend after all.

"I don't see any reason why it has to. We're both adults, we're both going into this with our eyes open. I'm not playing games, Grey, or saying one thing and expecting another. That's not who I am."

"I know it's not." He stared at me a moment longer, our bodies still leaned towards each other, the tension between us still intense as he mulled things over. "Alright. Let's get on home, then."

He didn't have to ask me twice.

~**Grey**~

I kept expecting to wake up at some point. It had to be a dream. In what world did the beautiful woman who lived next door to me get so turned on by the thought of my piercings that she suggested we hook up, no strings attached, so she could satisfy her curiosity?

That happened in movies, maybe, the adult ones, but not in real life. Definitely not in *my* life, where I hadn't hooked up with anyone in a very long time. It had been years since I'd spent a night away from Adele, and since I wouldn't bring a random woman into our home, it didn't leave a lot of options.

Billie wasn't a random woman, though. She understood exactly why we needed to be mindful of Adele. She knew the entire situation and it hadn't scared her off. Fuck, she'd even met Donna. I'd never imagined someone seeing the whole messiness of my life and still being attracted to me anyway. The women who flirted with me when I was out on a job didn't have a clue, and I didn't have the energy it would take to try to explain it, so I never engaged.

And she honestly thought I might not be attracted to her? How could I not be? How could *anyone* not be? Aside from being kind and caring and funny, the sight of her in that dress and boots had been doing things to my body all evening, no matter how I tried to pretend otherwise. My breath felt shorter when I looked at her, the blood in my veins felt hotter, and my cock seemed to take on a life of its own, making my pants a whole lot tighter. After sharing that electric kiss, it became a lot harder to ignore.

Though I knew I should keep my mouth shut and just accept my good fortune that she seemed to feel the electricity between us the same as I did, I couldn't help glancing over at her in the front seat of my van as we drove back to her house. "This won't get you into any trouble if it comes out, will it? I mean, with your job and all?"

Billie smiled as she looked out the window. "Apparently, there are no rules against teachers and parents dating. The policy doesn't specifically say anything about just having sex, but I assume it falls under the same area."

Did she know that off the top of her head, or had she been checking into it? Because of me? I didn't ask, preferring to imagine that she had.

"I'd appreciate if you didn't spread it around though, just in case," Billie added.

"Of course." I didn't have anyone to tell even if I wanted to.

"In that case, it shouldn't come out, then," Billie summarized, as if that put the matter entirely to rest.

I supposed it shouldn't, but I also knew that life had a way of taking unexpected turns. I didn't take anything for granted anymore.

At Billie's house, she walked straight in the front door while I hung back, waiting for Adele to come out. Tonia brought her out a moment later, my little girl running into my arms as soon as she caught sight of me, trying to tell me about her day all at once, so excited that I couldn't make out more than a few words.

"They all had a lot of fun," Tonia assured me as Billie joined her on the front step. "If you ever want to bring Adele over to play with my kids sometime, we'd love to have her. Maybe if you've got plans of your own sometime. You've got Cam's number, right?"

I did, and I also noticed how Tonia threw in the bit about having plans. Despite Billie's insistence that her sister hadn't been trying to set us up, I thought that might have been exactly what she wanted. It had worked out better than I could have imagined, so in reality, I owed Tonia a debt of gratitude for it, but keeping in mind Billie's instruction to pretend as if we hadn't enjoyed ourselves, I kept my expression neutral.

"I'm sure Adele would like that, but I'll be skipping any restaurant recommendations you make after tonight, if you don't mind."

Tonia's cheery smile faltered while Billie tried not to laugh. "You didn't like it?"

"I've never been so uncomfortable in a restaurant in my life." Technically, I didn't lie. I just left out all the good stuff that happened afterwards.

Tonia looked genuinely dismayed, throwing a glance back at her sister before her eyes returned to me. "Well, shoot. That's too bad. I'm sure the company made up for it though?"

She left that as a question, giving me the opportunity to say something nice about Billie, but I simply picked up my daughter and headed towards home. "Have a good night, ladies."

When I felt sure they couldn't see me, I let the smile I'd been holding in spread across my face while Adele told me all about her day in detail.

After I'd given her a bath and put her to bed, I glanced out my front window over to Billie's house. Tonia and Cam's SUV had disappeared and my heart, which had already been beating a little faster with anticipation ever since Billie and I kissed in the park, kicked into an even higher gear.

So far, I still hadn't woken up, so it seemed like this might actually be happening. All I had to do was send Billie a text and let her know she could come over.

First, though, I went into my new bedroom, trying to see it through a woman's eyes. I couldn't call it impressive. The little decorative skill I did have had all been expended on Adele's room and the living room. My own room came pretty low on my priority list. After a moment's thought, I pulled the sheets off my bed and replaced them with a clean set from the linen closet. If it couldn't be aesthetically pleasing, at least it could be fresh.

As I smoothed the sheets out over the mattress, the idea that Billie might actually be lying on them, naked, in a matter of minutes, still seemed impossible. Maybe I was in some kind of fever dream? Real or not, my body certainly liked the image my mind conjured. Just thinking about it had me hard. *Fuck*, it had really been a long time.

In the kitchen, I dug out a bottle of whiskey, looking for a little additional courage. After swallowing down a mouthful, I finally pulled out my phone.

All quiet here. You can come over anytime, if you still want to.

I stared at the words for a second, wondering when exactly I had become so unsure of myself. Encouraged by the warmth of the alcohol spreading through my veins, I erased the last five words.

All quiet here. You can come over anytime.

As soon as I hit send, time seemed to go into slow motion. Maybe she *had* changed her mind. Maybe she'd thought better of it. Maybe her sister had said something that talked her out of it. Maybe she'd be hit by lightning on her way over. Honestly, anything seemed more likely than the idea that Billie Callahan would be showing up at my door for a booty call in just a minute or two.

Every sound seemed heightened, every little creak taking on new significance until finally, a soft knock came from the front door. When I opened it, there she stood, still wearing her dress and boots, her blue eyes filled with a mix of anticipation and nerves that mirrored my own.

"Hi." Her sheepish greeting made me smile. Knowing that she felt at least a little awkward and unsure about our plans made me feel a whole lot better. We might not have any idea what we were doing, but at least we were in the same boat. Hopefully, we could figure it out together.

"Hi. Come with me."

Taking her small, soft hand in mine, I led her down the hall to my bedroom with her boots still on. As soon as the door had closed behind us to keep the world out, I pulled her into my arms.

~**Billie**~

I had never felt anything like the way I felt as I walked into Grey's bedroom. Adventurous and wicked, excited and terrified, curious and self-conscious, each emotion seemed to have a contradicting one that somehow heightened them both. I wanted him; I had no doubt in my mind about that, but I'd never done a one-night stand with someone I actually knew before. I had no idea what the next day would bring, and at that moment, I honestly didn't care. All I wanted was that night.

If Grey felt any of the same nerves, he didn't show it. His text message to me had been straight to the point and my body reacted to it immediately. I knew exactly what would happen if I went over there, and he didn't disappoint. When I arrived, Grey wasted no time with small talk. Taking me by the hand, he brought me to his bedroom and pulled me close, kissing me like he had in the park, except even more passionately.

Fuck, he knew how to kiss. With one hand on the back of my head and the other around my waist, he held me like something precious and fragile, but nothing in the way his mouth laid claim to mine showed any fear of breaking me. Every movement of his lips, his teeth, and his tongue felt possessive and confident, and the anticipation that had been building up inside me quickly reached a fever pitch. My whole body ached for him, every inch of me demanding attention, with the need between my legs the strongest of all.

"Wait." With a gasp, I pulled back, trying to clear my head. I wanted him, yes, but I didn't want to get so carried away that I didn't get a chance to appreciate what had started all of this in the first place. "I want to see your piercing."

Grey gave a disbelieving huff, shaking his head. "Trust me, Billie, we were getting there."

"I know, but I want to see it first." While I could still think clearly enough to appreciate it, I added in my head. If we waited much longer, I would be so desperate to have it inside me, I wouldn't be able to give it the attention it deserved.

His khaki pants had grown tighter than they were earlier, but he didn't start there. Instead, he unbuttoned the two buttons on his polo shirt and pulled it up over his head, revealing his tattooed torso to me again, along with the enticing nipple piercing that had featured in far too many of my daydreams lately.

Despite my eagerness to get into his pants, I couldn't help stepping forward and running my hands across the firm muscles of his chest, across the inked skin, my thumb brushing lightly over his nipple with the barbell through it. Grey's eyes closed as he exhaled, enjoying the feel of my fingers almost as much as I enjoyed touching him.

"You gonna let me finish?" he asked in a strained voice, and I smiled as I took a step back.

"Sorry. Go ahead."

My eyes were glued to his hands as they reached down to unbutton and unzip his pants. He pulled them all the way down, leaving his underwear in place as he stepped out of the tan pants and kicked them aside. The way his cock strained at the black fabric of his boxer-briefs left me in no doubt that he felt just as ready for this as I did, but I still couldn't tell what kind of piercing he had.

When he finally removed the last piece of clothing and I got my first look at him, my jaw dropped in both surprise and desire. *Holy fuck.* "You've got a Jacob's ladder!"

Grey almost smiled, his green eyes fixed on me as he carefully watched my reaction. "You do know your piercings."

I did, and I honestly hadn't been expecting that. I couldn't say *what* I'd been expecting, but I thought he meant piercing in the singular. Instead, a row of straight barbells lined the underside of his shaft, perfectly spaced along his not-inconsiderable length.

Needing a closer examination, I dropped to my knees in front of him. When he made no move to stop me, I gripped his shaft at the base and lifted it up to get a proper look. Six small metal rods pierced through him with round balls on either end, just as wide as his own width. Just the thought of having it inside me, of feeling those smooth metal balls against my internal walls as he moved within me had my thighs clenching tighter than ever.

Aside from what it would do to me, though, I was also curious about how it affected him. "Does it make you more sensitive?"

Grey inhaled deeply above me as his cock twitched in my hand, blood pumping straight to his head. "Yeah. It adds a whole other layer."

Was that why he did it, I wondered? As tempted as I was to ask, another thought tempted me more, and instead of posing the question to him, I leaned forward instead, close enough to run my tongue lightly along the ridge of his shaft, between the metal spheres of the barbells.

"Shit, Billie." Grey's grunt from above me turned me on even more. Emboldened, I pressed my tongue against him harder, flicking it over the metal and his skin as his hand threaded through my hair, his fingers pressing into my scalp.

As I reached the top of the ladder, I kept going, up to his head, swirling my tongue around it and sucking him into my mouth. His grip on my hair tightened, a low groan rumbling in his throat. With that sign of approval, I took him in deeper, reaching the first rung on the ladder with my lips.

"Wait, hold on." He pulled his cock back, out of my reach. "You keep doing that and this is gonna be over before it begins."

He must have been exaggerating, but he seemed serious about wanting me to stop, so I did. Gently, he pulled me back to my feet, kissing me again while his hands ran down my dress and around my back.

"Is there a zipper on this thing, or…" He trailed off, trying to figure out how to get my dress off, and I giggled as I shook my head.

"Just pull it off."

He did as I instructed, lifting it from the bottom and over my head. His hands brushing against my skin made me shiver, every part of me already on edge. When he had it off, he took a step back to place it on top of his dresser carefully, unlike his own clothes, and when he turned back to me, his eyes filled with appreciation as they roamed over my body, standing there in the middle of his bedroom in my bra, panties and boots. "Fuck, Billie, you're beautiful."

That was easily the nicest thing he'd ever said to me, and my whole body flushed at the compliment. My desire for him was becoming urgent, my body demanding satisfaction.

Grey was clearly on the same page. "You want me to use a condom?"

I shook my head. I had birth control covered and more than anything, I wanted to feel him and those piercings as fully as possible. "If you're okay without one, I am too."

"Good." With that, he pulled me back towards him, kissing me again, even harder that time. His big, rough hands skimmed over my skin as mine dug into his shoulders. It took him a moment's fumbling to get my bra undone, but he did, tossing it to the floor. As his hands cupped me, he lowered his mouth to my chest, running his tongue across my stiff nipple before sucking on it. My knees nearly buckled, but thankfully, Grey had it covered. In one swift, strong movement, he scooped me and placed me on top of his bed. The fresh lavender scent of his pillows seemed so at odds with the male specimen hovering above me that I nearly laughed, but as soon as his mouth found my breast again, laughing was the last thing on my mind.

As he continued to suck and tease me, one hand drifted down, slipping beneath the waist of my panties. As his fingers slid between my legs, they slipped through the wetness already gathered there, and he gave another deep groan of satisfaction.

"Fuck, you feel amazing. Warm and wet and perfect."

Again, his compliment had me blushing. "You feel pretty damn good yourself."

I could have almost sworn he smiled before his mouth found my neck, sucking on it hard as his fingers slipped inside me, and I let out a shameless moan of pleasure.

Grey's head immediately raised. "A little quieter, okay? I love hearing it, but we don't want to be interrupted."

Oh, fuck. I nearly forgot about Adele asleep just down the hall. "Right. Got it."

With that confirmed, he went right back to what he'd been doing, his mouth on my neck and his fingers inside me, occasionally slipping back out to rub over my clit while I did my best to whimper quietly, biting my lip to remind myself to keep it down. This man definitely knew what he was doing, and we hadn't even got to the best part yet.

We were about to, though. Obviously wanting it as much as I did, Grey sat back on his knees, pulled my boots off roughly, one at a time, and pulled my panties off too. With that, we were both finally naked, me dripping wet and his beautiful, pierced cock hard and ready, his head already glistening with a bit of precum.

"You still sure?" he asked me one last time, and when I nodded at him desperately, my legs instinctively spreading wider, he positioned himself against me, his cock pressing against my entrance as my anticipation built even higher.

Finally, after what felt like a lifetime, he leaned down over me again, his hands on either side of me as he pushed into me, slow and firmly, letting me feel every perfect inch.

When the first piece of metal entered me, my body clenched in surprise. It felt cold compared to the rest of him, firm and unyielding. He immediately pulled back, coating himself with my own natural lubricant before pushing forward again. As the rest of the ladder followed in, slowly, rung by rung, the only thing I could compare it to would be a ribbed condom, but much more intense.

"Is that okay?" Grey looked down at me with genuine concern in his eyes. Maybe I had begun to look catatonic with pleasure.

"Yeah," I managed to breathe. "It feels amazing. Don't stop."

Relief and lust filled his green eyes as he followed my instructions. With each thrust and withdrawal, I could feel every inch of him, filling me in a way I'd never experienced before.

It didn't hurt that his technique was just as good as his kissing had been. The ladder on a mediocre lover would have been interesting, but on one as confident and tuned into me as Grey turned out to be, it felt like heaven. I never wanted it to end, but my body had other ideas, my climax building quickly with him finally inside me.

With my last bit of strength, I wrapped my arms around his strong back and pulled myself off the bed so I could lick his pierced nipple, sucking it firmly into my mouth.

"Fucking hell," Grey muttered as his body contracted in pleasure, his orgasm hitting him at almost the same time mine did. There had been nothing drawn out about it; quick and dirty would be the best description, but falling back onto his soft, clean bed with his trembling body above me, I had never felt more satisfied.

I got what I wanted: I knew what his piercing was and how it felt, so that should be the end of it.

Why did it feel like a beginning instead?

~Grey~

That didn't take very long at all, but all things considered, I really couldn't complain. It had been such a long time since I did anything like that that it could have been over a lot quicker. When Billie took my cock in her mouth, down on her knees still wearing her dress and boots, I honestly thought I might come right there and then. I might never have been able to look her in the eye again after that.

At least I made it long enough that she got some pleasure out of it too, but the way she enjoyed herself was precisely why I lost control when I did. She made no secret of the fact that she found me sexy, especially my piercings, and the enthusiastic way she responded to them stood in complete contrast to the reception they'd received from the handful of other women who had seen them. Usually, the response ranged from trepidation to outright distaste, but Billie had the complete opposite reaction and I loved that they were a turn-on for her.

When we finished, I pulled out of her slowly, making sure not to hurt her now that the heat of the moment had passed. Or maybe I just didn't want it to be over; that was a possibility too. Still trying to catch my breath, I lay down next to her, surprised at how comfortable the silence between us felt. I'd expected the awkwardness to kick in almost immediately, but Billie didn't seem to be feeling any as she sighed in contentment, rolling onto her side to face me.

"What made you decide to get the ladder?" she asked me curiously. "How long have you had it?"

Obviously, her thoughts were still on my cock, and since mentioning the piercings had led to everything that just happened, I'd never been happier that I had them.

"I wanted them for a long time. I got this one at 18." I gestured down to my nipple piercing, which immediately brought to mind the way she'd just sucked on it without any prompting from me just before my orgasm. Obviously, she liked that one too. "And I had my tongue done at the same time but I got rid of that one when I started my own business and it put some of the clients off."

Her gaze immediately dropped to my mouth. "That's a shame. I've always wondered how it would feel to get oral from a guy with a tongue piercing."

Her bluntness was almost as much of a turn-on for me as my piercings seemed to be for her, and since we weren't holding back, I answered her honestly. "Well, I can't help you with that particular question anymore, but I don't think I'm so bad even without it."

I probably should have taken a taste of her while I had the chance. The foreplay had been pretty brief, and I couldn't help hoping that maybe, somehow, I'd get another chance sometime.

"I'm sure you aren't bad at all," Billie agreed, her blue eyes twinkling with both amusement and, unless I misread it, a touch of desire. Maybe she wanted a bit more too? "But back to the piercings: how did you go from this..." Her hand trailed gently over my pierced nipple. "... to this?"

With a featherlight touch, her fingers brushed over my still-sensitive cock, sending a delicious shiver through my body.

Clearing my throat, I tried to answer her question despite the distraction. "Like I said, I always wanted them. They increase the sensation for me, it's supposed to be good for my partner too, and I think they look good. There's no real downside."

None of that was a lie, but that night with Billie might have been the first time I truly enjoyed the experience of sharing them with a woman simply because of how excited she'd been about them.

Billie still had more questions. "Didn't it hurt?"

"They put six holes in my cock, Billie. Yeah, it hurt."

My deadpan tone made her giggle. "Alright, fair enough. I meant in the long term, though: how long did it take to heal?"

I'd never had anyone quite so interested before, but since she seemed so genuinely curious, I didn't mind answering. "A couple of months each time."

"Each time?" She glanced down at my cock again, her eyes wide as they returned to my face. "Did you have to do each one separately?"

"No, it only took two visits. They did three each time, and the first ones had to be healed completely before they put the second set in. No sex in the meantime."

Billie let out a low whistle. "I'm guessing you didn't do it while you were married, then."

Although she meant it as a joke, it hit pretty close to the truth. "No, I didn't. I wanted to but Donna never liked the idea so I did it after our divorce to 'celebrate my freedom' or whatever. Women get a makeover when they have a breakup, I got my penis pierced. Same difference, I guess."

Though she smiled at my attempt to make light of it, I could see the sympathy in Billie's eyes. "Well, I, for one, am glad you went for it. It doesn't sound like you regret it either."

"I don't. Especially not tonight."

That made her laugh, a warm, full sound that made the whole room seem cozier. "Good. I don't regret tonight either."

After placing a gentle peck on my cheek, she sat up and shuffled over to the edge of the bed, reaching down to grab her underwear off the floor. Although I knew why she had to go, I found myself wishing she'd stay anyway. The next day, we'd be back to neighbours and our parent/teacher dynamic, and I appreciated her in both of those roles too much to want to risk screwing it up, but fuck if it didn't feel nice to have her there in my room too.

"You should get a response to the IEP application this week," Billie told me as she pulled her dress back over her head, her mind clearly having moved on to the next day too. "There'll be an in-person meeting with the school board next and I'll be there too. We can prepare for it together if you want."

"That'd be great, thanks." I pulled a pair of flannel pajama pants from my dresser drawer so I could walk her back to the door. I'd rather be a gentleman and walk her to her own door, but I couldn't leave Adele alone in the house. Billie would understand that without me having to say anything.

When Billie had her boots back on, I opened the bedroom door quietly, making sure Adele's room was still dark and quiet before heading back down the hall with Billie close behind me.

At the door, there didn't seem to be any 'right' way to say goodnight after how intimate we'd just been. A handshake would have been awfully formal, but a kiss would be too familiar. I couldn't decide, so in the end, I simply gave her a nod of appreciation. "This wasn't the day I expected when I woke up this morning, but I'm not complaining."

Billie smiled her beautiful, easy smile. "You and me both. Goodnight, Grey."

"Goodnight."

With a cute little wave, she headed down the steps and across the lawn towards her own house. I watched her go until I couldn't see her anymore, and I waited at the open door a bit longer, until I heard her door open and close so I knew she was safely inside. Only then did I return to my room and my newly-christened bed, smiling to myself at all the new memories it held.

~**Billie**~

The encounter with Grey brought a smile to my face every time it crossed my mind over the next couple of days. I didn't see him Monday morning; he dropped Adele off at school himself every morning since I always went in early to prepare for the day. She came running into the classroom, eager to see me and ask about Charlie and Jenny again, giving me absolutely no indication that she knew I'd been in her house the night before.

It really was our little secret, which somehow made it even hotter to me. Maybe Tonia had been onto something when she talked about me being drawn to the taboo.

Monday afternoon, Grey was already home from work when Adele and I arrived, but he was on the phone when he answered the door. He gave me an apologetic shrug, mouthing to me that it had to do with work, and since I couldn't think of a good excuse to linger at his door and wait for him to finish, I simply waved goodbye and went home to my house alone. If I had thought he might contact me later that evening, I would have been disappointed, but I didn't expect it. I'd made it clear that I'd only been looking for a one-night thing, and he seemed to agree.

On Tuesday, when we returned home, Grey's driveway sat empty, which surprised me only because he had made a point of mentioning my weekly family barbecue several times. I felt certain he wouldn't have forgotten about it, and I still had half an hour before I usually made my way over, so I took Adele to my house instead to pass the time until her dad arrived.

The time for me to leave came and went, still with no sign of Grey, and I started to get a little worried, not for myself but that he might be in some kind of trouble. Just as I pulled out my phone to send him a text to see if everything was alright, a message came through from him.

I'm so sorry, Billie, I've been caught up in an emergency job. It will be another half hour at least.

His words were restrained, but I could imagine the frustrated set of his jaw as he punched out the words. Going back on his word didn't sit well with him, I knew that much about him already.

The solution seemed simple enough to me. *Don't stress about it. If it's okay with you, I'll take Adele to my parent's house with me. Charlie and Jenny will be there, she'll have a great time.*

I waited for his reply to come through, giving his assent, before I shared the good news with Adele. "How would you like to go and play with your new friends again?"

Her excitement had her bouncing so much that I had trouble getting her seat belt done up in the truck.

Her appearance at the barbecue would elicit some questions, without doubt, but with Tonia having met both Adele and Grey over the weekend, those questions were bound to come anyway. I already fully anticipated being the centre of attention that week even without Adele; at least with her there, some of the attention would be diverted from me.

Sure enough, as soon as Adele and I walked into the backyard, all chatter immediately ceased. "Hey, everyone." I gave the little girl's hand a squeeze, though it might have been more for my own sake than hers. "I brought a guest tonight, I hope that's okay?"

"Dell!" Charlie shouted out from across the lawn, his face lighting up at the sight of his friend.

"Charlie!" Adele's answering squeal was so full of joy that every single face broke into a smile as she let go of my hand and raced across the yard to join him.

After giving my mom and dad a hug, I went to join my sisters at the table. Cam and Jesse were hovering near the barbecue, as usual, and Jesse tipped his hat at me in greeting as I walked by.

"So?" Laura barely let me sit down before the questions started. "Any particular reason you have a child with you?"

My eyes darted over to Tonia curiously. "You haven't told her?"

My eldest sister smiled back gleefully. "I was going to wait until you got here, but this is so much better!"

"Tell me what?" Laura demanded. "What have I missed?"

"Billie's become a nanny for her hot single-dad neighbour!"

"What?!" Laura's jaw dropped as I shot Tonia a dirty look.

"I'm not a nanny. He's new in town and I'm just helping him find his feet."

"I bet you are. And maybe some other parts of his body too?" Laura's sly tone had Tonia giggling and me fighting to hold down my blush, trying not to show either of them how close to the mark she'd come. "How hot are we talking here?"

"Top tier," Tonia assured her. "Muscles for days and, unless I'm much mistaken, he's got his nipple pierced. We all know Billie loves that."

"How do you know anything about his piercing?" I had definitely *not* mentioned that to her during our conversation about Grey.

"I noticed it through that tight shirt he was wearing the other night," Tonia explained, and I had to admit that would have been possible. After all, I'd noticed it too. Her smile turned even more devious as she exchanged glances with Laura. "The question is: how do *you* know about it?"

Both of them turned to me expectantly while I tried not to panic. "Look, Mr Wright and I are just neighbours, and..."

"His name is Mr Right?!" Laura pretended to swoon into Tonia's arms before all three of us descended into uncontrollable giggles. My sisters were ridiculous and I loved them for it.

"What's so funny?" A new voice joined us, and immediately our laughter died off as we all turned in surprise towards its source.

"Dex!" Tonia jumped immediately to her feet to give our big brother a hug, and I pulled a chair over to make room for him. It had been so long since Dex had come to the barbecue that none of us had been expecting him.

"How are you?" Laura asked him as he took a seat. Of all of us, she saw him the least since she lived out of town and he'd stopped attending our weekly get-togethers.

"I'm fine, but don't change the subject on my account. What had y'all in hysterics?"

"It's not important," I quickly assured him, shooting a warning glance at my sisters to drop their interrogation for the time being. "We want to hear about you. How's the gallery doing?"

"It's fine," he repeated, his lips barely moving, he'd drawn them so tight. "Laura, how's the ranch?"

She smiled supportively. "It's doing great. This is the busiest time of year for us with guests, I've got another group arriving tomorrow. In fact, one of the guests a couple of weeks ago happened to come into the main house and he saw the painting you did of me and Jesse. I gave him your card, I don't know if he's been in touch…"

Dex interrupted her before she could finish, turning to me instead. "Billie, how's school?"

Stuttering over the change of direction, I did my best to answer him in a way that included him. "Uh, it's good. My new class is settling in really well now. If you wanted to come in and do an art class with them like you did last year, they would love that…"

His jaw clenching in frustration, Dex abruptly got back to his feet. "I'm getting a drink," he announced, leaving us all sitting there in rather stunned silence. Apparently, he really didn't want to talk about himself.

"Is that normal?" Laura whispered to us, concern written clearly across her face.

"Unfortunately, it's becoming more normal," Tonia explained, looking to me for confirmation and I quickly nodded in agreement. "He's been in a funk lately."

That was one word for it. We all watched as he went over to the cooler and grabbed a beer bottle, slamming it against the edge of the deck to pop the cap off. Cam and Jesse both wandered over to talk to him and he seemed to be starting to relax until the kids' game got a little too close to them.

Looking over her shoulder at Charlie as he chased her, Adele didn't see Dex in front of her until it was too late. I saw the collision coming a moment before it happened but not in time to warn either of them. She plowed into the side of his legs, hard, sending him off balance as the beer in his bottle flowed over the rim, drenching both her and him as they staggered sideways together.

"What the hell?" Dex roared in irritation, looking down at the small, beer-soaked child at his feet. "Whose kid is this? How many fucking kids do we need around here?"

His angry tone combined with the shock of the impact and the liquid soaking into her clothes and hair made Adele burst into tears as all the adults stared at Dex in shock.

Instantly, I was on my feet, scooping Adele up from the ground to comfort her. "It's okay, sweetheart. It wasn't your fault. Are you okay?"

She continued to wail as all the colour drained from Dex's face, the situation slowly sinking in as he realized exactly what he'd just done.

"I'm sorry, I... Jesus. I'm sorry. I... I should go."

The bottle slid from his hand, hitting the ground as the remaining liquid inside poured out, soaking into the lawn. No one tried to stop him as he disappeared back into the house, Adele's tearful sobs still filling the air.

"I'm going to take her home," I announced to everyone else as my mom quickly retrieved the beer bottle from the ground before any of the kids could pick it up. Charlie watched the entire commotion with big eyes while Jenny ran over to Tonia for comfort, clearly upset by the whole thing too even if she didn't know exactly what happened. Baby Randy in Jesse's arms began to cry too, picking up on Adele's unhappiness. "She'll need a change of clothes."

"Of course," my mom quickly agreed. "I'll get you a towel for now, come into the kitchen."

I did my best to comfort Adele as I sat her on the kitchen counter, my mom helping to clean her up as much as we could. Laura came in a few minutes later with some food that they'd packed up for us. By the time we got back in my truck, Adele's sobs had turned to sniffles, and I tried to explain to her that sometimes, people said things they didn't really mean when they weren't feeling well. She replied that she didn't like the 'bad man', her eyes filling with tears again at the thought of him.

Grey's van was parked in his driveway when we arrived back at my house, the door to the back of the van open. He seemed to be organizing his supplies, and he looked up in confusion as he saw us pull in.

"That was quick," he said, coming over as I got out of the truck and giving me a friendly nod. "I just got home, I thought you'd be a while still..." He trailed off when I didn't answer, or perhaps he saw something in my expression that gave him a clue that something had gone wrong. "What happened?"

Not wanting him to panic, I gave him the information as quickly as I could. "Adele's fine, but there was a little accident. She's a bit upset and she needs a change of clothes."

Grey nodded again as he came around the passenger side of the truck with me. "Sometimes, she forgets to ask to use the bathroom in a strange place, we're working on it."

I realized belatedly that he'd grasped the wrong end of the stick when I said 'accident'. "No, that's not it, she..."

He pulled the door open before I could finish, and as soon as Adele saw her daddy, she burst into tears again. In a second, he had her seatbelt off and picked her up to comfort her, and as the smell reached his nose, he turned to me in bewilderment. "Why does she smell like beer?"

"There was an accident," I repeated, trying not to grimace at what I needed to tell him. "She ran into my brother and he accidentally spilled his beer on her. He raised his voice to her, which upset her. He's not usually like that, he's been going through a rough time..."

"Are you kidding me?" Grey's eyes flashed with anger, just as they had the night we met. His arms tightened around Adele as she continued to cry against his chest. "You're supposed to be watching out for her!"

The implication that I'd been negligent in some way both shamed and frustrated me. Maybe I could have kept Adele closer to me, but I couldn't have predicted Dex's outburst. He'd never done anything like that before.

"Accidents happen," I reminded him, trying to stay calm even as his expression grew stormier. "She's not injured, and we already had a talk on the way home about how angry words can hurt."

"Save your teacher bullshit," Grey hissed, covering Adele's ears as he swore. "She hasn't got enough to deal with? She trusted you."

"I know that, and I'm sorry, Grey. Here, we brought some food home that you can have for dinner since she didn't have a chance to eat." I couldn't change what happened; I could only accept the responsibility and try to make amends as I grabbed the container out of the truck and held it out to him.

"You *don't* know. You have no idea." Ignoring the peace offering in my hand, he turned and took Adele back into his house, leaving me standing there alone on my driveway and his van wide open on his. When a few minutes passed and he didn't reappear, I went over and closed the door to his van before heading inside my house with my Tupperware container full of food.

Though I had no appetite anymore, I forced myself to eat anyway. So much for any breakthrough Grey and I made over the weekend towards being friends or maybe even more. His grumpiness had returned in full force, and that time, I had to admit it had some justification. He blamed me, but I knew that deep down, he also blamed himself, and his anger came mostly from that place. He felt the weight of the world on his shoulders, trying to protect his daughter from a world that could too often be cruel to her, and although I'd offered to be an ally, I'd let him down.

I could see his side of things perfectly well. What I couldn't see was how to earn back his trust, or exactly why it mattered to me so much that I did.

~Grey~

Adele's tears quickly dried once we got inside. She loved having a bath, and with me sitting on the floor beside the tub, we gave ourselves bubble beards and she painted on the tile with her bath paints. Before long, her usual good spirits returned in full force. By the time she ate supper in her pajamas, which made her giggle, and we cuddled on the couch to watch her favourite show before bed, she seemed to have forgotten all about her earlier sadness.

My emotions took a lot longer to sort through.

I didn't think I'd said anything untrue to Billie. She had a duty to look out for Adele's wellbeing, not only physically but emotionally as well. Being yelled at by a stranger would frighten any child, and Adele had always been even more sensitive to other people's moods than most children. Billie might not have been able to prevent the physical accident, but she shouldn't have had Adele around someone who would yell at her in the first place. I had trusted her to be able to make those kinds of judgement calls.

And yet, though I thought my feelings were justified, I also knew I could have been more tactful in my reaction. That conversation had been the first one Billie and I had after having sex, and all I'd done was criticize her. Had I been on my own for so long that I'd forgotten what having a real conversation looked like? I could have let her know my concerns calmly rather than snapping at her, and the unhappiness in her pretty blue eyes haunted me as I tried to get to sleep that night.

How many times could I push her away before she decided not to come back again?

After all of that, I couldn't expect her to watch Adele the next day like nothing had happened so I made sure I was at the school in plenty of time to pick my daughter up at the end of the day, even though it meant sitting idle for an hour before the end of the day since I didn't have time to complete another job. The teaching assistant from Adele's class saw me waiting with the other parents and brought Adele out to me a few minutes later. I didn't see Billie at all.

In Adele's school bag, I found a note with an appointment time for Friday afternoon for Adele's initial IEP meeting. The note was in Billie's neat handwriting but it stuck to the essential information with no personal touches at all.

A couple of times in the evening, I glanced out the window at Billie's driveway to see if she'd come home yet. I didn't know what my plan would be when she did; would I go over there and apologize? Or at least try to talk things through more calmly? I didn't know and probably wouldn't know until it happened, but even by the time I put Adele to bed, Billie still hadn't appeared. I lifted some weights in the guest room to try to burn off my nervous energy, but it didn't help much. My mind continued to race in bed just as it had the night before.

On Thursday, I collected Adele from school again, and that time, she protested my appearance. "I stay with Ms Cally-lan," she reminded me.

"Not today, sweetheart." I was glad to know she still wanted Billie to watch her and that she didn't associate any negative memories about what happened with Billie herself, but I still didn't feel right about it until Billie and I had a chance to talk things through.

Just before supper, someone knocked on our door, and my heart immediately beat a little faster. Usually, Billie would be home by then, so maybe she had decided to make the first move. It wouldn't be an easy conversation, but it needed to happen, so I would rather get it over with.

However, when I opened the door, there was no sign of Billie. Instead, a man stood there in a t-shirt and jeans, tattoos on his arms, a piece of paper in his hands and a nervous look on his face.

"Yes?" The only people who had been to my house since we moved in were Billie and her brother-in-law, Cam, and I didn't expect anyone else.

The man at the door greeted me a lot like Cam had. "Hey. You're Grey?"

"Yeah." Since he knew my name, it didn't seem like a cold call, and I had only one other idea about who he might be. "Are you another Callahan relative?"

A brief, so-quick-I-almost-missed-it smile flashed across his face. "That's right. We're like an infestation: you get one, you get us all."

At that point, it didn't sound like much of an exaggeration to me. "What can I do for you?"

"My name is Dex. I'm Billie's brother, but more to the point, I'm the jerk who upset your little girl the other night. I came to apologize to her, if that's okay with you."

Instantly, my guard went up, as high as it could go. "I'm not sure she'll want to see you."

Although Dex grimaced, he held his ground. "I know. If she doesn't, that's okay, but I have to try."

"Did Billie put you up to this?" Not having spoken to her in two days, I had no idea what had been going on in her head.

"No. I mean, she helped me out by telling me about you and Adele, but she doesn't know I'm here right now. Look, I owe you an apology too. I've already apologized to Billie. She brought Adele to what should have been a safe space and I ruined it for her. I'm not here to make excuses. There's no excuse. I just want to say I'm sorry."

His words sounded sincere, and a memory came back to me, words I'd almost forgotten I'd heard when Billie told me what happened. She said her brother had been through a rough time lately, and I sure as hell knew what that felt like. I also knew what it felt like to lose control and regret it afterwards, and reluctantly, my resolve began to soften.

"Hang on. I'll go and see if she wants to talk to you." Leaving him at the door, I went to the living room where Adele was cooking some play food, getting ready to feed her dolls dinner. "Hey, sweetheart. Come here for a second."

She immediately ran over to me as I knelt down to speak to her.

"Do you remember when you went with Ms Callahan on Tuesday to see Charlie and Jenny, and the man got mad at you and made you sad?"

She nodded soberly, assuring me she did. She had mentioned it again the night before, so I knew she really did remember.

"He's here to say sorry. Do you want to see him?"

"No!" Her immediate and forceful declaration made me smile. She had every right to say no and I loved that she would stand up for herself, but I made her a counter-offer anyway.

"Well, I'm going to go talk to him for a minute. You can come with me if you want and you don't have to say anything if you don't want to, or you can stay here and not see him. It's up to you."

She thought about it seriously for a moment before making up her mind. "You carry me."

"Sure thing." I scooped her up, even more proud of her for being brave, and headed back to the front door. "Adele, this is Mr Callahan. He's Ms Callahan's brother."

Though she kept her head against my chest, I could feel her face turn just enough that she could see him. "Brother?" she repeated curiously in a loud whisper. She knew the word but I didn't know for sure how much she understood the concept.

"That's right. Charlie is Jenny's brother, and Mr Callahan is Ms Callahan's brother, even though they're grown up now." I gave Dex a nod. "Go ahead."

He spoke to her calmly and plainly, in words she could understand. "Adele, I'm sorry for yelling at you. I was mad about something else and I got mad at you because of that, and that's not fair. I know you didn't run into me on purpose. I'm sorry, and I'd really like to be your friend. I heard you like to draw so I brought you a picture that I hope you like."

That last sentence definitely got Adele's attention and she raised her head from my chest to look at me curiously. "Picture?"

"Don't look at me, I don't have it. Ask Mr Callahan if you can see it."

She turned to face him warily, her curiosity outweighing her fear. "What picture?"

He turned over the piece of paper in his hands to show her and my jaw nearly dropped to the floor. A pencil sketch of Adele herself, it looked so lifelike and detailed, it could have almost been a photo.

My little girl's eyes immediately lit up and she reached for it, leaning so far over that I nearly dropped her. Dex handed her the paper and she brought it right up to her face, staring at it in awe. "Daddy, she's me!"

"She sure is." Unexpectedly, I found my throat closing up with emotion as I gave Dex a nod. "That's amazing."

Somewhere in the back of my brain, I remembered Billie mentioning her brother was an artist. It didn't seem like she'd been exaggerating.

Dex brushed the compliment aside, continuing to address Adele. "I hope you like it. Maybe we can draw or colour together sometime. I'd really like that."

Adele didn't say anything, still staring at the picture in wonder, her little fingers touching her pencil reflection tentatively, as if the girl on the page might come to life at any time.

"I'll ask her about it later," I promised Dex. "I think your apology's accepted though. She's a pretty forgiving kid."

He gave an appreciative nod. "Kids usually are."

Sensing he had something more he wanted to say to me in private, I put Adele down and told her to take the picture to her bedroom. When she'd gone, holding it carefully out in front of her, Dex spoke again.

"I know an apology isn't enough, so I want you to know I've signed up for therapy. Anger management and that kind of stuff. I can't take back what I said to her, but I'll do my damnedest to make sure nothing like that happens again."

"I appreciate that." He was making it damn near impossible for me to be able to hold a grudge. "Maybe you can teach me some tricks when you get it figured out. I'm not always the best at keeping my cool either."

Dex gave me an understanding smile. "It's tough when things don't turn out the way you planned and there ain't no one you can blame or anything you can do about it."

He had that right. I didn't want to pry into his own circumstances, but it sounded like he got it. "Thanks for coming over."

"Literally the least I could do," he countered, and though I didn't agree with that, I was glad he felt that way. "Nice to meet you, Grey. I hope we see more of you and Adele around."

"I'm beginning to feel like I don't have much of a choice about that."

Dex laughed at my sarcasm, though I hadn't been entirely joking. "You might be right. Have a good night."

With a nod, he headed back to his truck parked on the street while I glanced over at Billie's driveway. Her truck was there too, so she must be at home. If Dex had been man enough to come over and apologize, maybe I could summon the same courage too. Two days without talking to her already felt like far too long. I didn't have a fancy handmade gift to smooth things over, but I hoped she'd give me one more chance anyway. Hopefully, it'd be the last time I'd have to ask.

Chapter Ten

~Billie~

When I glanced out the front window before heading to the kitchen to start making supper, I was *not* looking for Grey. I kept telling myself that, though realistically, I had no other real reason to look.

Why did I care? What did I think would happen? He'd obviously decided the accident with Adele meant he no longer trusted me to look after her, without even giving me a chance to fully explain what happened. On Wednesday, I kept her back at the end of school in the classroom with me, as usual, expecting I would take her home until my teaching assistant came back inside.

"Mr Wright is here for Adele."

"Oh." I couldn't stop my exclamation of surprise. "Did he ask to speak with me?"

She shook her head. "No, he just asked for Adele."

Adele didn't like having to go when she'd just got set up at the table with some crayons and paper, but her dad's wishes obviously took priority over mine, so I got her ready and sent her home.

The next day, I prepared her to go home along with the other children, despite her protests, and when my teaching assistant returned alone, I had to accept that it seemed Grey really had made up his mind to end our arrangement unilaterally.

If he hadn't talked to me before making that decision, he had no reason to come over that evening either, and even though I knew that, I couldn't help looking out the window anyway. If he *did* turn up, I had a few things I wanted to say to him about using his words.

When I glanced outside, though, I didn't see Grey. What I *did* see was Dex's truck parked on the street. In confusion, I stepped closer to the window, looking for the truck's owner, but he was nowhere between the truck and my house. Instead, he appeared a moment later, coming from the direction of Grey's house, got in his truck and drove away, all without coming to see me.

Though I didn't know exactly what he'd been doing over there, I could guess. I'd spent the whole previous evening with my brother and my sisters. Tonia and Laura both dropped everything to head over to Dex's house, and while I had no plans to drop, I went along too.

Dex might not have been *happy* to see us, exactly, but he accepted our presence there with good grace. After getting us all a drink as we settled down in his living room, with one of his beautiful portraits of Shawna on the wall watching over us, he explained what his day had been like.

"I took the day off from work and went to see the head of my support group. She referred me to a grief and anger specialist and my first appointment is in a few days. I think I need some help dealing with everything I'm feeling. It ain't getting any better."

We'd gone over there to try to convince him that he needed some help, but it seemed our efforts weren't needed. He'd already figured it out himself.

Over our beers, he asked me about Adele and Grey, and I told him the whole story, other than what happened between me and Grey on Sunday evening. His questions focused on Adele specifically and what she liked, what would make her smile, so I suspected he planned to try to make it up to her even though he didn't tell me that in so many words.

We stayed for hours, ordering pizza and wings and catching Dex up on everything that had been happening in all our lives, laughing and teasing each other as usual. Though the spark in his eyes he used to have never quite showed up, it felt closer than it had in a long time.

With all that in mind, it didn't surprise me that he'd gone to see Grey. It did, however, remind me of the advice my sisters had given me the night before.

"Who does he think he is?" Tonia demanded when I told them all about Grey's reaction when I brought Adele home from the barbecue. "Must be nice to never make mistakes so that you can look down on anyone who does!"

"Oh, come off it, Tonia," Laura shot back, rolling her eyes. "If your babysitter brought Jenny home doused in beer, you'd lose your freaking mind."

"I would not..." Tonia began her sentence indignantly but as soon as she really stopped to think about it, she had to concede that point as the rest of us snickered. "Okay, maybe I would."

"*And* you'd never forgive them," I pointed out. "I think that might be where Grey and I are. Adele means everything to him and I screwed up."

"*I* screwed up," Dex corrected me. "Do you want me to talk to him on your behalf?"

"No." I quickly shot that idea down. My whole family harassing Grey wouldn't help matters at all. "You can talk to him if you want, I can't stop you, but please, leave me out of it."

He promised he would as Laura offered her own opinion. "I get why he's angry, but it sounds like he keeps doing this. You start to get closer and he finds a reason to push you away. I'm not saying he didn't have a reason this time, but in the wider context, it looks like a pattern. Maybe he's just not ready for a relationship."

"Who said anything about a relationship?" That word had never been mentioned, not to my siblings and definitely not between me and Grey.

"I'm reading between the lines," she informed me wryly. "And I've been there, Billie. Jesse was sure he didn't want a relationship and when they've got that in their heads, there ain't much you can do about it. Jesse had to figure it out for himself, and I think Grey does too. In the meantime, take care of yourself. Set boundaries that *you're* happy with. If it hurts when he pushes you away, maybe don't let him get too close in the first place. Or, if you really can't resist, make it clear there are consequences to treating you that way. You don't deserve to keep getting bulldozed while he tries to figure out which direction he's going in."

The idea that Grey would *ever* want a relationship with me still seemed pretty far-fetched, but Laura did have a point. Even if we were only friends, Grey needed to work on his communication skills. If he kept behaving like a child, maybe I needed to treat him like one. One thing I did have was a lot of experience working with kids.

As Dex drove away, I went to my kitchen and pulled out one of the meals I'd prepared in advance for the week. I'd just put it into a bowl and in the microwave when I heard a knock at my door. Thinking that maybe Dex had changed his mind and come back, I left my food, went to the door and opened it without hesitation, only to find Grey and Adele standing on my step.

"Hey." Grey gave me a tentative nod, holding Adele's hand as she bounced in excitement next to him, a piece of paper in her other hand. "Have you eaten?"

"What?" His question made no sense to me. He hadn't spoken to me in two days, and *those* were the first words out of his mouth?

"Supper," he explained, looking more uncomfortable with each word he spoke. "We wanted to invite you over, if you haven't already eaten."

"Why?" He still wasn't making any sense in the context of the last conversation we'd had.

"Look at my picture!" Adele couldn't contain herself any longer as she held up the paper in her hand to show. As my eyes fell on the unmistakable lines of one of my brother's sketches, I had to smile. So *that* was why he'd asked me to show him a photo of Adele.

Immediately, I crouched down to get a better look. "Wow! She's almost as pretty as you are!"

Adele giggled in delight, quickly pointing out all her favourite parts of the picture while Grey stood there, unable to get a word in.

"So, supper," he finally managed to say when Adele had to stop to take a breath. "You said we could prepare for the meeting together, right?"

Shoot. I *had* said that, and with the meeting coming up the next day, I still thought it would be a good idea. I supposed I had no real reason to decline, though I would have to keep my guard up, as Laura said. "Right. Just give me a second and I'll come on over."

He could have called or texted me an invitation, but he came over because he knew that with Adele right in front of me, I'd have a harder time saying no. I saw his game and I intended to call him out on it, just as soon as we were alone.

All in all, I had quite a few things I wanted to say to Grey Wright, and it seemed like he'd just given me the perfect opportunity.

~**Grey**~

Billie behaved just the same with Adele as she always had, not putting my little girl in the middle of the awkwardness between us in any way. I could hardly get a word in edgewise over supper as the two of them talked about Adele's new picture and all the fun things Adele could draw with Dex when they got together. Adele insisted on having the picture beside her while we ate, and although the meal didn't hold the potential for disaster that chilli did, it still made me nervous.

"Why don't you put it away until after supper? You don't want it to get dirty, sweetheart."

The bottom lip came out, and Billie immediately took her side. "She's being careful. Adele, if you bring it to school tomorrow, we can laminate it for you and then you don't have to worry."

Outnumbered, I swallowed my objections and bided my time until I could speak to Billie privately. With her attention on Adele, I didn't get much of an indication of how upset she might be with me. She accepted the invitation to come over, which I took as a good sign, but that probably had more to do with Adele than with me. I had no illusions that a dinner invitation on its own would make up for the way I'd spoken to her.

After supper, I sent Adele and her picture into the living room to play while I cleared off the table and pulled out my copy of Adele's IEP application and the notes that Billie had given me about it. "What do I need to know for tomorrow?"

Patiently, Billie ran through what the meeting would be like. "When Adele's a bit older, she can take part in these meetings herself to give her opinions about what she needs and wants in the classroom. I actually recommend having her there because it helps everyone in the room remember that we're discussing a real person and not just a budget. But for this first one, I can bring her with me to say hello at the beginning and send her back to class so she doesn't get bored. I think between you and me we can paint a pretty good picture of her."

She had thought of everything, putting Adele first in every instance, and I knew she would fight just as hard for her as I did. So, why hadn't I given her the benefit of the doubt the other night? With every calm, considered word Billie spoke, my reaction seemed less reasonable, especially in light of Dex's apology.

"I think that's it," Billie announced when we'd gone through everything she thought I should know. "You'll do great, Grey."

If I did, it would be mostly because of her. "I'm going to get Adele ready for bed but there's something else I want to talk to you about. Do you mind staying a little longer?"

With her agreement, I left her there while I got Adele changed into her pajamas and her teeth brushed. After that, we always read a story, but that night, she wanted to make a change. "Ms Cally-lan read it?"

"What's wrong with my reading?" I tickled her as I asked the question, making her giggle.

"Ms Cally-lan does voices," Adele explained.

"Does she?" I had to admit that intrigued me. "Well, let me ask her."

Billie glanced up from the paperwork she'd still been flipping through at the table when I reappeared in the doorway. "You've had a special request for a bedtime story, if you don't mind."

"Well, normally, I charge a fee for home visits," Billie teased me. "But I guess I can make an exception."

I hung back at the door while Adele showed Billie her bookcase and they picked out a book together. With Adele tucked into bed, Billie sat on the side of her bed and read her the story with a different voice for each character, just like Adele had said. My daughter listened with rapt interest, giggling and gasping at all the right places. I'd never seen her look at Donna with quite so much adoration.

Billie read it twice, at Adele's request, but she drew the line at a third time. "You need to get some sleep for school tomorrow. We get to feed Mr Buttons tomorrow, remember?"

Whatever that meant, it seemed to work as Adele immediately squeezed her eyes shut. Billie stepped out of the way while I went in to kiss my daughter goodnight, and we headed out into the hall together as I turned Adele's light off. "Mr Buttons?" I asked curiously after the door was closed.

"Our class snake."

I nearly choked in surprise. Adele definitely hadn't told me about a snake. "What happened to class rabbits? That's what I had growing up."

Billie gave me a wink that immediately had my body thinking all sorts of things it shouldn't. "I prefer things that are a little more edgy."

She definitely did have tastes that differed from the stereotypical elementary school teacher, I had to admit, as the memory of her on her knees, licking her way along my piercings, popped back into my head.

"And you named the snake Mr Buttons?" I asked, trying to keep my mind focused where it should be.

Billie laughed. "The kids named him. One of them thought the patterns on his skin looked like buttons."

That actually made some sense.

As we reached the living room, I gestured towards the couch. "Please, have a seat." She did as I requested, crossing her legs and waiting for me to speak, so I did my best to remember the words I'd been rehearsing in my head all evening. "Listen, Billie, I'm sorry for the way I spoke to you on Tuesday. I'm still not happy that it happened, but I know you didn't put Adele in that situation intentionally. I could have handled it better."

She nodded slowly as she considered my words. "And?"

And? What did that mean? "Excuse me?"

"And," she repeated, enunciating it clearly as if I simply hadn't heard her. "I appreciate the apology, but this keeps happening, Grey. The first couple of times, I accepted your apology, but if you really mean it, then this time, I want more."

"More?" The only experience I had was with Donna, who would only accept my apologies if I bought her something to go with them, but I didn't think Billie was talking about gifts. What did she want, then?

Billie nodded, her expression still open but firm. "Some kind of plan to prevent it from happening again. An awareness of why it happens in the first place. A promise that you can do better."

"Are you talking to me like one of your students?" I had the distinct impression that I'd just been called into the principal's office for a lecture.

She didn't deny it. "If that's how you're going to act, that's how I'm going to treat you. Just because you're older than me doesn't mean you can't still learn. When my students have an argument, this is how they have to apologize: they say they're sorry, they explain why they made a mistake in the first place, and they say what they'd do differently next time. Why don't you give it a try?"

"Billie..."

I didn't even know what protest I planned to make, but I never found out because she didn't give me a chance. "I'll go first if that makes you feel better. Grey, I'm sorry that Adele got upset at my family barbecue. I assumed because I knew everyone there that nothing could go wrong. If I could do it over again, I would introduce Adele and Dex so he knew she was there and they wouldn't surprise each other the way they did."

It did actually make me feel better to hear it all laid out like that, and it reminded me of Dex's apology too. He'd explained his reaction and told me what action he'd taken in the meantime. Billie used this method with her students, but maybe she'd learned it at home.

I supposed I *could* give it a try.

"Alright. I'm sorry that I snapped at you. I was angry. Next time, I'd try to talk it out with you rather than just blaming you."

Billie didn't look as impressed as I hoped she would. "That's a start, but *why* were you angry? Besides the obvious, I mean. Adele was upset, and that upset you, but why did you get *so* angry, and why did you direct it at me?"

It had been a long time since anyone had asked me those kinds of questions or forced me to examine my own feelings. It felt uncomfortable, and my instinct was to push her away again, but I recognized that wouldn't get me anywhere. I'd invited her over because I wanted to make things better between us and getting defensive wouldn't help. Instead, I took a deep breath and tried to come up with an answer that would satisfy her.

"I guess I was angry that I can't always protect Adele. No matter how much I want to, there's always going to be times when it's out of my hands, and as her daddy, that frustrates me."

Billie exhaled slowly, giving me a nod of encouragement. "I can understand that. That's a normal way for any parent to feel, I think, and when you've got a child with additional challenges, it must be even stronger. But why did you direct that anger at me? Why is it my fault?"

"It isn't," I quickly assured her. "I guess I just got angry with you because you were there, and that ain't fair to you either."

"No, it's not," she agreed quietly. "I'm on your side, Grey."

"I know that. I do. I guess it's just..." I tried to dig even deeper, like she wanted me to. From the first night we met, Billie had brought out my defensive side, and she was absolutely right, it wasn't her fault. So why did it happen? I could really only think of one reason. "You're pretty damn near perfect, Billie. You've got it all together while I'm just barely holding on. Maybe I'm jealous?"

"You want to be me?" The idea seemed to amuse her, but it wasn't exactly what I meant.

"No, I think you do a pretty good job of being you." I couldn't stop my eyes from dropping to her body, remembering the sight of it in my bed the other night. "It's more like I'm jealous of the man who gets to be with a woman like you. The man I could have been, if things were different."

Billie's eyes went wide, the amusement disappearing off her face instantly. "What?"

That was a damn good question. What exactly had I meant by that? That was the problem with speaking from the heart; sometimes, it said things my brain would have thought better of. Had I just crossed a line? From the look of disbelief on Billie's face, it seemed I might have, but now that the words were out there, I didn't really want to take them back.

Not when they were true.

~Billie~

It wouldn't have surprised me if Grey kicked me out of his house when I insisted on a real apology and some accountability for his actions. From experience, I know how quickly his mood could shift, and though he'd invited me over to try to smooth things out, he might change his mind. So, while it would have disappointed me if he snapped at me again, it wouldn't have been entirely unexpected.

What he actually said, though, came as a complete shock.

I'm jealous of the man who gets to be with a woman like you.

What did that even mean? It sounded like a compliment, a pretty significant one, but it also made no sense to me. He'd confirmed over the weekend that he found me attractive but he'd never hinted at wanting anything more than the hook-up we had. Then, out of the blue, he called me perfect? What did he mean by 'be with me'? And if he wanted to be with me, why couldn't he?

I had so many questions, I wasn't sure where to start.

"I didn't mean to make you uncomfortable," Grey apologized, looking down at his hands as he sat on the sofa, leaning forward with his elbows on his knees, his whole body tense. "You asked me why I get angry and I think that's part of it."

"I'm not uncomfortable." Confused, yes, but the idea of being with Grey in any capacity, no matter how he meant it, appealed to me. I couldn't deny the way it made my heart beat a little faster and my stomach flutter with both anticipation and desire, remembering the solid feel of his body beneath my fingertips and the sensation of that incredible pierced cock inside me. The memory turned me on, sure, but it definitely didn't make me uncomfortable. "I just don't really understand what you mean. Why couldn't the man you are now be with a woman like me?"

I tried to keep the question vague, like we weren't talking about us specifically, in the hopes that he'd elaborate a little further.

Grey let out a sharp, sarcastic laugh with no real humour in it. "I'm a mess, Billie. I couldn't keep my marriage together. I chose someone who failed as a mother in almost every way to be the mother of my child. What does that say about my judgement?"

I didn't see how Donna's failings were his fault, or how he could have possibly known in advance how she would react to the situation they found themselves in. "You can't blame yourself for someone else's actions, no matter how close you are to them. Plenty of people's marriages end for all kinds of reasons. It doesn't mean they don't deserve another chance."

He continued like I hadn't spoken. "And I'm going to put my daughter first every time, no matter what. A woman like you deserves someone who would make you the centre of their world and I can't do that. I already got a centre and that isn't going to change."

Did he honestly think I would expect him to prioritize me over his daughter? "Just how high-maintenance do you think I am?"

That drew a genuine, surprised laugh from him as he glanced over at me. "It ain't that."

"Then what is it? You haven't given me a good reason yet. Nothing you're describing sounds like a dealbreaker to me."

"You don't mean that." He sounded pretty sure of my feelings on the subject, ignoring what I actually said. "You're so young. Your life is just getting started. You don't want to be saddled with all my problems."

We'd moved from talking about a 'woman like me' to talking about me, I'd noticed, but I didn't think Grey had done it intentionally. He seemed to have convinced himself that I was out of his league for some reason, despite the fact that I'd very willingly gone to bed with him just a few days earlier. Maybe he needed a reminder of that fact.

"What makes you think you know exactly what I want? There's a lot about me you still don't know. You seemed surprised by my class snake, and you weren't expecting your piercings to be an aphrodisiac for me."

"Fuck." He groaned the word as if he were in pain. "You really just say whatever's on your mind, don't you?"

Plenty of people told me I was too blunt at times, but Grey didn't seem to be suggesting it was a bad thing. "I do, which is why you don't need to try to guess what I want. I don't need you to tell me because I already know."

Leaning closer to him, I slid my hand over his thigh as his eyes closed, his self-control wavering. "What do you want, Billie?" he asked in a whisper, his voice tight.

"I want you to trust that I want to help you."

My hand slid a little higher as Grey inhaled. "I do trust you."

"If that's true, why didn't you leave Adele with me yesterday or today?"

"I just didn't feel right about it until we had a chance to talk. I knew I owed you an apology. I'm not completely clueless, even if I act that way sometimes."

Those words came as a relief, but at the moment, my thoughts were definitely elsewhere as my hand moved even higher, brushing lightly across the growing bulge in his jeans. "Good. In that case, I accept your apology. And right now, I'd like to finish what I started the other night, and give you the best damn blowjob you ever had."

His whole body seemed to clench, an obvious sign of his arousal that sent an answering wave of heat through me. "That seems a little unfair to me," he pointed out through gritted teeth. "I'm the one who screwed up, and you want to reward me for it?"

"I believe in positive reinforcement," I teased him, my chin resting on his shoulder as my hand continued to move across the front of his jeans. "You're much more likely to remember this lesson if it's a positive memory for you."

Grey turned to look at me, his face just inches from mine, his green eyes dark with desire. "I'm pretty sure it'd be a memory I wouldn't forget."

That look told me all I needed to know, and my body hummed with excitement at the thought of getting him naked again. I hadn't been expecting it at all when I went over there that evening, but I had no intention of turning back. "In that case, what are we waiting for?"

Chapter Eleven

~Grey~

I never knew what would come out of Billie's mouth next. I'd just told her all the reasons she shouldn't get any more involved with me than she already had, and instead of heeding my advice, she doubled down. Offering me a blowjob in return for honestly addressing my emotions seemed like a massive overpayment, but coming from her, what man would be crazy enough to turn her down? Sure as hell not me.

Just like I had on Sunday when she first came to my room, I had to wonder if all of this was a dream, but the warmth of Billie's hand in mine as she pulled me to my feet suggested otherwise. Looking almost as excited as I felt, she led me down the hall, already knowing her way around and fully taking charge of the situation.

With the door firmly closed behind us, Billie slid one hand around the back of my neck, pulling my head down to kiss me at the same time that her other hand ran across the front of my jeans again. I groaned into her kiss, my body giving in to the promise of pleasure even as my mind still struggled to accept it.

Ever since she touched my thigh out on the sofa, my cock had been begging for attention. My jeans had never felt so tight, and every bit of pressure from her hand sent another wave of anticipation through me.

I'd never had a blowjob with the ladder in, not all the way to the end.

The only women I'd been with since my divorce had been one-time encounters, on the very rare occasions I got someone to watch Adele. With just one shot to shoot, I couldn't waste it on something designed far more for my enjoyment than my partners. I considered myself more of a gentleman than that.

Billie, on the other hand, wasn't a one-time thing. We were already on our second time, and she seemed completely determined to focus on me while I had no real will to resist her. Hopefully, she'd allow me to return the favour, but first, I planned to enjoy every damn second of what she had in mind.

"Where are you most comfortable?" she murmured as her hands went to the button of my jeans, undoing it and pulling the zipper down as I sighed in relief. "Sitting down? Lying down?"

"I'll... uh, I'll sit, I guess." That would keep my knees from buckling but also allow me to watch her, since the sight of her with my cock in her mouth would fuel my fantasies for a very long time to come.

Working together, we got my pants off in record time, and I pulled my shirt off too, leaving me naked while she remained fully clothed. It didn't matter; she would look good no matter how much she wore, and as she pushed me playfully down onto the edge of the bed, my cock was already about as hard as it could get.

At least, I thought so, until Billie pushed my knees apart and kneeled down between them, and another rush of blood flowed straight to my groin. "It looks just as good as I remembered," she said, her eyes on my cock as she licked her lips in anticipation.

Fuck, she turned me on. I'd never known anyone so straight to the point. "You've been thinking about it?"

Billie's blue eyes glanced up at me, amused and excited. "You have no idea."

No, I didn't, but as she bent down and licked me slowly from base to head, her tongue pressing down on each piercing in turn, I lost the ability to think entirely. No ideas of any kind were in my head, nothing but an awareness of her and her tongue and how she had me completely and utterly at her mercy.

As soon as she reached the tip, she immediately went back down again, her tongue flicking from side to side between the rungs of the ladder, teasing and stimulating the sensitive skin around each piercing, and as much as I wanted to watch her, I couldn't stop my eyes closing as the pleasure overwhelmed me. "Fuck, Billie."

She didn't seem to be in any hurry. Her tongue explored every inch of me, down to my balls where I inhaled sharply as she took them into her mouth, and back up to my head where she sucked me in so firmly that her cheeks hollowed, making me groan again.

When she began to take me in deeper, I reached down to gather her hair in my hand and keep it away from her face, partly for her benefit and partly for mine. I didn't want to miss a second of that incredible view, watching my cock disappearing into her mouth, slowly at first until she adjusted to the piercings and faster once she figured out how to avoid them with her teeth.

As she fucked me with her mouth, her hand reached down to stroke beneath my balls and my orgasm began to build, fast and hard. "I'm close," I warned her, not sure how she intended to finish me off.

Billie didn't stop. Taking me in as far as she could, I hit the back of her throat right as my control broke. The most exquisite pleasure flooded my body as I released into her mouth, my vision turning black even as I tried not to take my eyes off her.

Her mouth never left me. Her movements slowed as she swallowed but she continued to suck me, her tongue pressing gently against me until I'd completely finished. Only then did she release me, placing my cock back down with a satisfied hum as she pressed a kiss on my thigh.

"Well, that was fun."

My eyes opened in time to see her grinning up at me, looking incredibly pleased with herself. I was pleased with her too. Fuck, I'd never felt anything so incredible.

"Give me a second," I requested, my body still feeling weak from the incredible rush she'd given me. "When I catch my breath, I want to have some of that kind of fun too."

Billie caught my meaning instantly and her cheeks began to flush a pretty shade of pink. "You don't have to. There's no expectation on my part, Grey."

I knew that. Billie didn't do anything expecting something in return; that wasn't her style at all. "I know, but I've been thinking about it too. You wouldn't want to leave me hanging, would you?"

Her eyes flared with anticipation as she heard the conviction in my voice. I truly meant it, and thankfully, that seemed to come across. "Well, in that case, let me help you."

While I watched, Billie removed her own shirt and jeans, and her pretty underwear too, leaving her standing there beside the bed just as naked as I was, all soft skin and enticing curves, the most inviting sight I'd ever seen.

"Lie down." My voice sounded thicker as I moved out of the way to make room for her. With her head on the pillows, I pulled her hips down closer to me and spread her legs. Though I hadn't been kidding about thinking about her, far more than I should have, my fantasies still didn't compare to the real thing.

My mouth watered at her scent, my whole body flushed with anticipation over the chance to bring her even a fraction of the pleasure she'd just given me, and when I lowered my head to get my first taste of her, I let out a deep, rumbling groan. "You shouldn't have let me do this, Billie. I'm never going to be able to forget how good you taste."

Her thighs clenched around my head. "Good," she laughed breathily, her voice softer than usual. "You'll know how I feel, then."

As I set to work properly, I paid careful attention to Billie's reactions, both her verbal ones and the clues that her body gave me. I'd always been mechanically-minded, looking for cause-and-effect solutions to any problem, and by studying the effects of my actions on her body, I could figure out how to maximize Billie's enjoyment to get us to the end we both wanted.

She loved when I ran my tongue around her entrance, her hips pushing forward to encourage me as I teased her. Her clit brought the most immediate results, and the more turned on she got, the rougher she wanted me to be. My tongue flicked over her hard and fast as I added my hand to the mix, my calloused fingers pressing into her warm wetness, the feel of her body from the inside starting to send the blood flowing to my cock again so that by the time her legs started to tremble, I was half-hard again.

"Yes, Grey, fuck, yes, there." She gasped out the individual words as her hands pressed into the mattress on either side of her, and I dug deep to go even faster with my fingers, sucking her clit hard until her body contracted around me. Immediately, I lowered my mouth back to her entrance, dipping my tongue inside to savour the taste of her while I could.

Though I had no idea what came next, I knew one thing for sure: that was an apology I would never forget.

~**Billie**~

Ever since Grey told me that he thought his oral sex game was still pretty good even without his tongue piercing, it had crossed my mind way more often than it should, sometimes at completely inopportune moments. He didn't strike me as the kind of man to boast about his skills without a good reason, and I'd just confirmed both that opinion of him and his original claim. He was *damn* good.

Though I truly hadn't been looking for payment in kind when I gave him the blowjob, I appreciated his eagerness to do it anyway, and I sure as hell enjoyed the results. So, when he raised his head, trailing his lips up my stomach and gently over my breasts as my body bathed in the bliss of its orgasm, I pulled him the rest of the way up so that his lips connected with mine. My taste lingered on his tongue, just as his did on mine, mixing together in the heat of our kiss.

Each ridge and contour of his firm body called to me as my fingers trailed down his chest and stomach, his body hovering above me, and when I reached his cock and found him hardening again, I sighed in satisfaction. "Feels like we're not quite done yet."

Grey's green eyes looked down into mine, still full of desire. "If you ain't in any hurry, I think I still got a bit more apology left in me."

His phrasing made me giggle as I gave his cock a gentle squeeze, feeling it pulse beneath my fingers as the blood returned to it. "In that case, I definitely accept."

He kissed me again while I stroked him, getting him even harder, and when he felt ready, Grey slid his cock into me, using my own wetness to provide the lubrication. As good as that felt, though, I had something different in mind.

"Do you mind if I change the angle? I want to see how the ladder feels in a different position."

Grey huffed in amusement. "You can do whatever the hell you want, Billie."

He said that, but I didn't want him to feel like I was just using him for his cock. As sexy as I found it, I also cared about him having a good time. "I want you to enjoy it too, though."

A deep groan rumbled in Grey's chest. "Trust me, you don't have to worry about that. What do you want to do?"

With his assistance, we rolled over so that I was on top, and I climbed off of him. With Grey's curious eyes on me, I turned around and straddled him in reverse. As I sank back down onto him, I let out a moan of satisfaction that echoed back to me from the man behind me.

"Is that different?" he asked, his voice tight.

"Yeah." My breathless voice barely sounded like me. "It feels good. It's okay for you?"

A strangled laugh was his reply. "Yeah, Billie. It's okay."

Slowly, I began to ride him, my body lifting and falling onto his cock as each inch of him stroked me from inside, his natural size already good on its own and the piercings rubbing along the opposite wall from when we were in missionary. I tried to savour it, memorizing the feel of him, but soon, my need grew too strong, my body craving another release, and my movements grew quicker and more frantic.

Grey's need was building too, I could tell by the grunts and groans from behind me and the way he pulled my hips down onto his waiting cock every time I lifted myself up. When he laid a firm smack across my ass in the heat of the moment, I gasped in surprise and pleasure.

"You like that?" He double-checked just to be sure, and I nodded firmly.

"I like... all of it." Not the most articulate statement I'd ever made, but my brain was barely functioning by that point. Every part of my body seemed focused on the pleasure building inside me instead.

When I felt my peak approaching, I reached down to my clit to help me get there, and though Grey couldn't see what I was doing, he obviously knew anyway, and my boldness seemed to rub off on him. "Rub it for me," he commanded, his fingers digging into my hips tighter than ever. "Come all over my cock, Billie. Let me feel it."

Fuck, yes. My body jolted as my orgasm hit, and my hand immediately moved lower, grabbing onto his balls as his cock drove into me again. They tightened in my grip as Grey groaned, and a moment later, he came too, his cock pumping inside me as I stopped moving, gasping for breath and my mind reeling.

I'd had pretty good sex before. I thought it had been pretty good, anyway, but no one had ever turned me on the way Grey did, the way it did when he went from my grumpy, closed-off neighbour to a giving and sexy-as-fuck lover. After our first night together, I tried to convince myself I could be satisfied with the memory of it, but after getting another, even better taste, I knew immediately that I would want more.

And why not? What was stopping us?

I just had to tempt fate with that thought.

Still sitting astride him, his cock still buried deep in me, it took me a second to recognize the sound of the doorknob starting to turn. Grey heard it the same time I did, and we shared a quick, panicked look before I climbed off him as fast as I could and dove onto the floor on the far side of the bed. Stifling a groan of pain as the carpet burned against my knees, I could see Grey grab a pillow from beneath his head and place it over his groin just in time as the door creaked open.

"Daddy?" Adele's voice sounded sleepy and confused as my heart pounded with adrenaline. "I hear noises."

Shit. Yet again, I'd forgotten about being quiet, and it didn't seem like Grey had been thinking about it either.

"Sorry, sweetheart." Grey cleared his throat as he tried to sound casual. "I had my phone on too loud."

Thankfully, she seemed to accept that readily enough and moved on. "I need to pee."

Obviously, Grey couldn't get up in his current state, but he remained calm. "Sure. You go on to the bathroom and I'll be right there to help." The room went silent, which I assumed meant she'd left, and a moment later, Grey looked down at me over the side of the bed. "You okay?"

"Yeah, I think so." My knees stung a bit, but at least we hadn't been caught. "Go ahead and look after her."

He climbed off the bed on the other side and picked his jeans off the floor as I stood up. Pulling them on, he gave me a nod. "I'll keep her in there for a few minutes so you can get dressed and go."

Oh. I hadn't been planning on leaving immediately, since it felt like we hadn't fully finished our conversation earlier, being interrupted by our 'apology' instead, but I supposed we shouldn't push our luck. "I'll see you tomorrow, I guess."

His attention had already left me, his gaze flitting to the hall. "Yeah, good. See you."

He headed out the door as I put my own clothes back on, trying to ignore the disappointment that bubbled up inside me. When I was dressed, I stuck my head out the door tentatively, looking down the hall towards the bathroom. The door was closed, the light on inside, so I crept quietly back to the front door, got my shoes, and snuck outside to go back home.

~Grey~

That had been way too close. By the time I got Adele back into bed, my heart rate had only just started to come back down. Adele didn't know the first thing about sex and I had no intention of her introduction to it being to walk in on me in the middle of it. She didn't even find it odd that I'd been lying on top of my bed with only the pillow covering me when she came in. She had no clue what it meant.

We'd talked about private parts of the body and all of that, and she knew no one should be touching her in those places. We had that conversation regularly, unfortunately, just to make sure she still remembered it, since girls with her condition were even more vulnerable than other children to being abused. It made me sick to even think of it, but I had to, and I had to talk to her about it too.

However, when it came to sex in a reproductive sense, or just part of a healthy, happy life, we hadn't broached that topic at all yet, and I'd be happy to wait a few more years before we did. Since my sex life had been pretty nonexistent, it hadn't been all that hard to avoid.

Billie had changed that, just as she'd changed a lot of things.

The meeting at Adele's school was scheduled for the next afternoon, so I had time to run some errands in the morning after I dropped her off for the day, some over the phone and some in person. I wouldn't risk getting caught up in work and being late for the meeting, so I gave myself the day off, dressing up in the same clothes I'd worn to take Billie out for supper. I didn't own a lot of clothes that weren't t-shirts and jeans, but maybe I needed some more to go along with all the other changes in my life.

After lunch, I headed over to the school where Mrs Harris, the vice-principal who'd helped me on Adele's first day, came to meet me at the reception. Together, we went into a fairly nondescript meeting room with white walls, a window on one side, and a round table in the middle, around which sat three other people I'd never seen before. Mrs Harris introduced them to me: the tall man in the suit represented the school district, the younger man in a polo shirt and khakis similar to mine worked as the school's special needs coordinator, and the woman in a blouse and skirt was the school's educational psychologist. I'd never heard of that job before until Billie had told me about it.

Everyone seemed friendly and open, asking me about the move to Houston while Mrs Harris brought me a coffee. One chair at the table remained empty but not for long, as the door opened behind me and I turned around to see Billie and Adele walk in.

"Daddy!" Adele's eyes lit up when she saw me there, confused about why I'd be there but still full of excitement. Pulling loose from Billie's hand, she ran over to me and threw her little arms around me.

"This is Adele," Billie introduced her to the room, her smile full of affection.

The people around the table all asked Adele some age-appropriate questions about school and what she liked and didn't like about it. Ms Callahan got an enthusiastic thumbs up from her, but she couldn't think of anything she didn't like. She was such a good kid and I couldn't be prouder, even though I knew just how little of it had to do with me.

Once all the questions were answered, Billie left to take Adele back to the classroom and returned a couple of minutes later, taking a seat next to me, looking comfortable and confident in the situation. The supportive smile she gave me made me feel more confident too.

"What do you see as Adele's strengths, Mr Wright?" the man from the school district asked me.

I could talk about that topic for days. "She's got the best heart. She sees the best in everyone, even when they don't deserve it, and she wants everyone to be her friend. Even if you screw up, she'll forgive and give you another chance. Also, she really loves to learn. She's been so excited about coming to school, and Ms Callahan's made it such a good experience for her. She adores Ms Callahan."

Billie's cheeks turned pink from the praise as everyone looked over at her.

"And what are her biggest challenges?" the man followed up.

"Well, I reckon it's the flip side of that. She's too trusting and doesn't pick up on signals from other kids when they're not interested in her or just not being nice. She doesn't have a lot of personal boundaries. And as much as she loves to learn, she wants to do things her way and she can be a bit stubborn at times."

Billie backed me up when they asked her the same questions. "Mr Wright summed it all up very well. The biggest challenge for me is when we switch between activities in the classroom. Adele needs some help to make the transition and leave one thing behind to focus on the next thing. At the moment, it's taking up my time or my assistant's time, which delays the whole class. A dedicated aide would be able to help with that while I keep the whole class moving forward."

She outlined a few other ways the additional support could help, speaking frankly about Adele's challenges, and though I didn't particularly like hearing it all laid out that way, I understood why she did it. She'd warned me that we need to paint a picture of her worst days to make sure Adele would be supported properly, even if most days, she needed less help than that.

The other people around the table gave their opinions as well, and by the time we were done, it felt like we were all mostly on the same page. The special needs coordinator said that there were two other students in Billie's class who had been identified as needing a bit of extra support but not as much as Adele, so he recommended a full-time aide for the classroom who would be primarily working with Adele but could assist the others where needed. That sounded fine to me, and when Billie gave her agreement as well, I knew it must be the right call.

When the meeting drew to an end, Billie got to her feet. "Please excuse me, I'm going to get back to my class before the end of the day."

I'd hoped to have a chance to speak to her before then, but it didn't seem in the cards. Instead, after I'd said my goodbyes to everyone, I went back to my van to wait for the bell. When the end of the day rolled around, I returned to the schoolyard with the other parents, but when Adele's teaching assistant brought her out instead of Billie, I had to say something.

"I'd like to have a word with Ms Callahan, if she's available."

She asked me to wait there, and before long, Billie came out, looking curious and confused. "I'm sorry, did you want me to keep Adele? I thought since you were here, you'd be taking her home with you."

She seemed a little more distant than usual, but I put it down to the fact that other parents were all around us. Seeming too familiar with each other might invite some questions.

I lowered my voice accordingly. "I am taking her home, but I wanted to take you out to dinner tonight as a thank you for all your help with the meeting. I couldn't have done it without you."

Billie glanced around, reinforcing my suspicion that she didn't want us to be overheard. "Thank you, Grey, but that's not necessary. You absolutely could have done it without me, and besides, it's my job."

She had gone above and beyond her job for me and Adele and she knew it. "I'd still like to have dinner with you."

"You made me dinner last night," she reminded me. "That's more than enough."

Why was she making this so difficult? It seemed I would have to spell it out for her. "Billie, I'm sorry we got interrupted last night. I went out first thing this morning and bought a lock for my bedroom door. On top of that, I talked to Cam, and Adele's going to their house for a sleepover tonight. I'd like to take you to dinner as a thank you, and the rest of the evening after that is wide open. Now, would you please let me take you out?"

Chapter Twelve

~Billie~

Grey's dinner invitation caught me completely off guard. Based on the way things had ended between us the night before and his pattern in general, I expected him to be cool with me that day and I did my best to prepare myself for it. Laura had been absolutely right: every time we started to get close, he'd pull away. I didn't think he even knew he did it but I'd noticed the pattern just as my sister had, so I behaved the way I expected him to treat me, keeping things polite but casual.

The way he acted during the meeting seemed to back that up. He hadn't looked directly at me very much, but he'd been nervous, which I understood. We were talking about his daughter's education; it couldn't be a bigger deal, and after all our preparation, I was proud of how well he spoke on her behalf. When he praised me in particular, it pleased me more than it should have, but I still kept my hopes in check. Expressing his appreciation for my work with Adele was one thing and letting me deeper into his personal life was another thing entirely.

However, when he called me outside after the end of the school day and told me he'd bought a lock for his door *and* made arrangements for Adele to stay at Tonia's house that night so that we could have the whole evening to ourselves, I finally realized that he didn't intend to pull back at all. He couldn't be making it clearer that he'd enjoyed himself the night before and wanted more of the same.

Maybe he really had taken his promise seriously when he said he would try not to take his frustrations out on me anymore. Maybe this invitation meant more than just a thank you, as he'd claimed? Maybe something had shifted between us? Those were a lot of maybes, but I wouldn't know for sure what his invitation meant unless I accepted it. Besides, I couldn't deny the rush of heat through my body at the idea of spending the night with him, unrestricted, with no need to rush or keep quiet, so in the end, it didn't feel like a very difficult decision at all.

"How should I dress?"

A relieved and satisfied smile spread across Grey's face when I stopped resisting. "Casual. I'm planning on changing into my jeans when I get home, and the place I had in my mind ain't fancy."

After our restaurant experience the previous weekend, I didn't want anything fancy anyway, and from the smile in his eyes, I could tell he felt just the same. "Alright. I've got to finish up here for the week, but I'll be home and ready by seven."

"Perfect." His pleased expression pleased me too as he turned to his daughter. "Adele, do you want to go and play with Charlie and Jenny tonight?"

"Yeah!" Her enthusiastic response made us both smile. In her mind, she'd just won the lottery, even though by the sound of things, her dad and I would be the ones getting lucky that evening.

Back in the classroom, I pulled out my phone from my purse where it stayed all day, and sure enough, I had a message waiting from Tonia. *I hear we're babysitting tonight. Any particular reason Mr Wright wants the house to himself?*

She obviously thought she had it all figured out so I sent her back a sarcastic reply. *Maybe he's decided to join a heavy metal band and needs somewhere to rehearse.*

Oh, I think he'll be playing a tune tonight all right, she replied.

What does that even mean??

Giggling at my sister's continuing texts, which grew more and more outlandish by the minute, I managed to get through my preparation for the next week. I'd just finished doing one last check when Debbie Harris appeared at my door.

"Hi, Billie. The meeting went well this afternoon."

"It did." It sounded like my request for an additional aide in the class would be approved, which was great news not just for Adele but for the class as a whole. However, I didn't think Debbie had made the trip to my classroom just to give me her opinion on the meeting. "What's up?"

With a sigh, Debbie came into the room and shut the door behind her. "I just want to give you a heads up about one of the parents in your class. Apparently, there's been some talk."

I hadn't expected her to say anything like that, and my confusion showed. "What talk? Where?"

"On a parent chat group. I'm not in the group, for obvious reasons, but I have a friend who is and she keeps me updated about any potential trouble."

"You've got a spy in the parent chat group?" I knew she had her finger on the pulse of the school community, but that was still impressive.

"Not a spy," she protested before changing her mind with a shrug. "Well, kind of. Most of the time, I stay out of it, but if she sees something brewing, she'll give me a warning."

"And there's a parent in my class who's not happy? About what?"

I honestly couldn't imagine what would have upset anyone so early in the school year. There hadn't been any major incidents in the class, no bullying or fighting between the kids and nobody getting into any big trouble, which were usually the situations where parents got concerned.

"About Adele." Debbie's grimace made it completely clear she didn't agree with whatever had been said, she was just passing it on. "I guess her daughter said something about how Adele gets to stay after school with you and this mom took it to mean she's getting some kind of preferential treatment. Upon questioning, the daughter also said that Adele gets more of your attention in class than the other kids. To be fair, I don't think that's how her daughter meant it at all, I think her mother twisted her words. The mom has grumbled about it a few times, wondering why 'kids like that' can't go to their own school."

Although I knew that attitudes like that still existed, it frustrated me beyond measure that someone still felt comfortable voicing them in a public forum, let alone a parent of one of the children in my class who might pass those toxic opinions on to her child.

"Hang on, it gets worse," Debbie warned me. "The only reason I'm mentioning it to you is that apparently, she saw you and Mr Wright speaking after school today and is now convinced that the two of you are having a torrid affair and that's why Adele is getting special treatment. She went so far as to say the school shouldn't be hiring single women as teachers because they care more about finding a partner than they do about the kids."

That was utterly ridiculous, and Debbie obviously agreed, but the woman hadn't been far off the mark with the conversation between me and Grey. Were we really that easy to read?

"Plenty of people stood up for you, including parents from last year's class, and so far, nobody has agreed with her overall premise, but I thought you should be aware of it."

"I thought you said there was nothing in the policy against teachers dating parents," I reminded her.

"There isn't. Policy-wise, she hasn't got a leg to stand on, but she's trying to claim some sort of moral high ground. I'm not telling you what to do, Billie. If there *is* something going on between you and Mr Wright, that's none of her business, nor mine either. I just don't want to leave you in the dark about what's being said, and to let you know that if you need any kind of support, you can always talk to me."

"Thanks, Debbie." I really did appreciate her offer, even if the whole thing felt absurd to me. My personal life had nothing to do with how I did my job, and what she saw as 'special treatment' for Adele in class was only her getting what she needed. Adele staying with me outside of school hours didn't impact on the other kids in any way. Hopefully, if we got an aide specifically to support Adele, it would address any concerns about my attention being divided, but I had my doubts. She'd probably just see that as another example of Adele getting more than her daughter did. Some people just needed something to complain about.

In any case, I had no intention of letting some self-righteous woman I didn't even know ruin my night. After turning off the lights in my classroom, I headed home to get changed and ready for an entire evening with Grey, just the two of us, with endless possibilities.

~Grey~

Cam couldn't have been kinder when I called to ask about Adele going over to their place for the evening. Originally, I only planned to ask if they would watch her over dinner and I would pick her up afterwards. I didn't want to impose too much and even asking for that much didn't come naturally to me. I offered to bring some take-out for the whole family along with me to sweeten the deal.

"Tonia has the whole week's meal plan prepared in advance and there's always extra," he told me with a laugh. "Don't worry about food, and you don't need to rush back from your dinner either. In fact, if Adele's okay with being away from home, she could stay overnight if you want."

As a natural extrovert with an adventurous streak, Adele had never gotten homesick. I sometimes wished she'd be a little *less* eager to run into new situations, but at least in this case, it worked to my advantage. "Are you sure it wouldn't be too much trouble?"

"Not at all. We'd love to make it up to her for what happened at the barbecue."

Since Dex's visit and apology the night before, Adele seemed to have already forgotten all about that, so a sleepover for that reason didn't seem necessary. However, the prospect of having a whole uninterrupted night with Billie proved too tempting to resist and I found myself agreeing. When I saw the look of appreciation in Billie's eyes when I explained the situation to her, it made me mighty glad I had.

Cam and Tonia invited me into their beautiful ranch-style house when I dropped Adele off so I could see where she'd be sleeping and put my mind at ease about leaving her there. If anyone had told me a month earlier that I'd be leaving my daughter overnight in Houston with people I'd only met twice, I'd have laughed in their face, but Cam and Tonia had honestly won me over that quickly. As much as it had to do with them being great people, it probably came down more to the fact that I knew they had Billie's trust. For me, that was the deciding factor.

"If you want to call and talk to Adele at any point, go right ahead," Tonia encouraged me. "We'll send you some photos too so you can see her for yourself."

"Thanks." Maybe I still looked a little nervous about the whole prospect, enough to make her offer to keep me updated. "She'll be fine, I know. I'm the one who'll be anxious."

"Don't be. Just relax and enjoy your evening."

The smug smile on her face suggested she had a very good idea what kind of evening I had in mind with her sister, and she didn't seem to have any objections. They were a very open family, apparently. My sister and I were definitely not *that* close.

When I got back to my house, Billie's truck was in her driveway, and my heart rate immediately kicked up a beat as I pulled into my own drive. What the hell was I doing? I hadn't asked a woman out in years. The dinner that Billie and I went out for the previous weekend didn't count, since I hadn't planned it in advance. It had been thrust on both of us, and though it worked out better than I could have ever dreamed, the evening ahead of us felt different since the whole thing had been my idea.

Well, almost the whole thing. Cam had helped me out with picking a place to go since I didn't really know Houston at all. I told him I wanted something low-key and casual, something closer to a small-town bar than a five-star restaurant, and he told me he knew the perfect place. I sure as hell hoped it wouldn't be a repeat of our previous dinner out, but I trusted Cam, especially when he told me he knew Billie would love it.

What was I hoping to get out of the evening, though, besides a chance to thank Billie for her help and, hopefully, another incredible night with her? If we did end up in bed together again, which seemed more than likely, that would be three times in a week. At what point did it stop being a casual experimentation and turn into something else?

Whatever the answer was, I wouldn't figure it out sitting in my truck in the driveway. Since it hadn't quite reached seven o'clock yet, I went back inside my own house for a while, checking that everything was clean and tidy for Billie to come over afterwards. Although she'd been in my house several times, she'd never stayed over, and I wanted her to be comfortable if she did that night. She'd never had breakfast there, never showered there, and just the thought of doing both those things with her had my cock stirring. Fuck, I was looking forward to being able to really take my time with her.

At last, the clock ticked to seven, and I headed next door. Billie had obviously been waiting for me since she opened the door before I could reach it, standing there in the same boots she'd worn the other night and a different dress, just as pretty as the other one. With her hair down and her blue eyes shining, she looked so damn good that I was tempted to call off the dinner part of the evening entirely.

"Everything go okay with Adele at Tonia's?" she asked before I could get a word out, stepping out her front door and locking it behind her.

"Yeah, fine. Adele will have a great time. She probably hasn't even noticed I'm gone yet. You look wonderful, by the way."

I didn't mean it to sound like quite so much of an afterthought, but Billie didn't seem to mind. "Thanks. I like this look on you too." Walking straight up to me, she slid her hands up over my shirt, brushing against my nipple piercing as she went, and curled her hands around the back of my neck to pull me down for a kiss. Short and sweet, it only lasted a couple of seconds before she released me with a smile. "Let's go."

Good Lord, she was making it difficult to remember why I had suggested going out at all.

"How was work today?" she asked once we were settled in my van, heading to the place Cam had suggested.

"Actually, I took the day off on account of the meeting."

"How was work yesterday, then?" she asked instead.

My eyes darted over to her for a second, trying to figure out why she was asking. "Pretty routine. Nothing out of the ordinary."

She kept trying. "What's a routine day like? I don't really know what's involved in your job other than coming to the rescue of people like me who don't know where to turn their water off."

Although she laughed, it wasn't really a laughing matter. She was lucky she hadn't done more damage than she did. "That's the bulk of it. Sometimes, I'll work on new builds or renovations, but a lot of it is emergency response."

"Grey." Billie turned to me with an exasperated sigh. "I'm looking for a little more detail. The first job you had yesterday, for example: what did you do, exactly?"

I glanced back over at her, still unsure about her motivation. "It's not very exciting."

"Says who? I'm interested."

She did seem to be. I supposed I'd gotten used to Donna not caring about the ins and outs of the job, finding anything not directly related to her own interests a little tedious. Sometimes, she'd listen, but it always felt like a chore, and eventually, I stopped sharing. I didn't want to bore Billie either, which must have been why I tried to give her vague, short answers that would allow her to move on, but she wasn't having it.

"I can tell you over dinner if you really want to know."

"I do," she promised. "I'll hold you to that."

Luckily, it didn't take too much longer to reach the restaurant Cam had suggested. It definitely had a country vibe, with a large, semi-circular bar facing a small dance floor at the front of the place, and a quieter sit-down section in the back with booths and tables where we could eat. There was even a mechanical bull in the corner, but it sat quiet for the moment. The place seemed to be filled with locals rather than tourists, and a lot of people seemed to know each other. It was just what I'd had in mind.

"Are we dancing later?" Billie teased, gesturing towards the dance floor as we passed. A few couples were two-stepping, but it was still early in the evening. Things hadn't really picked up yet.

"I guess that's up to you. I could be persuaded."

"Really?" Her eyes were almost comically large as she looked up at me. "I was kidding, I didn't think you were a dancer."

"Why not?" I challenged, and she could only shrug.

"You're full of surprises, Grey."

As we slid into a booth and picked up the menus, I hoped she meant that in a good way. I knew I did when I returned the sentiment. "I could say the same about you."

~Billie~

At first, Grey was so reluctant to talk about his work, I would have almost thought it involved highly classified information or some kind of state secrets. However, once we had our ribs and beer, he finally began to loosen up, and when he realized he had my full attention, he started to add some colour and detail to his stories, describing not only the actual jobs but the clients he worked for in such sharp, clear terms, I could practically see them standing in front of me.

A shudder worked its way down my spine when he told me about being called out to a farm outside his hometown where a snake had managed to get into the pipes, followed by a laugh when he described his reaction. "When I opened up the pipe and found two eyes staring back at me, you ain't never seen a man move so fast as I got across that room."

"I don't feel quite so stupid about forgetting to turn the water off now," I said when he described how someone had inadvertently mixed up the sewage and freshwater pipes when trying to do their own repair.

"You still make the list," Grey teased me, his tone deadpan but his green eyes twinkling in amusement. "If you grew up on a ranch, didn't your daddy or your big brother ever teach you the basics?"

"I'm the baby in the family," I reminded him. "I was spoiled rotten. Everyone did things for me."

"I wouldn't call you spoiled." Grey's immediate defense of me made me smile, even if he had it wrong.

"When it came to chores, I definitely was. I didn't have to do half of what my big brother and sisters did. It had a downside too, though; I always got told I was too young to do the fun things they were doing. It took a long time for me to really feel as grown-up as the rest of them, but with my job and my own house now, in the last couple of years, it finally feels like we're equals."

"I understand," he assured me. "My sister's always been the one who had everything together. When I talk to her, I still feel like a kid sometimes."

We chatted some more about older siblings and other things we had in common, the conversation flowing easily, and I could hardly believe the guy sitting across from me was the same one who seemed barely able to tolerate me a few weeks earlier. He still hadn't said anything about wanting any kind of relationship with me beyond friendship and the occasional hook-up, but as dinner drew to a close, it felt possible in a way it hadn't before.

"Do you want to have a quick dance before we go?" he asked once he'd paid the bill, refusing my attempts to chip in my share.

My head turned towards the dance floor, which had filled up quite a bit since we came in. "How do you know how to dance? I need this story."

For the first time since we sat down, he looked a little uncomfortable, but he answered me anyway. "Donna insisted that I learn. For a while there, we had weddings to go to every other weekend, it felt like, and she wanted to make a good impression."

From the short time I spent with her, that didn't really surprise me. She seemed pretty concerned about appearances. "Can I ask a really rude question?"

Grey's eyebrows raised curiously, a smile pulling at the corner of his lips. "I didn't realize you needed permission."

"Hey, I'm not usually rude! Blunt, yes, but not rude."

He conceded that point with a shrug. "What is it?"

I still tried to phrase it in the least rude way I could, but I had to ask. "Why did you marry her?"

Despite my warning, Grey's eyes still widened in surprise. "You really aren't pulling any punches."

"I know how it sounds, but I'm genuinely curious. She must have some good qualities for a guy like you to fall in love with her. I know I've only seen part of the story, so tell me the rest: how did you guys end up together?"

His grip tightening on the bottle in his hand, Grey lifted the bottle to his mouth, though there wasn't much left in it. "If you asked anyone in town back when we were in high school, they'd have said she settled for me. She was pretty and popular and I was the quiet guy who sat in the back of the class and never said much. Didn't play any sports, wasn't great at tests. I didn't have a lot going for me."

As usual, he was being pretty hard on himself. He had plenty of good qualities too. "But she saw something in you?"

"Yeah, I guess so. I don't know why she asked me out in the first place, but she did. She'd take me out shopping and tell me which clothes to buy and how to fit in better. I guess she was building the boyfriend she wanted, just like when she made me learn to dance, but she wasn't mean about it. In fact, we had a lot of fun. She painted a picture of this perfect life that we'd have, and it matched up pretty well with what I wanted, at least on the surface. It wasn't until later that I realized that, deep down, our priorities were pretty different."

That was by far the most he'd ever opened up to me on a personal level, and as much as I appreciated the insight it gave me into his past, I didn't want to push my luck. With a smile, I did my best to lighten the mood instead. "And your piercings didn't match up with her vision?"

Just as I hoped, the mention of his piercings turned his gaze more heated. "No, I guess not. Lucky for me, they match mine perfectly. Now, are we dancing, or are we heading back home?"

As much as the idea of getting back to his place appealed to me, I wanted to see him dance after all that buildup. "One quick dance and we can go."

Sliding out of the booth, Grey offered me his hand, and he didn't let go of mine until we reached the dance floor. Turning to face me, he lifted our joined hands up while his other hand slid around my waist. "Just follow my lead."

I considered myself a decent dancer. My daddy might not have taught me about turning off the water supply, but he'd taught me how to two-step. At the very least, I was good enough to know that Grey made an excellent partner. With his strong arm around me, he led me across the floor, twirling and stepping around the other dancers with a sure and steady confidence. Most people on the floor knew what they were doing, but we definitely held our own.

One dance turned into two, and then three, both of us enjoying the music and the feel of our bodies swaying in time to it and in tune with each other. My hand that had been resting on his shoulder slid upward, curling around the back of his neck and running gently through his hair, and I could feel his body beginning to react as his hips pressed against me.

"Time to go," Grey murmured in my ear as the third song drew to an end. "I'm just going to use the restroom real quick. You okay here?"

With a nod, I sent him on his way, making my way to the edge of the dance floor to watch the other dancers. He hadn't been gone much more than a minute before another man stepped into the space beside me, tall and lean with a big belt buckle and a cowboy hat on.

"You looked great out there," he complimented me, raising his fingers to the brim of his hat in greeting. "Fancy another spin round?"

I gave him a friendly smile, but shook my head. "No, thanks. I'm leaving in just a minute."

"Well, we can dance for a minute, can't we? No point just standing here."

"Thanks, but no."

That should have been the end of it, but he didn't let the matter drop, probably having had a bit more to drink than he should.

"Come on, I ain't gonna bite. Just one dance." His hand slid around my waist as he nudged me towards the floor.

"I don't think my date would like that very much," I warned him, planting my feet firmly to stop our movement.

"Well, he ain't here right now, so..."

He didn't get to finish that sentence before a rough hand grabbed hold of the front of his shirt and pulled him away from me. "Actually, he is." Grey's face had taken on the stormy expression I'd seen a few times, but never directed at anyone else. "And the lady said no."

The other man immediately put up his hands in surrender, obviously not liking his chances as he got a look at Grey close up. "No problem. I heard her."

"I don't think you did." Grey took a step closer to him, making the man flinch, and I nearly stepped in to break things up before they got out of hand. Before I had to, though, Grey turned to me. "You ready?"

"Absolutely." As soon as the word was out of my mouth, he put his arm around me, not giving the other man a second glance as he led me to the door.

That display of testosterone sent a molten wave of desire through my body, making my knees weak, even though I knew it shouldn't. By the time we pulled up in front of his house, I wanted him more than ever. Good thing there was nothing to stop me from having him.

Chapter Thirteen

~Grey~

The adrenaline that kicked in when I saw the stranger hitting on Billie still ran through my veins as we got back to my house. As soon as I came back from the restroom, I saw him standing too close to her, and something deep inside me flared up, that same impulse I felt anytime I heard anyone making ignorant comments about Adele, that urge, almost a need, to protect and defend my own. I got there just in time to hear her saying that her date wouldn't like her dancing with anyone else, and she had that right. The sight of his hand on her waist brought out every possessive instinct I had, and I couldn't stop myself from pulling it off of her. If he hadn't backed down so quickly, I would've done whatever was necessary to protect her.

Except that Billie wasn't mine, not in that way. We were on a date, sure, but I had no claim to her beyond that.

I half expected her to tell me off when we got back in the truck for stepping in when she was doing a perfectly fine job of defending herself, but she didn't. It wouldn't be something she'd keep to herself if she felt that way, so when she didn't say anything about it bothering her, I had to guess that it *didn't* bother her. And what did that mean?

We should talk about that, and about how much I enjoyed our date in general. Talking with her over dinner came so easy, I could almost forget all the reasons that she wouldn't want to get too close to a guy like me. Billie deserved better than me, but when she turned to me with lust in her eyes as soon as we were inside my front door, I couldn't find it in me to remind her of that fact.

At that moment, all I could think about was being inside her again.

With a slightly mischievous smile, she ran her hands over my chest just like she had when I picked her up in the first place. "You know, with the whole house to ourselves, we don't need to go to the bedroom. We could make some new memories for your new house wherever you want."

A dozen potential locations immediately sprang to mind, her directness providing my imagination with ample ammunition. "What'd you have in mind?"

She reached behind me just to make sure I'd locked the front door, which I had. "How about we start in the living room?"

Start. It sounded like her expectations of the evening were exactly what I'd been hoping for too. The sight of her in that dress and boots and the way she felt in my arms on the dance floor had my cock begging to be put to use, and as soon as we stepped into the living room, I knew exactly what I wanted to do.

Billie melted into my embrace as I pulled her tightly towards me, kissing her with all the pent-up possessiveness brought on by her encounter with that random man at the bar. My hand threaded through her hair, clenching it in my fist to hold her head steady while I took possession of her mouth, kissing her so hard it felt like all my breath came from her. There wasn't room between us for it to come from anywhere else.

My other hand trailed down her body, from her face down over the neckline of her dress, and I let out a groan as I felt her stiff nipple through the fabric of her dress. "Fuck, Billie. You don't have a bra on."

"I know," she teased me. "I left it off when I changed. It didn't magically disappear."

"Why?" Even though I hadn't noticed all evening, the thought of her out in front of those other men who might have even accidentally touched her had my blood pumping faster again.

"To give you a nice surprise when we got home."

Another groan rumbled in my chest at the thought of her getting ready for our date and thinking about that. About *me*. All my jealous energy dissipated, the blood rushing to my cock instead as I pulled the front of her dress down to expose her bare breast to me.

Billie gasped as my mouth connected with her nipple, sucking it in hard while my tongue teased the tip of it. My hands travelled up beneath her dress to her ass at the same time, checking to see if she wore any panties, not sure whether I wanted the answer to be yes or no.

Relief settled in my chest when my hands hit the lacy fabric. As sexy as the idea might be, in reality, I didn't want her running the risk of flashing that gorgeous pussy at anyone else. For that night at least, it was all mine.

I didn't have enough hands for everything I wanted to do all at once. Pulling her panties down came first, but I left them around her thighs, going back to her dress to slip it off her shoulders and get her other breast out, transferring my mouth to the second one before going back to her underwear and tugging it the rest of the way off. Billie's hands were on my shoulders, clinging to me as I tossed her panties aside and ran my hands back up her thighs, my mouth still on her nipple.

"Oh, God," Billie moaned as my fingers slipped between her legs, dipping inside her for a bit of moisture before sliding over her clit. "Your hands feel so good."

"Really?" I couldn't help asking out loud, releasing her nipple as I glanced up at her. "They're not too rough?"

The scars and calluses on my hands from the kind of work I did had left them a little worse for wear, and I'd never had a woman tell me she liked that before.

Billie laughed, her hips tilting towards me to increase the friction. "I like things a little rough."

From the way she responded to my cock, I had to believe she meant that, and when I thrust my fingers deep inside her, taking her nipple back between my teeth, Billie's moan confirmed she had absolutely no complaints.

With one hand gripping her ass, the other pumping inside her and my mouth still focused on her breasts, Billie couldn't move, and I brought her as close to the edge as I could before I couldn't take anymore. "I want to feel you coming on my cock."

A whimper left her lips as she gave her breathy agreement. "Me too."

Not wanting to waste any time, I got my jeans undone as quickly as possible, pulling them and my underwear down to my knees before taking a seat on the sofa. Billie still had her dress and boots on, the top pulled down to expose her breasts and nothing on underneath as she climbed on top of me, straddling me as I spit on my hand to coat my cock.

When she sank down onto me, her pussy warm and wet and tight around me, my fingers went back to her clit and my mouth to her nipple, biting and pressing down simultaneously, and Billie's body almost immediately jolted in response, her orgasm hitting her fast after all that buildup. Feeling her pulsing around me as she came had to be the best fucking thing I'd ever felt.

While she recovered, I pulled my shirt off, and the spark in her eyes as they drifted across my chest let me know she was definitely up for more. With my hand in her hair again, I pulled her down to kiss her, our tongues tangling until her hips started to move against me again. At that point, I pulled her dress off too, up and over her head, leaving her in just her boots as she sat astride me, my cock still buried deep inside her.

When she began to ride me, slowly and deliberately, her breasts rising and falling just in front of my face as her body stroked the length of my cock, it was my turn to moan. "I'm never gonna be able to sit on this couch now without picturing this."

Billie laughed again, her head falling forward and her hair spilling down around her face and over her bare shoulders. "Good."

"Good?" The word came out choked as she quickened her pace and my orgasm started to build, faster and faster.

"Good," she repeated. "You need some happy thoughts, Grey, and I assume this is a happy one."

"You're fucking right it is," I managed to say before my body took over, my eyes closing as my pleasure reached its tipping point and I came deep inside her, every single part of the experience permanently imprinted on my mind for all time.

~Billie~

Although I was close, I hadn't quite managed to come a second time when Grey's orgasm hit. I could feel him pumping inside me as I sank down onto him, his piercings rubbing against my inner walls in a way that was just on the right side of intense.

I loved to see him lose control and I loved the way that he groaned when his pleasure overwhelmed him. With him pinned on the couch between my thighs, I had a perfect view.

Most men I'd been with before, as soon as they had their orgasm, that would be it. If I hadn't come yet, some would make an effort to help me get there, but their enthusiasm always took a significant dip. If I *had* already come, they would consider their work done, no matter how close I might be to arriving again.

With that experience behind me, I didn't expect Grey to be any different, but when he opened his eyes again as his orgasm subsided, those green eyes staring up at me in wonder, he immediately asked the question: "You didn't come again, did you?"

I could have lied and said I did, but lying had never been my style. "No, but it's okay. We'll have another chance later on…"

My words turned into a squeal as Grey's strong hands went to my waist, lifting me off of him and tossing me down onto the sofa next to him with just the right mix of roughness and tenderness. "No it's fucking not okay. I don't leave a job half done, Billie."

Next thing I knew, his fingers were back inside me, taking the place of his cock. They must have been coated with the cum he'd just left there, pushing it deeper inside me as he fucked me firmly with at least two fingers, maybe even three. The thought made me shiver even before he lowered his mouth to my sensitive clit, his tongue flicking eagerly across it while his fingers pumped into me.

His consideration and determination to make sure I was completely satisfied turned me on nearly as much as his actions, and my need quickly built again. "Yes, Grey, fuck. Nearly... just... there."

My words trailed off into incoherence as my body gave in, my orgasm washing over me and flooding me with pleasure from head to toe.

"Yes, there." Grey sounded gratified from between my legs as the last echoes of my satisfaction rippled through me. "That's better."

It certainly was. I couldn't remember it ever being better.

"I guess we should, uh, clean up a bit." He looked sheepishly around the room at our clothes, tossed all over the place as if we'd been unable to help ourselves, which wasn't far off the truth. "Do you want something else to wear?"

It sounded like he'd just realized I might need a thing or two if I were staying the night, but luckily, I'd already considered that. "I have a small bag just inside my front door. I'll go and grab it now."

Grey looked simultaneously impressed with my forethought and offended at the idea that I would go and get it myself. "I'll get it. Where are your keys?"

I directed him to my purse that I'd left by the front door, and he threw his jeans back on while I gathered up my clothes and went into the main bathroom. Toys lined the bathtub and there was a stack of board books next to the toilet, making it crystal clear that a child lived there. Although Adele was having her own fun that night, if Grey and

I were going to keep hooking up, or whatever the hell we were doing, we would eventually need to talk about what it meant and how it might affect Adele. She was top of my mind, just as she was for Grey.

He knocked on the door a few moments later. "I've got the bag, it's just here in the hall for you."

"Thanks." I could hear the creak of the floor as he went down the hall to his bedroom, and I grabbed my bag from where he'd left it. Inside were my toiletries, everything I needed for my bedtime and morning routines, along with both comfortable pajamas and a sexy pair, depending on what the situation called for. Since I had a feeling we weren't done just yet, I put the sexier pair on as I brushed out my hair and washed off my makeup. He would see me without it in the morning anyway, so I might as well get the shock over with.

Leaving the bag in the bathroom when I'd finished, I returned to the living room to find Grey sitting on the couch, his phone in his hand, wearing a pair of grey sweatpants and a fresh t-shirt. His feet were bare, and his lips parted as he glanced up and saw me in the pale peach-coloured lace-trimmed nightie.

"Fuck." His voice immediately sounded tighter again. "I was just gonna call Tonia and say goodnight to Adele, but now, my mind is elsewhere."

I gave his arm a teasing swat as I sat down next to him. "Can I say goodnight to her too?"

He looked down at the neckline of my nightie, his gaze lingering there a moment longer than necessary. "I was going to video call."

"Just keep the camera from the neck up." It didn't seem like rocket science to me.

"Right. Yeah." Clearing his throat, he placed the call, and after a couple of rings, my sister's face appeared on the screen.

"Hi, Grey! Perfect timing, the kids are just having their bedtime story. Oh, and hey, Billie."

Only a few strands of my hair were visible on the screen, but she guessed my identity anyway so Grey obligingly turned the phone to include me in the shot as I answered her. "Hi, Tonia. We just got back from dinner. I wanted to say goodnight to Adele too before I go home."

Her smirk told me she didn't buy that for a second. "Uh huh. Well, she's right here, hang on."

We were treated to a view of Tonia's ceiling as she walked down the hall to Charlie's room, where sleeping bags had been set up in a circle on the floor, all three kids having a campout indoors. At that moment, Cam sat among them, Jenny in his lap, Charlie on one side and Adele on the other, all caught up in the story he read to them.

"Adele, Daddy wants to say goodnight," Tonia told her, her voice coming from farther away as she held the phone out to the little girl.

An excited squeal preceded Adele's appearance on the screen, holding it so close that we could only see one of her eyes. "Daddy! We had pizza and ice cream and popcorn and movies and games and Charlie is a tree and..."

"Whoa there, hold on," Grey chuckled, enjoying his daughter's excitement. "You can tell me all about it tomorrow, okay? I just wanted to say goodnight and I love you. Ms Callahan is here too."

The eye on the screen moved even closer. "Ms Cally-lan is a baby!"

"What?" Grey and I looked at each other in confusion as Tonia laughed in the background.

"I showed her some pictures of you as a baby," my sister explained as I rolled my eyes. Of course she did. My sister never missed a chance to tease me.

"I'd like to see those myself sometime," Grey said, joining in on the joke, his eyes still on the screen. "Alright, you go on back to your story and I'll see you tomorrow, sweetheart."

"Night, Daddy!" The little face disappeared, the phone doing dizzying somersaults before Tonia's face reappeared, moving back into the hall.

"So, she's doing just fine," Tonia summed up with a laugh. "Nothing for you to worry about."

"Thanks, Tonia. I really appreciate it." Grey couldn't have sounded more sincere. "Y'all have a good night."

"Not as good as yours, I'm betting. Goodnight!" Tonia hung up before either of us could respond.

"I'm sorry about that," I apologized as a reflex. Not everyone appreciated my family's particular brand of in-your-face bluntness.

"It's okay." Despite those words, Grey's good humour seemed to disappear as he put his phone back down. "I'm sorry she's giving you a hard time, but I understand why you don't want her to think there's anything going on."

"What?" He seemed almost upset, but I had no idea why.

"You told her you were going home," he reminded me, still looking down at the phone in his hand.

"I did, but..."

Hang on. Did he think I was embarrassed to be spending the night with him? That I didn't want people to know? That wasn't it at all.

"Grey, you've seen how Tonia can run with something, and when it comes to what's going on between us, I don't even know what it is yet. I don't want her making assumptions and plans and whatever else she gets into her head until I know for sure what's happening. That's the only reason I said that. I still don't even know for sure if you're going to be talking to me tomorrow. I don't know what you think this is or what you want it to be."

His eyes moved up to my face as I spoke, his green eyes looking dark and intense. "What I want and what I *should* do are two different things entirely."

He seemed so damned convinced of that when it didn't seem clear to me at all why that should be the case. "Maybe they don't have to be? If you tell me what you want, I'll tell you what I think. You know I won't hold back."

He acknowledged that with a nod, but as his gaze dropped down to my body again, he seemed to get distracted.

"I don't know about you, but I usually like to take a shower before bed. Maybe you want to join me, and we can have a talk afterwards?"

It felt like he just wanted to delay the conversation we needed to have, but when the distraction he suggested sounded as tempting as that did, I couldn't bring myself to refuse. "That sounds pretty damn good to me."

Grey's smile returned as he got to his feet, pulling me up with him. "Let's go and get you wet, then."

~Grey~

Billie knew as well as I did that I was stalling, but as we made our way to my bedroom, stopping to grab her bag from the main bathroom along the way, she didn't protest too much. It seemed like the idea of showering together appealed to her as much as it did to me, and I hadn't been able to think about much else since she appeared in that pretty nightie of hers, the fabric just barely covering her and the peach colour looking warm against her tanned skin. Although it looked beautiful on her, I couldn't wait to take it off.

When we got to the bathroom, she reached into the shower to turn the water on, adjusting the temperature to her liking, and I couldn't resist the chance to tease her. "Careful, now. Don't break anything."

She shot me exactly the look I expected, disapproving and a tiny bit embarrassed. "You think you're funny, don't you? Just wait until you have a teaching emergency and I have to bail you out."

She already had, in a way, but I kept the joke going as I pulled my shirt up over my head. "A teaching emergency? What would that look like, exactly?"

Her eyes drifted down as I pulled my sweatpants down, my cock already hard again for her. She looked so damn good, it would have been impossible not to be. "Well, I know how to turn a child's handprint into just about any kind of picture you can imagine. Surely that's got to be good for something?"

Her answer was so ridiculous that I had to laugh. "I'm sure that's a lot of help in an emergency." With me naked, her nightie had to go next, and though I had just seen her naked in the living room, she somehow looked even better there in my bathroom. "I'd rather that my hands do this."

Giving her that warning, I stepped towards her, backing her into the shower until her back hit the tile wall while I swung the door closed behind us. The shower was only meant for one so we were squeezed in there pretty tight, but I didn't mind. I wanted to be closer to her anyway. When she had nowhere to go, I reached down between her legs to find her clit again.

"Mmmm." Billie hummed in pleasure as her arms wrapped around my shoulders. "All that working with your hands has paid off."

"I'm glad you think so, but this is a hell of a lot more fun than my day job. The two things don't really compare."

Her hand went to my cock, wrapping around it as I continued to tease her, kissing her neck and her shoulder as the water rained down on us.

"Your shampoo is in your bag?" We had better shower before we got too carried away, and Billie nodded as she tried to catch her breath.

It only took me a second to step out of the shower and grab it. Pulling the showerhead off the cradle, I used it to wet Billie's hair gently, keeping the water out of her eyes as much as possible. "Maybe you should have been a hairdresser," she teased me, sighing happily as I started to massage the shampoo into her hair, my fingers pressing against her scalp.

"You ain't seen pictures of Adele when she was little and I cut her hair. If you had, you wouldn't suggest it."

"Why did you cut her hair?" Billie's eyes were closed, her voice curious.

A lump formed in my throat as the memory came back to my mind. "Donna didn't like to take her to the hairdresser, said she hated everyone staring. I thought she meant for Adele's sake, but now, I ain't so sure.

In any case, I'd cut Adele's bangs when her hair got too long and got in her eyes but it wasn't always the straightest since she didn't like to sit still."

If Donna'd had her way, Adele would have never been seen in public at all, and everyone could forget that she'd ever had a child who didn't fit her idea of the life she deserved.

Billie couldn't be more different, standing up for Adele in the school and introducing her to her family without any hesitation at all, never treating her any different from anyone else. That was how it should be, obviously, but in my experience, what should be and what actually happened were two very different things.

My moody reflections could have brought the moment to a screeching halt, but Billie refused to let it. With her eyes still closed, she smiled softly. "You're a good dad, Grey. Would it be weird if I called you daddy too?"

I nearly choked on nothing at all, coughing as I laughed. "Yeah. That'd be weird. I ain't that much older than you."

"No, you're not."

As she grinned in satisfaction, I belatedly realized that she'd talked me into a trap, deconstructing one of my objections to the two of us having an actual relationship. The age difference didn't seem to bother her, but that was only part of it. It didn't just come down to a number. She was just starting out in life, her options still wide open, and I would just weigh her down.

Fooling around like we were, sure, I could do that. She wanted it and I sure as hell did too, so I didn't see anything wrong with it. But anything more than that, I couldn't quite wrap my head around. She deserved someone without any of the baggage I brought along with me, someone as light and happy and good as she was.

"Are you going to rinse me off now, or what?" Billie's blunt question made me realize I'd stopped moving, staring off into space as I got lost in my thoughts.

"See? I'd never make it as a hairdresser." Trying to keep the mood light just as she did, I moved on, rinsing her hair and putting the showerhead back before I took some soap in my hands and rubbed the rest of her body clean. No inch of her remained untouched, my fingers sliding over her smooth, soft, slippery skin, over her taut nipples, following the curve of her ass, until finally, I reached between her legs again. "You ready for me?"

"Always." Her breathy reply sent a rush of anticipation through me, the blood pumping to my cock as I lifted her up, letting her legs wrap around me as I pressed her back against the shower wall and guided my stiff cock into her for the second time that evening.

The steam of the shower was nothing compared to the heat in my veins as her body took me in, fitting me like a glove. Out on the sofa, she'd been in charge, but there in the shower, my feet planted firmly on the shower floor and her pinned against the wall in front of me, my cock buried deep inside her, she was completely at my mercy.

Even so, I only wanted to make her feel good. Since I needed my hands to hold her up, I'd have to rely on my words instead.

"If I were to get another piercing, where would you want it? What would you like to feel?"

Her body shivered at the possibilities, and at the reminder of all the metal that was thrusting into her at that exact moment. However, instead of answering me, she shook her head. "You'd have to heal for months, right? Which means no sex?"

"Depending on where I got it," I had to agree.

That was all she needed to hear. "Then no. I think you're perfect just as you are."

Even though I'd been trying to turn *her* on, I was the one who groaned before trying to return the compliment. "You feel perfect, Billie. The way your legs feel around me, the way you moan when I'm fucking you, the way you look when you come... there's nothing I would change."

That worked better as she bit her lip to try to keep from whimpering.

It didn't work. "Harder," she whispered, which made *me* groan again. "Fuck me as hard as you can, Grey."

My fingers dug into her skin as I gripped her tighter, getting some leverage to thrust into harder and faster, just like she wanted. I didn't say anything else and neither did she, both of us too focused on the sensations, the feel of my cock inside her, the sounds of our moans and sighs and the water from the shower, both of us breathing in the steam and heat and sweat as we worked towards our mutual release.

"Grey!" She spoke again just before she came, moaning my name as her legs trembled around me, and feeling her give in was all I needed to do the same. I came hard, just as hard as I'd been fucking her, harder for being the second time within the hour. I couldn't even remember the last time that happened for me. It must have been when I was younger than her.

My own body shaking from the exertion and release, I gently pulled out of her and placed Billie down on the floor. Wordlessly, she grabbed my shampoo from the shelf and washed my hair just as I'd done for her, and my body afterwards, taking extra care to clean around my piercings.

The water had started to go cool by the time I switched it off and stepped out of the shower to grab towels for both of us. "I'll let you get ready for bed in here," I offered. "Do you want anything to drink?"

"Just water, thanks."

After towelling off my hair, I threw on some flannel pants, leaving my chest bare, and went to the kitchen to get her a glass of water. It didn't take Billie long to comb out her hair and get her pajamas on, coming to join me in the bed with her hair still damp, looking just as beautiful in her cotton pajamas with her face bare as she did all dolled up in her dress and boots.

"Are we going to talk now?" she asked, her tone teasing as she took the water from me. "Or are you going to think of another way to distract me?"

"Are you complaining about that distraction?"

She laughed, shaking her head. "No, but you're stalling again!"

She was right, and she'd earned the right to talk about anything she damn well wanted. "Alright, Billie. I'm here and we're talking. What, exactly, do you want to know?"

Chapter Fourteen

~Billie~

Grey really didn't look thrilled about the idea of having 'the talk', and I thought I understood why. He and Donna got together in high school, and since they broke up, he hadn't had a serious relationship. From what he'd told me about Donna and what I'd seen for myself, I had my suspicions that they'd never really had a serious conversation about their relationship either. Things probably developed naturally to the point where they'd been together so long, marriage seemed inevitable.

I didn't really operate that way. Things were better when everyone was clear on what they wanted, and I'd given my sisters a hard enough time when they were in the early stages of their relationships to know that I couldn't avoid it any longer. After the last few weeks with Grey, the ups and downs, the getting closer and pulling back, and getting all the way to where he'd invited me to spend the night, it felt like we were right on the verge of something special. So long as we both wanted the same thing, I didn't see any reason we couldn't have it.

We just needed to take the chance together.

"I want to hear your thoughts first," I began. There were a few reasons for that: first, I didn't want to put any pressure on him, and second, I didn't want him to just agree with what I suggested if it wasn't really what he wanted. If he went first, he'd have to articulate his own thoughts and we could go from there. It felt much more productive.

"I think you're great, Billie, and sexy as hell. Obviously." His arm swept around in a circular motion, indicating his bathroom where we'd just satisfied each other in the shower and the bed with both of us in it. I had to agree that he'd proven beyond a doubt that he was attracted to me. "I respect you too. It ain't just physical."

That all sounded pretty good so far. "And?"

"And..." His grimace as he carried on didn't inspire a lot of confidence. "If another version of me met you, one who still knew how to laugh and take things easy and let things go, then he'd be all over you. I don't know how the hell you're still single, honestly. The men in Houston must be blind. Or crazy. Or both."

The words made me smile, but the sentiment behind them troubled me. "Don't worry about what might have been right now, Grey. Don't worry about what I want or need. Tell me what *you* want."

He took a deep breath, his green eyes fixed on me. "I want to keep having evenings like we just had."

That was better. "Good. I want that too."

"You didn't let me finish."

He said it sarcastically, but not as a joke. He still had more to say, and I had a feeling the rest of it wouldn't be nearly as positive.

"The fact of the matter is that I can't have evenings like this. I've got a daughter, and my Friday nights are usually spent right here in this house with her, watching My Little Pony on TV or playing with dolls, singing songs and reading books and going to bed at nine o'clock. You deserve someone to take you out for dinner and dancing every weekend and make love to you in every room in the house afterwards, someone who can give you all their attention and energy, and that ain't me, Billie. No matter how much I'd like it to be, it's not."

"You set me up." By agreeing that I wanted nights like the one we'd just had, I'd proven his point, at least in his eyes, but that wasn't at all what I meant. "I don't care about the dinner out or the dancing. They're both nice every once in a while but I don't need it every weekend. Having dinner with you and Adele last night and coming back here to your room was just as nice. It's the time we spend together that's important, not what we're doing."

From the way his face tightened, I could tell he didn't fully believe me, and I felt pretty certain Donna was to blame for him feeling that way. Going out and being pampered must have been things *she* cared about, but I wasn't her. When would he figure that out?

All I could do was to keep reminding him of it. "I'm not like the other women you've been with, Grey."

His amused snort made me smile. "That's for damn sure."

"I mean it. Each woman is unique, and you need to see me for me, and not some idea you've got in your head about what I am. I don't care what anyone else wants. I know what I want, and it's you. We could be great together, Grey. I know you know that, and I care about Adele too. You hit the jackpot here, but you want to throw your ticket away? What sense does that make?"

He couldn't help laughing at my metaphor, and encouraged by his good humour, I kept going.

"You can see it, can't you? The three of us hanging out in the park together or going to my family's barbecue? Those are the moments I want, not just the dinner and dancing."

In his eyes, I could swear he agreed. I could practically see the images there, the same as they were in my mind.

"Your 'mess' doesn't bother me." I used air quotes around the word 'mess', since he'd called it that. I didn't see it that way. "I met Donna and she didn't scare me. Tonia keeps pushing us together but I'm not going to let her call the shots. The mom from the school can rant all she wants. I don't care what any of them say; I'm only worried about you and me. And Adele. If we focus on that and no one else's expectations, I think this could be something spectacular."

The light in Grey's eyes slowly dimmed as I spoke, his eyebrows drawing together in concern as he listened to me carefully. "What mom from the school?"

Shit. I'd forgotten I hadn't told him about that yet, and I hadn't meant to bring it up in the middle of that conversation. It just slipped out as another example of the people we shouldn't be paying attention to. "Just someone who wants to make herself feel important."

Despite my attempt at deflection, he wouldn't let me gloss over it. "What did she say? Ranting about what?"

Keeping my tone as even as possible, I told him the basics. "Apparently, one of the moms of one of the other kids in my class has got it in her head that you and I are seeing each other and that Adele's getting special treatment because of it. It's ridiculous, I know it's ridiculous and so does the administration. It's nothing to worry about."

"The administration? Your boss knows about this?"

He looked more horrified by the second, and I quickly tried to reassure him. "I don't think the whole administration knows, but even if they do, it's not a big deal. There's no rule against teachers and parents dating, and I know that the other children aren't being disadvantaged by anything I'm doing with Adele. This woman's accusations are completely false."

"But she's making those accusations in public? Other people are talking about it? Fuck, Billie, and you let me take you out tonight? Are you crazy? What if people saw us?"

The dismay in his tone made me bristle. "So what if they did? I just said there's nothing wrong with it."

"Not technically, maybe, but a lot of people care more about how things look than whether they're technically right or wrong. What about your reputation?"

We were getting pretty far off track from the conversation I actually wanted to be having, but obviously, this had really upset him. His face had gone pale and he looked almost nauseated. "People know I'm a good teacher. That's what's important."

"What's the worst-case scenario?" he demanded, as if I hadn't said anything. "If this mom gets other parents on board, what's the worst that could happen?"

I hadn't really thought about that, but since it seemed to be so important to him, I tried to imagine it. "Well, I can't lose my job because, like I said, it's not against any rules. But I guess if she really tried and enough other parents got behind her, I could be reassigned to a different class."

I wouldn't be happy about that since I'd already grown fond of my class for that year, but it wouldn't be the end of the world. I could adjust, and it seemed a long shot to me that it would go that far anyway.

Grey seemed to feel otherwise. "So, you wouldn't be Adele's teacher anymore?"

"Not if I got reassigned, no."

His eyes closed in disappointment, or pain, perhaps. I couldn't be certain. "Well, there's your answer, Billie. We didn't need to talk about it after all. It's already been decided for us."

He had to be kidding. "Nothing's been decided! There are other good teachers at the school, and Adele would be fine with them if it came to that. I'm only going to be her teacher for this year anyway. Me being Adele's teacher and us taking a chance on a relationship aren't equal."

"You're right, they're not." Though he agreed with me, I knew he meant it differently than I did, and frustration filled me as he kept talking. "I told you I would always put her first and I meant it. She couldn't have a better teacher than you, and I won't put what I want ahead of that. I can't."

In his response, I heard the words he didn't say just as clearly as the ones he did: he wouldn't put his own desires first, even when Adele would only be mildly inconvenienced, and he wouldn't take what I wanted into consideration either. I had no problem with him putting Adele first when it mattered, but he seemed to lack perspective, seeing things in a completely rigid, black-and-white way.

Arguing about the specifics seemed pointless when he'd made his overall feelings completely clear, and a deep disappointment settled over me as I realized I might have been fooling myself all along. I thought he'd been coming around to the idea of how good we would be together, but even if his tone was different, it felt like the first night we met all over again. He'd put his concern for Adele above getting to know me or giving me a chance to explain, and I really should have heeded that red flag.

When it came right down to it, nothing had changed at all, and if he hadn't changed his mind after all our intimacies of the past week, I didn't know what else would persuade him.

"I think I should go home."

I'd imagined going to sleep next to him more times than I cared to admit, but with my body feeling like lead and my heart aching, it would be nothing like I'd imagined. At that moment, I'd rather be alone.

He didn't even try to stop me. "Maybe you should. I'm sorry, Billie. You're amazing, and you know I think that. This just wasn't ever a good idea, no matter how much I enjoyed it. We got carried away."

Maybe he was right. I'd been hoping he was someone braver than he actually turned out to be, but if he wouldn't fight for me even a little, maybe it wasn't a good idea at all.

I didn't even bother to change. In the darkness of the empty street, no one saw me sneak from one front door to the other in my pajamas, clutching my overnight bag, and no one was inside to see me lean back against the front door after locking it as tears rolled down my cheeks.

~**Grey**~

Silence had never seemed quite so... silent. From my bedroom, I heard the front door close after Billie's departure, and in its wake, the house felt so quiet that even my own heartbeat seemed loud.

I was never home by myself, hardly ever in the last seven years. Even when Adele slept, I remained aware of her, my ears tuned to any sound or cry or crash that might indicate she needed me. On the days when Billie had been watching her and I arrived home before her, I had a million things that needed to be done before she returned, preparing dinner and cleaning, filling the house with the clatter of pots and pans or the hum of the vacuum. Things were never just *quiet*.

I wished she hadn't gone, but I understood why she did. If our roles were reversed, I would have left too. I warned her that Adele's needs would always come first, but having a vague sense of that and seeing it in practice were two different things.

I meant what I said: Adele couldn't have a better teacher, and neither could the other kids in her class. Depriving not only Adele but all the other kids of being taught by her would be a level of selfishness I couldn't allow myself.

What Billie probably didn't see was that I'd actually been trying to put her first too.

No matter how she protested that it wouldn't affect her job, I knew how people could be. How the hell had this woman even found out about us in the first place? We'd only really hooked up in the privacy of my own home, and somehow, it had already become schoolyard gossip. How much worse would it be if we actually began dating in public? Billie risking her reputation and her entire career, a career she loved, over a relationship with me made no sense at all.

She didn't see it because she still lived in a world where everything worked out alright in the end, whereas I knew it didn't. Sometimes, things just went wrong and there wasn't a damn thing you could do about them, and I didn't want to be the reason that she learned that lesson. I wanted to keep that sunny optimism of hers intact, even if it meant I no longer got to enjoy it.

By cutting things off between us, Billie could keep the job she loved and Adele could keep her teacher and champion. Everyone got what they deserved.

The only one who lost was me, but I'd gotten used to being alone. Our brief interlude would be an amazing memory I could hold onto, something unspoiled and purer than my relationship with Donna had ever been. I could live with that. Somehow, I'd find a way.

As early as I dared in the morning, I sent Tonia a message to let her know I was on my way to pick up Adele.

There's no rush, she texted back. *She's still having fun. You've got a wonderful kid, Grey.*

I certainly did, and nothing warmed my heart more than when others noticed it too. *It's alright. I'm going to take her to the zoo today, we've been talking about it for a while.*

Okay, if you're sure. We'll see you soon.

When I pulled up, Adele and Charlie were playing in the front yard while Tonia and Jenny sat on the step. Adele waited until the van had stopped before she came over, just like I'd taught her. "Daddy, I'm going to the zoo!"

"I know, sweetheart, I'm the one taking you." Scooping her up, I held her little body tight as she wrapped her arms around me, breathing her in. I'd missed her like crazy even though she'd only been gone a night. How Donna could walk out of her life for good, I'd never be able to understand.

Tonia came over with Adele's bag, her eyes darting curiously to the van. "Billie's not with you?"

"No." I left it at that. If Billie wanted to share anything about our conversation with her sister, she could, but it wasn't my place. "Thanks again, Tonia. If I can ever return the favour, just say the word."

Her laugh sounded so similar to Billie's, it made my heart pang. "I'm not sure I dislike you enough to subject you to Charlie overnight, but we should definitely get them together again sometime soon."

"Sounds good." Giving Jenny a wave and Charlie a high-five, I took Adele back to the van and we headed to the zoo.

By the time we got home, Adele could barely keep her eyes open.

Between the excitement of the sleepover and the zoo, she'd worn herself out completely, and I fed her a quick dinner before putting her to bed early for the night.

Billie's truck was gone from the driveway the whole time, though I told myself I didn't check for it on purpose. I just happened to notice.

On Sunday, I woke up to another text from a Callahan, that time from Dex.

If y'all ain't busy today, you could bring Adele by my gallery so we can do some drawing together.

He'd obviously meant it when he offered to spend some time with her, and I appreciated him following through. Would Billie be there too? Did I want her to be or not? I couldn't even tell.

That sounds great. Let me know where and when,

Just after lunch, we pulled up outside a pretty blue storefront with the words A Work of Art over the door. I held Adele's hand tightly as we walked in and saw all the fancy-looking sculptures and paintings that she could knock over in her excitement if I let her run around.

"Howdy. How can I help you?" A woman I'd never seen before sat behind the counter at the back of the store. Even though I didn't recognize her, something about her seemed familiar anyway, and when she glanced down at Adele, her face lit up. "Well, hey there, Adele! You came to do some drawing, didn't you?"

As so often happened when the Callahans were involved, I felt a couple of steps behind. "I guess you know we're here to see Dex."

"I sure do. I'm his sister, Laura." As soon as she'd introduced herself, she turned towards the open door in the back, raising her voice. "Dex, your guests are here!"

Billie had mentioned Laura to me, and after finding her there, it seemed like I'd met the whole family. "I thought you lived on a ranch somewhere."

She laughed good-naturedly. "I do, I just took the day off today to help free Dex up so he could spend some time with this little lady. Dex!"

She shouted for her brother again just as he appeared in the doorway, wincing at the volume of her voice. "This ain't the ranch, Laura, I can hear you just fine."

"Well, you didn't answer me so how am I supposed to know?"

Dex showed us his workshop in the back where he had a project already set up for him and Adele to work on together. I hovered nearby for a while, not really sure what to do with myself, until Dex told me I could go. "We're fine here if you want to go sit out with Laura and have a coffee or something."

That sounded nice, actually, so after checking that Adele was okay for me to leave, I returned to the gallery which, unfortunately, didn't seem to have a lot of visitors on a Sunday afternoon. I couldn't see why not. The stuff looked really nice as far as I could tell, though I didn't know much about art.

"This one is gorgeous." I didn't even really mean to say the words out loud, but the statue in the front window was so pretty, I couldn't keep it in.

"That's Dex's wife," Laura explained, a wistful smile on her face. "He loved her so much."

"Loved?" I repeated the word without really thinking about it, curious about her use of the past tense.

"She passed away a couple of years ago. Cancer."

"Oh. Fuck. I'm sorry."

In the back of my brain, I remembered Billie mentioning that when she gave me the quick rundown of her entire family, and she'd also said he was going through a rough time when she told me what happened with Adele, but I hadn't fully connected the dots in my head. After getting to know him a bit more and seeing the beautiful statue, it all felt a lot more real, and I went over to sit down next to Laura before I could put my foot in my mouth any further.

"Yeah. It sucks." Laura's blunt response reminded me so much of Billie, I had to smile. "We promised her we'd help Dex find someone new, but it ain't going too well so far. Sometimes, you can't rush when a person's going to be ready to move on."

No, you sure couldn't. I knew that better than most. "It wouldn't be easy. For him, for sure, but for the woman too. It'd be hard to compete with the memory of someone he loved so much."

"What kind of women are you hanging out with?" Laura gave me an unimpressed look that reminded me once again of Billie. I could definitely see the resemblance now that I knew who she was. She looked more like Billie than Tonia did. "If a guy like Dex, who's capable of the kind of love he gave Shawna, fell in love again, it'd be just as epic. Different, of course, but just as good."

I supposed she had a point, but I still thought it might get complicated. "It's a lot of baggage, though."

"We've all got baggage, Grey, and sometimes, someone who doesn't have very much of their own has a little more room to help carry someone else's."

We moved on to talking about her ranch and other things, but those words stayed with me, lingering in my mind long after we'd gone home to hang Adele's artwork proudly on the living room wall.

I'd never thought about it that way before. I didn't want to weigh Billie down, but maybe the load wouldn't be as heavy for her as it was for me if we shared it together. Maybe she *wanted* to share it. A couple of times, I was almost tempted to go next door and ask her, until I remembered that I'd effectively ended things between us and she hadn't made any attempt to contact me all weekend.

I also remembered what Cam had told me about how, once Billie's trust had been lost, getting it back would be nearly impossible, and that time, I was afraid I really had gone too far.

~Billie~

My family only ever wanted the best for me, but they all had their own unique ways of showing it. First up was Tonia, who called me Saturday morning to ask why I hadn't come over to her house with Grey.

"You spent the night together, didn't you?" she asked me outright.

I stuck to a one-word answer, hoping she'd take the hint. "No."

Of course that didn't work.

"Why the hell not?" She sounded utterly perplexed. "When you spoke to Adele last night, I could have sworn you were on your way to bed. You like him, I know you do. I've never seen you light up when you talk about another man the same way."

Again, I answered as succinctly as possible. "My feelings aren't the issue."

Again, she wouldn't let it go. "But he likes you too, I can see it in the way he looks at you."

"He's attracted to me, sure, but not..."

"No, Billie." She cut me off that time. "I don't mean that he looks at you like he'd love to have you for dinner, even though he does."

Memories of Grey's tongue inside me came back so forcefully, my thighs squeezed together involuntarily, my body instantly reacting to the mere thought of it. Just what I needed: getting turned on by his memory when the real, live man wanted nothing more to do with me.

Tonia hadn't finished yet. "It's something else. It's like he can't quite make sense of you."

Despite everything, I had to laugh. "I think he finds our whole family a little perplexing."

"That's not what I mean. I don't know how to describe it, but it's like he thinks you're too good to be true, or at least too good to be true for *him*. If he's holding himself back, it's only because he doesn't believe it's possible."

If I wanted to end her speculation and the conversation, I would have to be blunt. "He told me flat-out that it's not going to happen, Tonia. He's made his decision."

"He might say that, but as long as he's breathing, nothing's ever final. I should know."

I had to concede that point. She'd sworn up and down that she would never, ever give Cam another chance, and there they were, married and blissfully happy with their two beautiful children. Our situations, however, weren't the same. "I don't plan to wait around six years for him to change his mind."

I meant it as a joke, and she took it that way, laughing off my sarcasm. "I don't think it'll take nearly that long, but I hear you, and you're right. You shouldn't have to wait. He should know a good thing when he sees it, and if he doesn't, then screw him."

Only Tonia could go from rooting for us to get together to turning on him in a matter of seconds if she thought he'd hurt me. She would have my back no matter what and I loved her for it, but at that moment, I still didn't want to go into details, the rejection too fresh in my mind. "Listen, I'm going over to help Dex at the gallery today and I've got to head out. I'll talk to you later."

That hadn't just been an excuse. With Dex cutting back on his staff's hours at the gallery, he needed some extra help, and while I was there, Dex asked me about Grey too, in his own way. "I'm going to invite Adele over here tomorrow to make something with me. Would you help me figure out what she'd like?"

Seeing my big brother making a real effort to fix his mistake only increased my admiration for him. "Of course."

During the day's quiet moments, we put together an activity I thought Adele would enjoy and which would challenge her but not to the point that she'd get frustrated with it. Once we'd got everything he'd need set up, we returned to the gallery, taking a seat together behind the counter, and Dex broached the subject of the little girl's father.

"Is everything okay between you two? You seem a little down today."

Did I? I thought I'd been doing a damn good job of hiding it. "It's fine. We've decided that we're just going to be friends."

"You've both decided, or he has?"

My brother could be pretty perceptive at times, and I found myself answering honestly. "He decided. I told him I wanted more and he said he didn't. Simple as that."

My brother's blue eyes were so full of understanding that tears sprang back to my eyes, even though I'd told myself the previous night would be the one and only time I ever cried over Grey Wright. "Doesn't sound simple at all to me. It's okay to be upset about it, Billie."

"Why should I be? There was never a relationship there to start with, so there's nothing to lose."

"That ain't true. You can grieve all sorts of things you never had. I miss Shawna and the life we had, but I also miss the life we mighta had. It's different but the grief is just as real."

The tears grew stronger, blurring my vision as I tried to blink them away. "You can't compare a crush I had for a few weeks with the love of your life, Dex."

"I can if I want to." He gave me a teasing, sympathetic smile. "One of the things my therapist said this week that really struck a chord for me is that my anger sometimes comes from thinking I'm alone, that no one else understands how it feels to be in my position, but that ain't true. The core emotions we all feel are the same, even if our situations are different. There's no contest and there's no prize for being the most miserable. I need to try to see my own emotions in the people around me, and that'll help me connect with people again. So, yeah, I think I can compare it. It hurts when you lose what you want, even if you never had it."

Put that way, I really couldn't argue. "Alright. It hurts and I'm upset. He said he has to put his daughter first, even though I never asked him not to."

Dex's brow furrowed in confusion. "But having you in her life would be the best thing for her. You'd never do anything to hurt her. How is that argument to not be together?"

"If you figure that out, let me know."

Thankfully, Dex didn't push any further, but I had to wonder if he'd said something to Laura because she texted me the next day.

He'll be ready when he's ready, Billie. Remember to protect your boundaries. If he comes around, make him come to you.

I hadn't followed her advice very well the last time she gave it to me, but I intended to try harder now that he'd made his own position clear. Friends and neighbours, nothing more.

When I got to my classroom on Monday morning, half an hour before the school would open, I sent a message to Grey himself. *Unless you don't want me to, I'm planning on bringing Adele home with me after school.*

He wrote back almost immediately. *That would be great. Thanks, Billie.*

At least we were still in agreement on that, and I had just slipped my phone back into my purse when the principal and vice-principal appeared at my door, their faces grim. "Billie, we need to speak with you."

Chapter Fifteen

~Grey~

Billie's text on Monday morning about watching Adele after school both surprised me and didn't surprise me at all. She wouldn't be the type of woman to take out any frustration she had with me on my daughter, so I hadn't expected her to take back her offer to help with Adele. I hadn't been sure if she'd even be speaking to me, though, after going the whole weekend without a word.

To be fair, I hadn't been in touch with her either. Somehow, I'd talked to every member of her family *other* than her.

When I dropped Adele off at school, I stood there as she went inside, watching her until I couldn't see her anymore just like I did every morning. Before I could turn to go, however, a woman I'd never seen before came up to me.

"Howdy. You're Adele's father, right?"

Instantly, my guard went up. Could she be the woman Billie had mentioned to me, the one who'd complained about our relationship? Why else would anyone be approaching me?

I kept my answer short until I knew more. "Yeah, that's me."

She stepped a little closer to me. "Do you have time to grab a coffee?"

That didn't shed any light on what might be happening, but a quick glance down at her hands confirmed she had a sparkly diamond ring on, along with a gold band. Chances were she wasn't flirting with me, but I still didn't know what she wanted. "Not really, ma'am. I'm about to head off to work."

"I thought that might be the case, but if you can spare even a few minutes, there's something you oughta know. It's about Ms Callahan."

That was exactly what I'd been afraid of, and I asked the next question through gritted teeth. "What about her?"

She leaned in even closer, casting a quick glance around before she did. "There's some talk going around about the two of you, and I thought you should know. My son was in Ms Callahan's class last year and she was the best teacher either of my kids have ever had. I don't want to see her get in any trouble."

If her son had been in Billie's class the previous year, that meant she probably *wasn't* the woman Billie mentioned to me, not to mention the fact that she was telling me about the rumours circulating about me and Billie. What did this woman know, and what information did she want to give me? It felt like it could be worth my time to find out.

"I could probably spare a few minutes. My name's Grey, by the way."

"Charlotte." She gave me a smile as she stepped back. "I know a place that the helicopter moms wouldn't be caught dead in. I'm in the green SUV over here, you can follow me."

She said nothing else before heading back to her vehicle, so I did as she said and followed her a few blocks away to a small, family-run cafe. Bright and clean but not at all trendy, its clientele at that time of day consisted mostly of elderly couples having their morning coffee. No other elementary school parents were in sight.

I ordered a black coffee, Charlotte had the same, and when the waitress walked away, Charlotte finally got down to business.

"I realize you probably think I'm crazy, whisking you off like this, but Keri-Lynn's got eyes everywhere."

"Keri-Lynn?" I hadn't come across that name before, but I could guess who she might be, and Charlotte quickly confirmed it..

"The source of the talk about you and Ms Callahan. Why don't I back up and start at the beginning?"

"I'd appreciate that."

The waitress returned with the coffee pot and we both fell silent as she filled our cups, but as soon as she'd gone, Charlotte started again.

"Keri-Lynn Keller is another parent. Her son is in the same fifth grade class as my oldest, so I've had to deal with her quite a lot over the years, unfortunately. Her daughter is in Ms Callahan's class this year."

"So, she's the one who's complained about Bil... Ms Callahan?"

I was jumping ahead of her story, and giving myself away by referring to Billie by her first name, but I couldn't help it. I wanted to get to the heart of things as quickly as possible.

Charlotte didn't seem put off by my interruption. "That's right. Just so you know the kind of woman you're dealing with: my son went to her son's birthday party a couple of years ago and told me that the birthday boy won all the party games because his mom would change the rules mid-game. She fixed every single game so her son would win. They were eight years old."

If I were being completely honest, it sounded like the kind of thing Donna might do. Definitely not out of the realm of possibility, at least, so I had a rough understanding of the kind of woman we were talking about.

As interesting as that might be, though, I wanted to get to the point. "What did she say about Ms Callahan?"

"Well, it starts with Adele."

I wouldn't have thought it possible for my back to be up any more than it already was, but the mention of my little girl did it. "What about her?"

She went on to tell me about the parent chat group she was in, not just for parents of Billie's class but for the entire school. "Usually, we just keep each other informed about things we need to know, but occasionally, there are rumours and complaints that go in there as well. About ten days ago, Keri-Lynn began to complain about Adele getting special treatment in class."

In disbelief, I listened as Charlotte read out some of the messages from her phone. This Keri-Lynn woman had posed it as a question at first: 'Has anyone else noticed...', but when no one backed her up, she got more aggressive until she was questioning Adele's right to be at the school at all.

"And people are agreeing with this bullshit?" I asked roughly, trying my best to hold back my simmering anger. Charlotte didn't deserve to be on the receiving end of my temper any more than Billie had, and I tried to remember the lesson Billie had taught me about that.

"She's got a whole little clique of moms who want to be on her good side, so they're backing her up in the most general terms. I don't think any of them actually agree with her, but they'll go along with her anyway. Honestly, it's like high school all over again. It's exhausting."

Charlotte went on to tell me how this eventually morphed into suggestions that Billie and I were seeing each other, and how I was essentially trading sexual favours to get my daughter extra attention. The whole thing was so ridiculous that I wanted to laugh, except that it wasn't funny at all. This woman was doing her damnedest to turn people against both Adele and Billie. She could say what she wanted about me, I couldn't care less, but she had crossed a line by going after the people I cared about.

"Here's the kicker," Charlotte warned me, handing the phone to me so I could see it for myself. "She posted these over the weekend and said that with this 'evidence', she planned to submit a formal complaint to the school first thing this morning."

On the screen, in a series of four photos, Billie and I were in each other's arms, smiling at each other, on the dance floor at the restaurant I'd taken her to on Friday. I *knew* that had been a bad idea. It sounded like this woman was insane enough to have followed us there.

Despite my frustration, I couldn't look away from the photos. Billie looked so fucking beautiful, I couldn't take my eyes off her, and I actually looked... happy. I couldn't remember the last time I saw that look on my face, not in pictures and not in the mirror either.

Charlotte summed up the situation bluntly. "Now, all I see there are two adults having a nice time, adults who ain't hurting anyone. Like I said before, my son was in Ms Callahan's class last year and he thought she was wonderful. So did I. She's a young, single woman who deserves a life outside of her job, and I don't believe for one second that she's letting any of the kids in that class down in any way."

"I'm sure you're right, but we both know that ain't always the way the world works." Finally, I managed to pull my eyes away from the photos and hand Charlotte's phone back to her. "What'll happen with this complaint?"

"Well, that's the main reason I'm talking to you. Keri-Lynn already posted that she has a meeting with Ms Callahan and the principal after school today to follow up on her complaint. I thought you might want to know."

I certainly did, especially since I didn't expect Billie to mention it to me. Why would she, after the way I'd pushed her away?

"Are you busy today, Charlotte?" I was supposed to go to work, but as a subcontractor working on a job-by-job basis, I could change my plans if something more important came up, and this definitely qualified. I just needed some help from someone who knew the players involved better than I did.

"I can make time, especially if it means bringing Keri-Lynn down a peg or two." A smile of satisfaction crossed her face as she leaned closer to me over her coffee cup. "What do you have in mind?"

~Billie~

Once the kids arrived and the day began, I didn't have a spare minute to stress over the upcoming meeting, but my feeling of dread about it didn't entirely disappear. It lingered in the pit of my stomach as a vague sense of uneasiness, reminding me that things could definitely be better. Not only had Grey decided he didn't want a relationship with me, but the worst-case scenario that had been the catalyst for that decision might be about to happen anyway if Keri-Lynn Keller got her way.

Rhonda, our principal, and Debbie, the vice-principal, had assured me the meeting would be informal and a chance to address Keri-Lynn's concerns before they got out of hand. However, despite their attempts at convincing me it wasn't a big deal, I could tell by their expressions that they didn't expect this meeting to be the end of things. From their past experience with her, they knew she didn't back down easily, and though they personally agreed that posting the pictures of me and Grey to the parent group had been an invasion of privacy, they had to admit that we had been in a public place, so technically, we couldn't do anything about it.

"We'll be there for back-up, but it'd be best if you and Keri-Lynn can sort this out directly," Debbie told me. "The less the school needs to be involved, the better."

So, it would be up to me to try to appease the woman who was at least indirectly responsible for convincing Grey to close the door on a relationship between us. The blame still lay primarily with him but she'd played a part, and the idea of having to suck up to her didn't sit right with me at all.

Despite all of that, I couldn't hold her mother's actions against Sophie Keller, and when the little girl proudly showed me the horse she made during our craft for the day, I praised it just like I would have for anyone. I didn't play favourites, no matter what her mother thought. I did, however, assign Sophie and Adele to work together that afternoon. She actually got along quite well with Adele, and if she told her mother about it, all the better.

"They're ready for you, Billie." My teaching assistant passed on the message when she returned from making sure all the children had been picked up at the end of the day.

"Thanks. I'll try not to be too long." In my absence, she'd agreed to watch Adele until I got back, and I didn't want to keep her any longer than necessary. Hopefully, I could defuse Ms Keller's indignation once we actually had a chance to chat face-to-face.

Rhonda, Debbie and the woman who must be Keri-Lynn Keller were all waiting for me in Debbie's office when I arrived. Sophie and an older boy who must also belong to the Keller family were sitting outside the office, waiting for their mother. Pasting my best friendly, unthreatening smile on my face, I walked in and held out my hand.

"You must be Keri-Lynn. I'm Billie Callahan."

"Ms Callahan." The blonde woman stood up to shake my hand, greeting me primly and refusing to address me by my first name though I'd called her by hers. That wasn't a great start. Perfectly made-up and wearing a dress that suggested she didn't spend a lot of time getting her hands dirty, she looked almost exactly as I imagined she would.

Taking the lead as Rhonda and Debbie had asked me to, I took a seat and jumped right in. "I understand you've got some concerns about the amount of attention that Sophie's getting in my class."

"Oh, this isn't just about Sophie," she protested, sounding scandalized at the idea that she would be there only on behalf of her own child. "Several of the other parents have concerns as well. I'm just here as a representative."

That wasn't what Debbie told me from the messages she'd seen in the chat group, but since we weren't technically supposed to know about those, I had to play dumb. "What concerns are those?"

Her voice was like honey mixed with venom, sweet on the surface but poison underneath. "Well, as I stated in my message to the principal, there's a concern that your inappropriate relationship with Mr Wright means that his daughter is receiving extra attention to the detriment of the rest of the class."

That was almost word-for-word what her complaint had said, and I latched onto one word in particular. "What exactly makes my friendship with Mr Wright inappropriate?"

She gave me a tight smile. "Well, it's not just a friendship, is it?"

I had no intention of letting her ruffle me. "I don't see how that's any of your business, to be honest, but even if we were dating, it still wouldn't be inappropriate. Isn't that right, Debbie?"

The vice-principal immediately backed me up. "That's right. There's no policy against teachers and parents seeing each other, Ms Keller."

"There should be," was her indignant response, and Debbie's lips twitched as she tried not to smile.

"We aren't in a position to discuss what the policy should or shouldn't be. I can only tell you what it is, and Ms Callahan is right: if she and Mr Wright were dating, there would be nothing inappropriate about it from the school's point of view. In the same vein, teachers can teach their own children and that's perfectly fine as well."

I thought that was a good point, but Keri-Lynn disagreed. "Well, that would be different because the teacher wouldn't be trying to impress anyone. The problem is that in trying to court Mr Wright, Ms Callahan will want to curry favour with him by giving his daughter preferential treatment. What's the school's *policy* on that?"

"What evidence do you have..." Debbie started to ask, but I cut her off with a different question of my own, keeping my tone as even and professional as possible.

"Ms Keller, I assume you're aware that Adele has Down Syndrome?"

"Of course."

"And are you aware that children with the condition sometimes need a bit of extra support to do the same things that neurotypical children take for granted?"

Obviously, she didn't appreciate the way I phrased that, her lips pursing in disapproval. "If that's the case, then she should be in a school more suited to her needs."

That, I believed, was the real heart of her complaint, and I did my best to address it. "This school is perfectly capable of handling her needs. We're in the process of getting approval for an additional aide who will be able to support Adele and the class in general. It just takes some time to put these things in place, so *if* Adele has received any extra attention from me over the past few weeks, it will be remedied as soon as that aide is in place."

"The school is going to use my tax dollars to provide an additional staff member just to help one child?" She managed to twist my words into something that sounded outrageous in her mind, getting more offended by the moment. "That's unacceptable."

Debbie threw me an amused glance before stepping in. "The alternative, Ms Keller, is that Ms Callahan gives Adele more of her own attention, which you've already stated that you find unacceptable as well. What would you find an acceptable solution?"

Put on the spot, she doubled down. "The child should go to a school that already had provisions for someone like her."

The way she never referred to Adele by name and talked about 'someone like her' told me all I needed to know about her views. I had it on the tip of my tongue to reply that Adele had every right to be at this school, just as much as her own children did, but Debbie shook her head at me, asking me to keep quiet, so I swallowed the words back down.

"That would be a matter to take up with the school board," Debbie told her. "Is there a solution we can come up with here today that would satisfy you?"

The words out of her mouth didn't really surprise me as she ignored every point I'd tried to make. "It still seems to be that having Ms Callahan teaching her lover's child is asking for trouble. Another teacher would be able to be more objective, so the other parents and I would like to have Ms Callahan removed from this classroom."

There it was: exactly what Grey had been afraid of.

"And you speak on behalf of the other parents in the class?" Debbie clarified.

Keri-Lynn raised her chin a bit higher. "Of course."

Though I didn't know if that was true or not, my heart sank anyway. If she really did have other parents on board, the administration might agree simply to avoid trouble. The squeaky wheel got the grease, and appeasing her might be easier than making an enemy of her.

However, Debbie only smiled. "Well, let's hear an opposing viewpoint, shall we?" Getting to her feet, she walked over to the door and opened it again. "Mr Wright? We're ready for you now."

As Grey walked into the room, I honestly didn't know who was more surprised: me or Keri-Lynn. What in the world was he doing there?

He gave me no indication, not glancing in my direction or Keri-Lynn's, addressing himself to the principal instead. "Mrs Jameson, I have something I think you oughta see."

He handed his phone to the principal as Keri-Lynn strained forward, trying to see the screen. "What is that?"

Grey looked over at her, his green eyes hard and determined. "That's a petition signed by every parent in Ms Callahan's class other than you, confirming they want her to remain as the class teacher."

What? How in the world had he managed that? I knew he would do whatever was necessary for Adele, but for him to go to those lengths truly surprised me.

Keri-Lynn looked just as flabbergasted as I felt. "That can't be true."

"Are you calling me a liar, Ms Keller?" His tone was the same one that he'd used on me the night we met, hard enough to make me flinch.

"It all seems to be in order, Ms Keller," Rhonda told her, not looking nearly as surprised as I expected her to as she weighed in for the first time since the meeting started. "As I see it, Ms Callahan hasn't broken any rules and none of the other parents have a problem with her staying in the class. If *you* have a problem with it, then perhaps the simplest solution is to move Sophie to a different class rather than disrupting everyone else."

Keri-Lynn looked around the room in dismay at the four completely unsympathetic faces, all united against her. "But... it's not just me."

"It seems it is," Grey told her. "And I suggest you don't interfere in my personal life again, not unless you want me to start following your husband around too."

I had no idea what that meant, but Keri-Lynn's face went pale as she got to her feet. "Well, I think that moving Sophie to a different class will be a good start."

That would be the most that happened and we all knew it, but she still had to try to save face.

"I'll have the arrangements in place by the end of the week," Rhonda told her, gesturing to the door. "Thank you for coming in, Ms Keller."

She beat a hasty retreat out the door, leaving me, Grey, Rhonda and Debbie all grinning at each other in relief.

"That went just about as well as I hoped," Debbie announced once we were sure Keri-Lynn was out of earshot. "Mr Wright, thank you for your contribution. Billie, you're free to go, we'll take care of things from here."

Grey and I stepped out into the empty hallway together, my head still spinning. "Well, thanks, I guess. I'm glad it's worked out that I can keep on teaching Adele."

His green eyes had lost the hardness they'd had in the vice-principal's office. Looking over at me, he looked almost nervous instead. "I didn't do it for Adele. Well, not just for her, anyway."

"What exactly did you do?" I blurted out, making him laugh.

"It's kind of a long story. Do you want to come over for dinner tonight and I'll tell you?"

That offer tempted me, way more than it should have, but I had to be sensible. I knew the pattern by then: we'd have a lovely evening, talking and laughing together, maybe ending up in bed together, and then he'd find another reason to push me away again. Eventually, I had to take a stand or things were never going to change.

"No, I don't think so. I'll go get Adele for you and you can take her home. Wait here."

With that, I walked briskly back to my classroom, ignoring the ache in my heart. He'd made his decision; all I could do was abide by it, no matter how much it hurt.

~Grey~

All the exhilaration and triumph I'd been feeling evaporated as Billie walked away from me, her smile tight and her shoulders hunched. I thought she'd be just as delighted as I was about our victory over the meddling Keri-Lynn, but if she felt any kind of relief or joy, she kept it to herself. She didn't seem to want to share her emotions with me at all, and though I completely understood why not, it disappointed me all the same.

After a few minutes of me standing awkwardly in the school hallway, Adele appeared, not with Billie but with the other woman who often brought her out. "Daddy, why are you here?" she demanded with a pout. "I go with Ms Cally-lan."

It sure didn't take long for my own kid to prefer her sweet teacher to me, and I could hardly blame her for it. I liked Billie a whole lot more than I liked myself too, at least at that particular moment.

Even though I didn't feel much like smiling, I put a smile on my face for Adele's sake. "Usually, you do. Not today, though. Come on, it's time to go home."

The day had been such a whirlwind, I was still processing it all as I made Adele supper that night. After I told Charlotte I wanted to hit back where it would hurt Keri-Lynn most, by going after the support of the same parents she had tried to sway to her side, Charlotte worked some kind of magic to get me the names and numbers of the other parents in Adele's class. I made all the calls myself, explaining who I was and why I was interrupting their day. Most of the parents were in the chat group so they already knew the background, and several of them told me how they felt Keri-Lynn had crossed a line in posting the pictures.

"Ms Callahan's lucky to have a champion like you," some of the moms told me, almost sounding jealous.

"You sound smitten," a couple of other parents laughed, and I couldn't really argue with that. I kind of was.

Several of them also told me how they'd heard about Adele from their own children, and what a great job Billie had done of making it clear to the kids that Adele was different from them but just the same too. None of them wanted Adele removed from the class, and none of them wanted Billie to go either. Getting the majority of them to agree to lend their names to my petition posed very little challenge at all.

A few were trickier. They were friends of Keri-Lynn, or wanted to be, and they were afraid that by supporting me, they'd draw her ire. The only thing that really swayed them was when I explained how I had the rest of the class on board, and we were going to be proposing that any parents who felt the same as Keri-Lynn be moved to a different class. Faced with that prospect, none of them wanted to lose Billie as their child's teacher, and so in the end, they all signed.

When I had all the names, I called the vice-principal to lodge my counter-complaint, and after she heard what I'd done, she invited me to attend the meeting too. The look on both Keri-Lynn and Billie's faces when I walked in was priceless, and it all played out just as I hoped, all except Billie's reaction at the end.

When I told her afterwards that I didn't only do it for Adele, I hoped she would read between the lines and realize that I wouldn't have gone to such efforts for anyone other than her. With every phone call I made, I tried to prove to her that I had her back. I wanted it to pave the way to asking her to give me one more chance at answering the question about what kind of a relationship I wanted with her, because after losing her sunshine in my life for the past few days, I couldn't remember how I ever lived in the dark and cold before. I'd do just about anything to feel her warmth again.

Hopefully, I hadn't missed my chance for good.

On Tuesday, I went back to work, still none the wiser about how to get Billie to talk to me again. The door that she'd always left open for me seemed to have closed, and I had no idea how to find the key.

Halfway through fishing out a wedding ring that someone had inadvertently washed down their sink, the solution came to me: her family barbecue.

Every Tuesday, Billie had dinner with her family, and though they would no doubt take Billie's side over mine, maybe if I could convince them that I had her best interests at heart, they could help me convince her to at least hear me out. They appreciated bluntness, so I laid it all out to Tonia as plainly as I could, giving her a call from my van between jobs.

"I screwed up. Billie ain't talking to me, and I need to apologize to her. Whether she accepts it or not, I need to let her know how I feel."

"What do you want me to do about it?" Tonia asked, her reply just as to-the-point as I expected.

"I was hoping you might invite me over to y'all's barbecue tonight and I can try and talk to her there."

Tonia let out a low whistle. "You really want to walk into the lion's den? We Callahans can close ranks pretty quickly if you mess with one of us."

"I got that impression," I told her drily, but I wasn't kidding. I knew that I'd be making enemies if I hurt Billie, but that was the last thing I wanted to do. "I know the risks, but I need to make her see that I'm serious, and what could say that more than taking my chances with the lions?"

Tonia had to agree I had a point, and she told me she'd talk it over with Dex and Laura and get back to me. An hour later, my phone buzzed while I was elbow deep in a clogged bathtub, and it nearly killed me to wait until the job was finished to find out what the Callahans' verdict would be.

Tonia's message could have struck fear into my heart, but when I read it, I only felt joy:

Here's the address. Come any time after seven, and don't screw this up.

Chapter Sixteen

~Billie~

My teaching assistant had to leave early on Tuesday afternoon for an appointment, so I took the children out to meet their parents at the end of the day, taking Adele along with me since she'd be staying with me until I went home.

Usually, the kids ran off to their parents and all I got from their moms or dads was a wave or a smile, but not that afternoon. One by one, they came up to me to tell me how pleased they were that Keri-Lynn had gone quiet on the parent group, how they supported me teaching not only their own child but Adele too, and how they hoped everything had been settled in my favour.

"This must be Adele," one mom said, giving the little girl at my side a friendly smile. "I've heard so much about her from my son. He loves it when he gets a chance to work with her, we hear all about it."

"It's wonderful that they get to learn that there are all kinds of people in the world," another mom told me. "Adele is a celebrity in our house."

Along with those comments, the other thing that kept coming up over and over again was how passionately Grey had spoken on my behalf.

"That man seems like a keeper," said one woman, not much older than me. "My husband would have never gone to all the trouble."

"You've sure made an impression on him," another mom laughed.

"I've rarely heard a man sound so devoted."

With each comment, I tried my best to smile and keep my responses polite but vague. They must have gotten the wrong end of the stick. Grey wasn't devoted to me, and he hadn't made those calls for *me*. Adele had been his motivation, as usual. He was a good dad and would always go to bat for her; no one could deny that. To think that it had anything to do with me as a person rather than as Adele's teacher would be pushing it.

Grey's van sat in his driveway when I got home, so I took Adele over there. At the door, Grey and I exchanged a few polite sentences about her day, but that was all. He didn't repeat his offer from the day before to spend time together, and if anything, he seemed a little withdrawn again, solidifying my conviction that I'd made the right decision. I didn't need to be constantly walking on eggshells, waiting to see what kind of mood he'd be in and how that would affect whether he wanted to be with me or not.

I'd made the right choice in deciding to keep my distance.

I just had to make myself believe it.

And I had to face my siblings' questions about it too, I suspected, as I pulled up to my parents' house a little later that evening for our weekly barbecue. The previous Tuesday, I'd brought Adele and Dex lost his temper, but it seemed impossible that had only been seven days earlier. So much had happened since then, ups and downs, highs and lows, hopes and disappointments. I almost felt like a different woman walking into the backyard, one a little bit wiser but a little bit sadder for it.

Everyone else had already arrived, and though they greeted me warmly as always, Laura was already in the middle of a story about her latest group of guests at the ranch, so after giving my parents a hug in greeting, I sat down at the picnic table with a beer to listen. She soon had us all in stitches, howling at her description of the banker who ended up hanging off his horse sideways, and though I laughed along with the others, my gaze kept returning to Jesse who watched his wife with so much pride and affection that it nearly brought tears to my eyes.

He'd tried to push her away too before he finally admitted he couldn't live without her. Laura said he just had to be ready on his own time and his own terms, with a little nudge from Dex to help along the way, but the idea that Grey might have a similar epiphany seemed incredibly unlikely. Not on a timeline that worked for me, anyway.

When Laura had finished, we moved on to talking about Tonia's business, and then to Dex's gallery, and though I was always interested to hear what my siblings were up to, I found it rather odd that no one asked me about Grey or my week. My usually nosy family were actually minding their own business, and I found it rather unsettling.

Just as Dex was finishing sharing his news, my parents' doorbell rang and Tonia immediately jumped up. "I'll get it."

That struck me as strange too. We weren't expecting anyone else, so the person at the door probably wanted to sell something; why would Tonia be so eager to go and deal with it? As she headed into the house, my parents both got up to bring the food over, telling the rest of us to stay put.

My question about Tonia's enthusiasm was soon answered when my sister returned, bringing behind her two very unexpected guests, at least to me. My jaw dropped as Grey and Adele followed Tonia out onto the deck, looking for all the world like they belonged there.

Ignoring me, Tonia took Grey over to my parents to introduce them, and Grey handed my dad a case of beer he'd brought while Adele and Charlie ran off together, eager to resume whatever games they'd been up to during their visit on Friday.

"You knew about this, didn't you?" I demanded, turning to Laura and Dex who both refused to look me in the eye. No one seemed surprised at all about Grey's appearance except for me, and since my siblings weren't talking, I tried their partners instead. "Cam? Jesse?"

"I mighta heard something about it," Cam mumbled, shooting Jesse a pleading look.

Jesse came to his rescue. "He just wants a chance to talk to you, Billie.

We all have your back, so if you want him gone, just say the word and we'll carry him outta here if we have to, but maybe you could hear him out first. We all make mistakes, it's how we deal with 'em that matters."

He and Laura exchanged an affectionate look, reminding me that if she hadn't given him a chance to make amends, they might have never gotten together to become the happy family they were. Tonia and Cam spent six years apart rather than just talking things out with each other. I supposed if Grey had gone to all the trouble of getting himself invited to the barbecue and braving my entire family, he must have something important to say.

After finishing up his conversation with my parents, Tonia brought Grey over to the picnic tables where the rest of us sat, and he gave everyone a nod of greeting. "Howdy. I think I've met everyone here except for you."

He gestured to Jesse, who got up and introduced himself, shaking Grey's hand firmly and whispering something to him that I couldn't quite hear. I didn't know when Grey and Laura had met, but they seemed to have since she greeted him along with everyone else. Somehow, I'd been left completely out of the loop.

At last, only when everyone else had said hello, Grey turned to me. "Hey, Billie."

My intentions of letting him speak quickly fell to the wayside, his casual greeting irking me more than I expected to. "Hey? That's what you've got to say to me? What are you doing here?"

Though he winced at my tone, he answered me readily. "Well, I wanted to talk to you and you weren't interested in coming over for dinner, so I thought I'd come here instead. Adele wanted to play with Charlie, so it's a win all around."

His hopeful smile had the corners of my mouth pulling upwards, but I forced myself to hold them down. "And which of my siblings did you wrangle an invitation out of?"

He shrugged. "All of 'em, kind of."

Tonia backed him up. "We all agreed, Billie. Now, I think Mom and

Dad need some help with dinner."

That was obviously a prearranged signal because everyone got to their feet en masse, heading over to the barbecue and the kitchen, out of earshot but close enough that they'd hear me if I called for help, leaving me and Grey alone together.

Grey shook his head as we both watched them go. "They're something else. I'm kind of growing fond of them."

"They'll eat you alive if I give the word. Just remember that." Having made my threat, I gestured to the bench on the other side of the table. "After going to all this trouble, I'm curious about what could be so important. What do you want to say to me, Grey?"

He folded his long legs beneath the table awkwardly, getting himself settled before he leaned forward and looked me straight in the eye. "I came here to ask you for another chance, Billie. I know I don't deserve one, but it's been four days since you left my bed and I ain't been able to stop thinking about it, so I'm doing what you told me to: I'm apologizing and I'm telling you how I'll do better next time."

Though my stomach fluttered, the promise in those green eyes almost impossible to resist, I did my best to keep my head anyway. "Apologies start to lose their value when you have to keep making them."

"I know that," he assured me, scratching at his chest nervously. "I hope this is the last one I need to make, so I'm gonna do my best to make it a good one. I'm sorry for pushing you away. I'm sorry for thinking I knew what was best for both of us without taking your feelings into consideration, and I'm sorry for letting my past affect the way I treated you. I've talked to a lot of people in the last few days. I talked to your family and I talked to all the other parents from your class, and I realized that pushing you away doesn't protect you like I wanted it to. I didn't want to dump all my problems and disappointments and failings on you, but I think maybe the problem is that I've been trying to carry it all myself for so long that I forgot how to let anyone help. I forgot how nice it can be to have someone to help carry the load."

I knew how heavily his failed marriage and Donna's parenting weighed on him but I didn't realize it had played that much of a role in his decision. My resolve softened, just a touch, as Grey continued.

"I ain't perfect, not by a long stretch, but somehow, you were willing to give me a chance anyway, a chance I never expected, and rather than accepting it for the gift it was, I kept looking for all the reasons why it wouldn't work. I don't want to do that anymore."

"What *do* you want?" He'd said a lot of things, but not the answer to the question I'd been trying so hard to get him to tell me the other night. If he still wasn't sure or if came up with more excuses about why he couldn't decide, I would know not to waste my time.

That wasn't what he did, though. Instead, he looked me straight in the eye and gave it to me plain. "I want to give this thing between us an honest chance. I want to put you first; not before Adele, necessarily, but in front of my fear and doubts, at least. I want to see what it could be like, because I have a feeling it might just be the best damn thing I ever had."

~Grey~

My chest felt so tight as I waited for Billie's response, it made it hard to breathe. After thinking it over long and hard, I'd tried to do exactly what I thought she'd appreciate. I tried to do exactly what Jesse advised when he shook my hand and told me to lay it all on the line, holding nothing back. I tried to be open and honest and vulnerable with her in a way I hadn't ever been with anyone else.

I tried, but I still didn't know if it would be enough.

"It doesn't need to be the best," Billie whispered, her blue eyes hopeful and conflicted and wary all at once.

"What?" As much as I wanted to understand, she'd lost me. I'd been trying to pay her a compliment by saying a relationship with her would be the best thing I'd ever found, not to mention I sincerely believed it to be true.

Billie had a different perspective, though. "There's no competition, Grey. You don't need to compare things to how they were with Donna. It doesn't need to be an either/or between me and Adele. You're allowed to have multiple good things in your life at once. Things can be wonderful and hard at the same time. I think... well, I think you've been functioning in survival mode for a long time, where things are just black or white, but the world has a lot more colours and shades than that. You don't need to be perfect. I don't expect you to be, and Lord knows I'm not. You just need to try, just like you're doing right now."

She really did see me, more than anyone ever had, and I could recognize the truth in what she said. "I don't know if I know how to let go of that survival mode. I used to be a lot more easygoing. I used to..."

"I don't care," she cut me off bluntly, and when my eyes widened in surprise, she laughed. "I mean, I care, but I don't want you to try to be something you're not or something you think I want you to be. We all grow up, we all change when life throws stuff at us. I'm not the person I was ten years ago and I don't expect you to be either."

"Ten years ago... when you were thirteen," I couldn't help pointing out, and she narrowed her eyes at me playfully.

"You can play the grumpy old man all you want, but I don't think that's really who you are either. There's a happy medium somewhere, and I think if you can find it, you'd be a lot happier, with or without me."

"I'd be a lot happier with you." The words popped out of me spontaneously, like a reflex, and I could see Billie appreciated them even if she shook her head at me missing the point. I tried my best to assure her that I did understand her. "I hear you, Billie. I do, and I think you're right. I've cut myself off from the world for a long time thinking that was the way to keep both me and Adele from getting hurt, but I've really just been treading water. Through you, I've met your family and some of the other parents that I'm gonna stay in touch with, and it's reminded me that there are good people out there, good people who want to help even when they've got their own stuff going on. It all started with you, and it all comes back to you too."

She chose to ignore my last statement, focusing on the other things I'd said instead. "I'm really glad you're building a community. You've got so much to give too, don't forget that. You can get help when you need it but you can give it too, and we all need to feel useful sometimes. What you did for me at the school was really incredible."

"Why do I feel like you're about to give me a gold star?" I teased her, not knowing if she was aware she'd slipped into her teacher voice.

"Would that turn you on?" she teased me right back, her eyes sparkling in amusement.

It felt so good to have her smiling and joking with me, but she still hadn't said if she'd give me another chance yet, so I tried to steer the conversation back in that direction.

"You don't have to do very much at all to turn me on. Everything about you is attractive to me. I think that's the only thing I've managed to show you properly without screwing it up."

"That is one thing you definitely do right," Billie agreed, the look in her eyes turning more heated. No doubt the same memories in my head were playing through hers too, and hopefully, those memories would work in my favour. On their own, they weren't enough, but they couldn't hurt either.

"You asked me before about what I could see for us, and the truth is that I was too afraid to let myself imagine it. But I'll tell you what I see now: if you say you'll give me one more chance, then we'll stay here at this barbecue as long as you want to, visiting with your family. Afterwards, you'll come home with me and stay the night. The whole night, with my bedroom door locked so we won't be disturbed. In the morning, we'll wake up together, I'll make breakfast and get Adele ready for school, and I'll kiss you goodbye, knowing that I'll see you again that evening. We could come to your house or you could come to ours or we could go out if you prefer; it doesn't really matter to me as long as I get to see you." I could see it all crystal clear in my head, like a memory even though it hadn't happened yet. "It ain't much, I know, but to me, that sounds pretty damn great."

"It sounds pretty great to me too." Billie's eyes were shining as she leaned closer to me across the table. "And you won't care if anyone sees us?"

"There's only one person in the world whose opinion matters to me, other than yours." Her brow furrowed in confusion for a second before I turned around, calling to my daughter. "Adele, come on over here for a second."

She came barrelling over, breathing hard from whatever game she'd been playing. "What, Daddy?"

"Would you like it if we went out for dinner with Ms Callahan tomorrow?"

She glanced over her shoulder at the deck, where dishes of mouth-watering food were just waiting to be served. "No dinner tonight?"

"No, I didn't mean... we can have dinner here tonight. But tomorrow, do you want to go out somewhere with Ms Callahan, just the three of us?"

"Okay. I have to go, Daddy, bye!"

She ran off before I could stop her, squiggling out of my reach as Billie laughed. "Not exactly a ringing endorsement there. She's much more worried about the food than about me."

It could have been better, but on the other hand, it totally worked. "I thought it was perfect, actually. It doesn't even phase her that we'd spend time together, she thinks it'd be totally normal. She loves you already, and it's never even crossed my mind once to worry that you wouldn't love her too. For some women, the fact that I've got a daughter at all, let alone one with additional needs might be a dealbreaker, but with you, I never worried about that. It's only been about whether I could be the man you need me to be, and I'm willing to try."

Billie's eyes had started to turn red, so I summed things up as quickly as I could.

"I've got no more arguments to make, Billie. That's my apology and that's my offer, and I just hope you'll say yes."

Pushing herself to her feet, Billie leaned further across the table until her lips connected with mine, taking me by surprise as pleasure and hope swelled inside me.

"Yes, Mr Wright," she whispered, her agreement the sweetest word I'd ever heard. "I'll give you one more chance."

~Billie~

Hoots and whistles from the deck interrupted my romantic moment with Grey, and I rolled my eyes as he laughed, rubbing a hand across the back of his neck sheepishly. "Shoot, I kind of forgot we weren't alone."

I had too, which shocked me. "I'm amazed they left us alone for that long. Usually, my family is much more in-your-face."

"Just like you are," he reminded me, a look of genuine affection in his eyes. "But there's nowhere else I'd rather have you be."

It really sounded like he meant that, and though I still didn't fully understand what had brought on such a big change of heart, I wasn't about to complain. It felt right. At that moment, everything in the world felt right.

My siblings drifted back over, bringing food with them as they sensed that our conversation had reached an end, at least for the time being.

"Glad we get to let you live, Grey," Cam teased, clapping him on the shoulder as he sat down next to him.

"For now," Tonia added, giving Grey a stern look that was only half in jest. "Jury's still out on the long term."

Grey took it all in good humour. "It is, but I'm liking my odds."

I liked them too.

The parents called their kids over to eat, and the little ones squeezed in at the tables where they could find room among the largest group we'd ever had at one of our regular barbecues. If our family kept expanding, we'd need a third table before long. Looking around the table at the happy couples, only Dex was still on his own, but he seemed a lot better that evening. Deciding to take responsibility and control over his emotions had really made a difference for him, and I hoped it would continue to do so.

Grey asked Dex about his situation in a roundabout way during a rare lull in the conversation. "I saw your sculpture of your late wife at the gallery. It's beautiful. She must have been something special."

Dex answered him with that same look of pride in his eyes he always had when speaking about Shawna. "She sure was. I'm really lucky to have had that kind of love in my life."

"You know, you're not exactly ancient yet," Laura pointed out, her hand resting on Jesse's knee. "It's not too late to find love again."

We all knew Shawna had wanted him to move on, but Dex just shook his head like he always did whenever anyone brought it up. "I'm not much use to anyone in the relationship department and I don't think I ever will be."

To my surprise, Grey spoke up. "I felt the same way after my divorce. I know it's not the same thing, but I felt like if I couldn't be the man I was before, it wouldn't be possible to be happy again. I'm learning that ain't true, though, not if you find the person who's right for the man you are now."

My sisters both beamed in my direction as I tried not to blush. Where did this open and talkative Grey come from? I had no idea, but I rather liked him.

We stayed until dessert, talking and laughing with my family, my dad doting on Adele while Cam, Jesse and Dex argued about who would be more likely to need to be bailed out of a plumbing emergency by Grey. As much fun as we were having, though, the words Grey had spoken earlier about how he saw the rest of the night going had lingered in the back of my mind, and eventually, I couldn't take it anymore. I wanted to make them come true, and when I caught his eye and asked him if he was ready to go, Grey's smile made it clear his thoughts were in perfect sync with mine.

We'd arrived separately, since I hadn't known they'd be coming, and so we had to drive home separately too. "Go and get what you need from your house," Grey told me as he opened my truck door for me. "I'll start getting Adele ready for bed. Let yourself in when you're ready."

I didn't think I'd ever been more ready for anything in my life, but I knew what he meant. He wanted me to stay the night, not to have to dash home in the dark as I had done every other time we slept together. He promised me that night would be different, and I was willing to give him one more chance to prove it to me.

It didn't take long to gather a quick overnight bag with my pajamas, toiletries and clothes for work the next day. By the time I slipped through the unlocked front door of Grey's house, locking it behind me, I could hear him and Adele in her room, and I stepped quietly down the hall, not wanting to disturb them.

"Ms Callahan's going to stay here for a sleepover," Grey was telling her. "Just like you stayed at Charlie and Jenny's on the weekend. She'll be here in a few minutes to say goodnight and she'll still be here when you wake up."

Not *just* like Adele's sleepover, I hoped, but I appreciated him putting it in terms she'd understand.

It did lead to one small problem though: "Ms Cally-lan sleepover with me!" Adele announced gleefully as I stopped outside the bedroom door, just out of sight, leaning back against the wall with my hand covering my mouth to keep from laughing. That definitely wasn't part of Grey's plan.

"No, she's going to sleep in my room," Grey corrected her. "And before you ask: no, you can't sleep there too. If you need something, you can knock on my door but you can't come in, okay? The door's gonna be locked. Those are the new rules."

"No new rules." I could hear the pout in Adele's voice and picture the way her lip must have jutted out as she said it, but I knew that Grey had no intention of backing down.

"That's the way it goes, kiddo. New house, new school, new rules. Lots of changes for both of us, but I think they're all pretty great ones. We were pretty darn lucky to move next door to Ms Callahan. You like her, right? You want her to spend more time with us?"

"Yeah!" Her enthusiasm returned in full force, and I poked my head around the door just in time to see Adele giving her dad a high-five, making my heart melt.

"Can I say goodnight?"

Grey jumped at the sound of my voice, nearly swearing but catching himself in time as his startled green eyes looked over at me. "How long have you been there?"

"Long enough." I shot him a warm, teasing smile, leaving it at that as I knelt down in front of Adele. "Do you want to pick a story for bedtime?"

After reading two books with Grey standing at the door watching us, I leaned down to give Adele a hug, and she wrapped her little arms around me tightly. "You stay tonight and forever," she instructed.

That was kind of my hope too. "Tonight for sure," I promised. "See you in the morning, sweetheart."

Once Grey had given her a kiss, we closed the door and he took my hand for the short walk down the hall to his bedroom. After making sure the lock was turned, he took me in his arms. "I know this ain't the first time we've done this, but it kinda feels like it anyway."

"I know what you mean." I'd been feeling it too. The first time we slept together, there hadn't been any pressure since we both expected it to simply be for fun. That night, it felt like the start of something bigger, but despite that, I still wanted it to be fun. "Just forget about tomorrow for right now. Tell me what you want tonight."

He cleared his throat as his gaze dropped down to my body. "Well, as good as all that food was tonight, it still doesn't compare to the taste of you. It's been way too long since I had you on my tongue, Billie."

Good Lord, that man knew just how to turn me on. "Is there something stopping you?"

He grinned back at me. "Not anymore."

Without warning, he scooped me up in those strong arms of his, and I squealed in surprise as he dropped me roughly onto the bed, his hands immediately going to my pants to get them off. Just as eager as he was, I pulled my shirt off and undid my bra while he pulled my pants and panties down, so that in a matter of seconds, I lay there completely naked, my whole body primed and pulsing and ready for him.

Grey looked down at me ravenously. "That's more like it. Now, let's see if I can remember what you taught me."

Spreading my legs with his strong hands, he dipped his tongue straight into my throbbing pussy as my back arched off the bed and I gasped in delighted surprise. "You definitely get bonus marks for getting straight to the point."

He chuckled against my skin. "Are you gonna give me a grade when I'm done here?"

I loved hearing him laugh. "If I can still think straight enough to grade you, I think you've failed."

"In that case, get ready to lose your train of thought, Ms Callahan."

He really had been paying attention the other times we'd been together. Everything I'd told him I liked, everything I'd responded to before, he remembered and did it even better than before. With his ring finger and pinky finger inside me, his index and middle finger rubbed along either side of my clit with each thrust while his tongue flicked over the top of it. It overwhelmed me in the best possible way, and his hums and growls of satisfaction at my body's response only made it better. I soon lost the power of speech, and all control of my body soon after that as a powerful orgasm gripped me, temporarily blinding me as pleasure filled me from head to toe.

"Holy... fuck..." I managed to gasp after a moment or two, when my heart had begun beating again. It felt like I'd actually left my body for a moment.

Grey pulled himself up from between my legs, looking supremely satisfied with himself. "I told you: I'm a problem solver, and keeping things wet is my specialty."

With a groan, I dropped my head back onto the pillow. "I've been waiting for the plumber pick-up lines. Took you long enough!"

"Is it still a pick-up line if I just made you come?" he wondered. "Seems to me we're past that stage."

We definitely were, and I wanted to be even further. "Would you get inside me already?"

He didn't need any further invitation, and as his cool metal piercings slid inside me, sliding easily through my own arousal, I let out a soft moan.

"I've mentioned how much I love your ladder, right?"

"Once or twice," he agreed, his breath shorter than it had been as he pushed further inside me. "I love that you love it and I love the way you feel against it."

He'd told me it made the sensations even better for him, and I believed it must be true. "Maybe I should get a piercing too. I could do my clit?"

His body shuddered against me, the idea obviously a turn-on for him, but ultimately, he shook his head. "That would mean no sex during recovery. Not sure I like that idea."

As he thrust into me again, harder, I had to agree. "Maybe somewhere else, then?"

"If you want to. You'd look amazing with any piercings you want, but you look fantastic without them too."

The look of desire in his eyes as he scanned my body, his own firm, pierced chest hovering above me, had me nearly melting again, and I let the subject drop as I focused on the feel of him inside me instead.

Since he'd already made me come, Grey didn't seem to be in any hurry. He took his time, bending down to suck on my breasts or my ear or to kiss along my neck, all while his firm cock continued to move within me. My legs wrapped tight around his waist as I thrust my hips up to meet him, my fingers running through his short hair and over his taut, firm shoulders. It felt timeless and natural and exciting and so damn perfect, it made me want to laugh and cry all at the same time, but I couldn't do either, lost in the pleasure he brought me instead.

Finally, he couldn't take it anymore, and his pace increased, his thrusts turning rougher as he pinned my arms down by my wrists. My legs began to tremble again just as he reached his limit, and we came together, drowning in the pool of our mutual pleasure before collapsing into a pile of tangled limbs and sweaty satisfaction.

"If I hadn't already accepted your apology, that definitely would have clinched it," I teased him once I got my breath back.

We took turns cleaning up in the bathroom and changing into our pajamas, and when we climbed into bed together, Grey's warm, solid body curled around me, I fell asleep with a smile on my face, knowing deep in my heart that we'd only just begun.

Epilogue

Nine months later
~Grey~

"Hey, Grey! Is everything set for this weekend?" Charlotte's cheery greeting as I walked into the schoolyard attracted the attention of half the other moms in the vicinity, and soon, I found myself surrounded.

"Is this it?"

"It's about time!"

"Does she know?"

Questions came at me from all sides, and I held up my hands to try to slow them down. "Hang on, you're all getting way ahead of yourselves. Billie and I are taking a trip for the weekend to celebrate the end of the school year. That's all it is."

No one looked like they believed me, and there was no reason they should. I was lying, plain and simple.

Charlotte had agreed to take Adele for the weekend so Billie and I could have some time alone together. In fact, when I'd put the request out to the parent chat group, a new group just for parents of kids in Billie's class, formed shortly after Billie and I got together and which did *not* include Keri-Lynn Keller, I had been inundated with offers. After my efforts in arranging the petition to keep Billie as class teacher, the other parents had all accepted me and Adele with open arms. We had a community of support I'd never expected to find when we moved to the city, and I knew that it mostly came just from being open to it. Once I stopped shutting myself off from the world, I found there were a hell of a lot of kind people in it.

That wasn't to say that people still couldn't be awful, because they could. We still ran into people who seemed annoyed by Adele's very existence and had to deal with rude comments when Billie and I took her out on the weekends, but Billie never let it slide, standing up for Adele as fiercely as if she were her own daughter. In fact, over the past nine months, Billie had been more of a mother to my little girl than Donna ever had, and I hoped she wanted to take on that role more permanently as part of the question I wanted to ask her that weekend.

Of course, the other parents had all guessed my intentions even though I'd denied it at every turn, not wanting word to get back to Billie. For the same reason, I hadn't asked Tonia, Laura or Dex to watch Adele; if they knew Billie and I were taking a weekend away, they'd no doubt guess why. As much as possible, I wanted to keep it a surprise for her and make the weekend as special as I could.

When the bell rang, the kids all streamed out the front door, eager to get their summer vacation started. Joy and excitement filled the air, matching my mood exactly, and when Adele came running over to me with all of her school supplies, I could hardly believe how much she'd grown. With all the love and support around her, she'd truly blossomed.

"I'm going to miss you," her aide, Danielle, told her, crouching down to give Adele a big hug. "Have a wonderful summer and I'll see you in the fall."

Danielle would move to third grade with Adele, so she'd have a familiar face with her even though her teacher would be new. As much as she would miss Billie, I knew she'd be just fine. The other kids would look out for her too. She had so many friends, I couldn't keep track of them all. As I took all of her things from her, kids I'd never seen before waved and shouted goodbye to Adele as they went past.

I got down to eye level with her too. "Alright, sweetheart. Mrs Brown has your bag for the weekend. If you want to talk to me or Billie, you just tell Mrs Brown and she'll call us, okay?"

"Okay, Daddy. Bye!"

She ran off without a backward glance, as independent and trusting as always. I gave Charlotte and her two kids a wave before they all headed off together.

Meanwhile, I headed into the school, following the now-familiar path to Billie's classroom. I often came to pick her up at the end of the day, so all the staff greeted me with friendly smiles as I went, all looking just as excited about the end of the school year as the kids were.

When I got to Billie's classroom, however, I found her sitting at her desk, wiping tears from her face. "Billie? What's wrong?"

She looked over in surprise at the sound of my voice before rubbing her cheeks dry even more firmly than before. "I'm fine. Sorry. I didn't think anyone would see me."

"You're not fine. Why are you crying?"

She gave me a sheepish shrug, looking just as beautiful as always. She'd recently had her brown hair cut shorter and I loved it on her. I couldn't think of any way she wouldn't look incredible. "I'm just going to miss my class, that's all. What are you doing here? Where's Adele?"

She got up as I walked over to her, leaning down to give her a kiss and wipe away one last stray tear that sat on her cheek. I had told her that I'd pick Adele up that afternoon and take her home so Billie could work on cleaning things up in the classroom, but that had been a decoy. "She's staying with Charlotte Brown all weekend."

Billie took a step back from me, her face a picture of confusion. "What? Why?"

"Because you've worked damn hard all year and you deserve a break. It's a bit of a drive so we should go."

"Go where?" Billie still looked utterly bewildered. "You've lost me, Grey. What's going on?"

Taking a deep breath, I backed up a little. "I know it's hard to be spontaneous when we've got Adele to think about, so I asked Charlotte to watch her for the weekend. I've booked us a hotel in San Antonio so we can just go and enjoy a couple of days on our own. No work, no kids, no family; just you and me. Is that alright?"

Her blue eyes melted into the look of appreciation I loved so much. "That sounds amazing. How long have you had this up your sleeve?"

"A while," I admitted. "And don't worry about the classroom, I can come and help you with it when we get back. For once, you can skip out early."

To my relief, she agreed, and when we got out to her truck, she was surprised to see the two packed suitcases already inside. "I'm impressed. This is a whole new side of you."

She had that right. With Donna, I never would have planned anything like that, not daring to make any decisions without consulting her, knowing I wouldn't hear the end of it if I did things wrong. She'd even picked out her own engagement ring, but with Billie, I knew she'd appreciate the effort even if things weren't exactly what she would have chosen.

I couldn't ever be the man I'd been before, but I didn't have to be. Billie loved the man I had become, and I liked him too, especially when he got to be with her.

The drive was full of conversation and laughter and a few more tears as Billie recounted her last day and all the things she would miss about her outgoing class. She was a damn good teacher, I knew that right from the start, but as glad as I was that Adele got to have her for a year, I was so much happier that she would continue being in our lives once the year had ended.

We went straight to our room when we arrived, ordering room service so we could make full use of the uninterrupted time alone with a bed and a bathtub big enough for two. In the morning, we went out for breakfast and for a walk around downtown. To her, it seemed like our route was random, but I actually had a destination in mind, though I tried to act surprised when I saw the piercing and tattoo parlor.

"Look at this: it must be a sign. All year long, you said you'd get a piercing over your summer break and here we are."

After a lot of deliberation, she'd decided she'd like to get her nipples pierced, and I loved the idea too. She just wanted to wait until she was less likely to have children running into her all day while they were healing.

Billie peered into the store, a mix of excitement and trepidation on her face. "Really? You want to do it now? I thought I had to have a consultation first."

Some stores liked to do that, but I'd already called ahead and checked that it would be okay. "Well, let's see what they say. We're here, so why not check?"

She didn't seem to be onto me as we headed inside together. As arranged, the woman said she could do Billie's consultation and piercing right there and then, but that it would take a while. Billie looked over at me in indecision. "Is this really how you want to spend our day?"

"If it's something you want, then yes. I can always get a tattoo while I wait, I've been thinking of getting a new one anyway."

With no more excuses, Billie agreed, getting more excited all the time as she headed off to have her consultation. Meanwhile, I sat down in the tattooist's chair as he pulled up the design I'd sent him ahead of time.

"You sure about this?" he asked good-naturedly. "It's pretty permanent."

"I'm sure." I didn't have a doubt in my mind.

By the time Billie came back from her piercing, walking a little stiffly but looking pleased with herself, I was almost done.

"And?" I asked her eagerly. "How did it go?"

"Not bad," she assured me. "No worse than the time Bobby stabbed me in the groin with his pencil crayon."

The tattooist looked up in surprise as I laughed. "Bobby's an 8-year-old in her classroom, and it was an accident," I explained so he wouldn't get the wrong idea.

"Are you almost done?" Billie asked, trying to resist the urge to peek until I said it was okay.

"Nearly. Actually, maybe you could help with the last bit."

She gave me a curious, confused look. "Help? How?"

"Come over here and see," the tattooist invited her, getting up from his stool so she could take his place.

As Billie rounded the chair to get a closer look, I watched her face closely, waiting for the moment she'd realize what was going on. The tattoo was a simple one on the left side of my chest, just above my heart: five words with two checkboxes underneath, one for yes and one for no.

She squinted at it as she sat down for just a second before her eyes widened and she looked up at me in hopeful disbelief. "Are you serious?"

"I can't actually see it," I pointed out. "But if it says, 'Billie, will you marry me?' then yeah: I'm serious."

"He wants you to check yes or no," the tattooist helpfully explained. "He said you could put a gold star in the appropriate box."

"A gold star, huh?" Although she teased me, I could hear the joy in her voice and see it shining in her eyes too, letting me know even if I hadn't already guessed which box she would choose.

With him guiding her hand, Billie helped to ink the final part of the tattoo, placing a small gold star in the 'yes' box, and holding up a mirror to my chest to show me the finished result.

Though I was meant to stay still, I couldn't help it; I sat up and pulled her into a deep kiss right there and then. "I love you, Billie. Thanks for not giving up on me."

"I love you too, Grey. Thank you for keeping your promise to keep trying. And thank you for giving me the best proposal story ever!" She was both laughing and crying as she pulled back to look at her handiwork again.

"If this doesn't show that I'm in it for good, nothing will," I pointed out, grinning just as wide as she was. "Now, let me get finished up here, and we can head back to the hotel. We still got a whole night here and a whole lot of celebrating to do."

Four months later
~Billie~

When Grey and I walked into our wedding reception, hand-in-hand, the cheer that went up nearly took the roof off the school gym. Every student from the three years I'd taught there had been invited, along with their families, not to mention our own families and friends. The room barely looked like the gym at all, decorated in a beautiful fall theme by my brother and sisters. When I told them that I wanted to be married before Christmas and that I wanted to incorporate the school that had played such a big part in bringing Grey and I together, Tonia took it as a personal challenge to get everything organized. As usual, she exceeded all expectations.

Holding her dad's other hand, Adele greeted the assembled crowd with a wave befitting a queen, as if the applause were entirely for her. She hadn't stopped grinning since she woke up that morning, excited to wear the pretty dress she'd been admiring in her closet for weeks.

"I'm the flower today!" she squealed in excitement as she jumped up into bed with me and Grey, having knocked on the door first like Grey had taught her.

"The flower *girl*, sweetheart," Grey corrected, not able to keep the smile off his face either. He leaned over to whisper in my ear, his stubble tickling me as it brushed against my skin. "I'm afraid she might actually think she's going to turn into a flower."

"Close enough," I assured him before pulling Adele into my lap, sitting so she could see both me and Grey. "You're going to do amazing today, but there's something I want to ask you about first."

Though I didn't expect her to say no, my heart beat a little faster anyway. Over the last few months, Grey had gone through all the necessary legal steps to have Donna relinquish any parental rights to Adele. When she dragged her feet on signing the final papers, Grey went to see her in person, the first time he'd seen his ex-wife in more than a year. He returned with the signed documents and a frown on his face. "She didn't even put up a fight," he grumbled. "She doesn't even miss her."

Even though he'd gotten the result he wanted, it still stung him anyway, and I understood that. With some gentle prompting from me, we talked through why it bothered him and how to let it go. Rather than taking his frustration out on me as he would have, once upon a time, we worked through it together, just as he'd promised me he would always try to do.

Since then, we'd organized all of the adoption paperwork needed to make Adele officially my daughter, and all that remained was to get her agreement. Between us, Grey and I had decided that doing it on our wedding day made the most sense; that day, we would truly become a family, all three of us.

"You know how Daddy and I are getting married today, right? He's going to be my husband and I'll be his wife."

Adele nodded in confirmation. We'd had that conversation a few times before, about what a wedding was besides just an excuse to wear pretty dresses.

"Well, that means I'm going to be part of your family. Daddy's already your daddy, and I would really like to be your mommy, if you'd like that too."

My lungs seemed to stop working as I waited for her answer, no air going in or not. I knew she loved me, but honestly, she loved everyone, and giving me the title of Mommy was a pretty big deal. Grey told me that she hadn't asked about Donna in several months, but he suspected if she were to see her, she wouldn't hold any kind of grudge, and I believed it too. Adele didn't have a vindictive bone in her body.

She obviously hadn't been expecting the offer, and she looked over at Grey in uncertainty. "I get to choose Mommy?"

Grey nodded, as encouraging as he always was with her, and he did his best to explain things in terms she'd understand. "Isn't that lucky? Most people don't get to choose, but you do. So, if you could have anyone in the whole world be your Mommy, who would you pick?"

In the whole world? That might be pushing it. She might choose someone from one of her favourite TV shows, or one of her friends' moms, or hell, even one of my sisters. She loved them both too, and Laura was a current favourite since we'd spent a bunch of time at the ranch over the summer. She'd drawn a picture of Laura and her horse and it currently hung beside her bed where she said goodnight to it each night.

But she didn't choose any of those. Instead, she looked back at me, her grin taking over her whole face.

"Billie!"

She launched herself into my arms with such force that I tumbled backwards, and only Grey's quick reflexes stopped my head from smacking into the wall and leaving me with a concussion for my wedding day. With happy tears in both our eyes, we kissed our little girl, and when we signed the marriage certificate and registration at the ceremony, we slipped the adoption papers in too, signing everything all together as part of the same ceremony, so by the time the minister announced us as husband and wife, we were more than that.

We were a family.

At the reception, Tonia had arranged different activities to keep the kids entertained, so Adele ran off to join her friends while Grey called out after her uselessly, "Don't get your dress dirty!"

I just shook my head. "Let her get it dirty. I've never minded a little mess."

Those green eyes of his turned back to me, full of love. "No, you never did."

The receiving line went on for ages, with the parents of all the children giving us their best wishes. They knew me on a professional level and Grey on a personal one, and it felt like we had our own little town right there in the city. Even Keri-Lynn Keller came. Her youngest child, Eddie, was in my class that year. After her failed complaint the previous year, Sophie had been moved to another class and I didn't hear a word from Keri-Lynn until a few weeks before school started in the fall. She showed up at the front door of Grey's house where I had moved in fully a couple of months earlier.

"I'm glad I was wrong," she claimed. "Everyone says you were a great teacher, and I just wanted to check that if Eddie were to be in your class this year, you'd be able to overlook any prior misunderstanding between us."

I wouldn't exactly call it an apology, but I suspected I wouldn't get a better one, so I answered her truthfully, if a little pointedly. "I always treat all my students the same, Ms Keller, no matter who their parents are."

She actually had the decency to blush a little bit.

Grey had a few dealings with her too, along with other parents from the school, and although he couldn't say for sure if her views had changed, at least she kept them to herself. Sophie and Adele were back together in the same third grade class that year, and when Keri-Lynn arrived at the front of the receiving line, she surprised us by mentioning Sophie's birthday party the following week. "We'd love to have Adele there."

"That sounds great," Grey told her, and when she'd moved on, he offered me a wry explanation. "Adele never holds a grudge and she's about the happiest person I know, so I figured I could take a page from her book. Sometimes, people deserve one more chance."

Grey's sister, June, and her partner, Richard, had flown out from California for the wedding, and June hugged me so hard, I nearly lost my breath again. "I tried to get him to leave Texas after the mess with Donna," she whispered to me. "I'm so glad he didn't. He was meant to stay here and meet you. I knew it the first time he talked about you."

I didn't know if she meant that seriously or if it was just something people said. "How did you know?"

She laughed into my ear. "He has a tell. When he's talking about something he really cares about, he'll scratch his chest, just above his heart. He has no idea he does it, so if you ever want to know if something's important, keep an eye out for it. That's my wedding gift to you."

Finally, bringing up the rear, the Callahan family arrived as one big unit, though with one person fewer than at our peak. My dad had a second heart attack in the spring, five years after the first one, and he couldn't cheat death twice. Dex had been there to help my mom through it, and along with the therapy he still attended, it seemed to give him a new purpose. He walked me down the aisle in my dad's place that afternoon, and overall, he was a lot more like the old Dex we used to know, though he still refused all our attempts to try to set him up with someone new.

I'd mentioned to Grey once how sad the idea of my brother spending the rest of his life alone made me, but he said he wouldn't count on it. "No matter how sure he is, someone might come along and blow him away. With the right woman, I could see him having a change of heart, just like I did."

When my mom reached me, she held me tight for a long while. "I can't believe my baby's all grown up and married."

"I'm not the baby anymore," I couldn't help pointing out, though I knew that to my whole family, I always would be.

"No, not anymore," my mom agreed, stepping back to include Grey in the conversation too. "You know, Jim had a dream just before he died. I didn't tell you about it then because I didn't want to put any pressure on you, but he dreamt that he was here at your wedding."

Tears immediately sprang to my eyes as Grey reached over to take my hand. "I'm sure he is," Grey said.

My mom smiled in agreement. "I think so too, but that wasn't the important part. He said you told us at the reception that you were pregnant, so I have to ask: any news, Billie?"

Grey laughed, and I did too, though my laughter was a little more uncertain than his. The truth was my period *was* a little bit late, but I'd been putting it down to stress over the wedding and the new school year. Maybe my daddy was trying to tell me something?

The thought stayed in my head throughout the reception, and when Grey and I finally said our goodbyes, leaving Adele with Tonia so that we could have our wedding night on our own, I asked him if we could stop at the drugstore on the way home.

Still in my wedding dress, I attracted a few looks as I led Grey over to the pregnancy tests and picked one out. "Really?" he asked in surprise and curiosity.

"I'm not sure, but maybe. We might as well find out." We had already talked about it. I wanted more kids, without question, and Grey was coming around to the idea, at least enough that he agreed we could stop the birth control and see what happened. That had only been a month earlier, though; I expected it to take a lot longer before we saw any results.

By the time we got home, we were both a bundle of nervous energy, and once Grey had helped me out of my dress, I went into the bathroom to take the test. In my lingerie, I returned to the bedroom, sitting down on the bed next to Grey, who had taken off his suit jacket and tie, as we waited for the results.

"Would you like a boy or a girl, if it's positive?" I asked him, trying to help pass the time.

"Honestly? It doesn't matter one bit to me. I'm going to love our baby no matter what, and I know you will too. That's one of the reasons I married you, Billie Callahan, because I know I'll never have to doubt it."

"Wright," I corrected him. "Billie Wright, remember?"

He kissed me so hard and deep that by the time we came up for air, the test was ready. Holding Grey's hand, I flipped it over so we could both see the little plus sign that greeted us, and I honestly didn't know how much more happiness I could take. My heart felt ready to burst.

"It looks like one of your marks on your class assignments," Grey pointed out. "I guess that means we passed?"

With a laugh, I threw my arms back around him. "We definitely did. We thought we were getting a family of three today, but we're actually a family of four. I'd say we got ourselves some extra credit."

Our joyful embrace quickly turned more heated as we remembered that, despite everything else, we were still celebrating our wedding night. No matter what else might change in our lives, one thing had remained constant since the first night he took his shirt off in front of me: Grey Wright was the sexiest man I had ever met, and I couldn't feel any luckier that he was mine.

~~THE END~~

The Callahans

You can read about the other Callahan siblings in their own books:

A Matter of Time - Tonia's Story
A Piece of Land - Laura's Story
A Work of Art - Dex's Story

More from the Author

Contemporary Romance – 18+

Callahan Series
A Matter of Time
A Piece of Land
A Change of Heart
A Work of Art

Christmas in the City Series
Mistletoe Mistake
Candy Cane Challenge
Tinsel Temptation
Gingerbread Gamble
Stocking Standoff
Eggnog Experiment

Standalones
Leading Lady
A Set of Three
Charity Case
Hired Lover

Contemporary Romance – New Adult/Clean

It Figures duet
It Figures
Figuring It Out

Historical Romance – 18+

Lady in Waiting Series
Lady in Waiting
King in Training
Princess in Hiding

Paranormal Romance – 18+

Cold Lake Pack Series
The Curse and the Prophecy
The Spell and the Legacy
The Dream and the Destiny

Mismatched Mates Series
Mismatched Mates
Misguided Motives
Mistaken Meanings

Serena's Story
The Alpha's Second Chance
The Returned Mate
The Vampire's Consort

Sacrifice Series
Blood Donor
Life Giver

Paranormal Romance – New Adult/Clean
The Alpha's Prey

Keep in touch

Daily updates from my works-in-progress, bonus chapters and more can be found on my Ream account, Chilli & Chocolate, along with Emma Lee-Johnson:
https://reamstories.com/chilliandchocolate

You can find and follow me on Facebook at:
facebook.com/melodytyden

Join the Facebook group Melody's Romance Corner for fun games, interaction with the author and exclusive news and excerpts.

You can also sign up to my newsletter at www.melodytyden.com for all the latest news.

www.ingramcontent.com/pod-product-compliance
Lightning Source LLC
Chambersburg PA
CBHW072048110526
44590CB00018B/3085